# Ethnic and Racial Studies Today

Edited by Martin Bulmer and
John Solomos

Routledge

London and New York

First published 1999
by Routledge
11 New Fetter Lane, London EC4P 4EE

Simultaneously published in the USA and Canada
by Routledge
29 West 35th Street, New York, NY 10001

Typeset in Sabon by Routledge
Printed and bound in Great Britain by
Creative Print and Design (Wales), Ebbw Vale

*British Library Cataloguing in Publication Data*
A catalogue record for this book is available from the British Library

*Library of Congress Cataloging in Publication Data*
Edited by Martin Bulmer and John Solomos
Ethnic and racial studies today
Includes bibliographical references and index
1. Race relations – Study and teaching.
2. Ethnicity – Study and teaching.
3. Minorities – Study and teaching.
I. Bulmer, Martin. II. Solomos, John.
HT1501. E75 1999                                          98-30802
305.8' 0071–dc21                                          CIP

ISBN  0–415–18172–0 (hbk)
ISBN  0–415–18173–9 (pbk)

# Contents

vi  *Contents*

# Contributors

**Linda Martín Alcoff** teaches philosophy and women's studies at Syracuse University. She has published *Real Knowing: New Versions of the Coherence Theory* (1996) and papers in *SIGNS*, *Radical Philosophy*, *Philosophical Topics* and elsewhere. She is working now on a book titled *Visible Identities: Race, Gender, and the Self.*

**Gargi Bhattacharyya** is a Lecturer in the Department of Cultural Studies and Sociology at the University of Birmingham. She is the author of a number of articles and *Tales of Dark-Skinned Women* (1998). She has also written about aspects of her research and teaching.

**Alastair Bonnett** is a Lecturer in Human Geography at the University of Newcastle, England. He is the author of *Radicalism, Anti-racism and Representation* (1993) and two forthcoming books: *Anti-racism* and *White Identities: An Historical and International Introduction.*

**Martin Bulmer** is Foundation Fund Professor of Sociology at the University of Surrey and Academic Director of the Question Bank in the ESRC Centre for Applied Social Surveys, London. Previously he taught at the University of Southampton, the London School of Economics and the University of Durham and has been a visiting professor at the University of Chicago, as well as briefly a member of the Government Statistical Service. Since 1992 he has been editor of the journal *Ethnic and Racial Studies*. His recent works include *Directory of Social Research Organisations*, second edition (with Sykes and Moorhouse, 1998) and *Citizenship Today: The Contemporary Relevance of T. H. Marshall* (editor with T. Rees, 1996).

**Karen Henwood** lectures in the School of Psychology at the University of Wales, Bangor. She has done research in the areas of psychology, race and racism; women's relationships; and qualitative research methods. She has published in a range of psychology and interdisciplinary social science journals, including: *Feminism and Psychology*, *Theory and Psychology*, *Ethnic and Racial Studies*, *Journal of Ageing Studies* and *British Journal of Psychology*. She has edited a volume on *Standpoints* *and Differences: Essays in the Practice of Feminist Psychology* (jointly edited with Chris Griffin and Ann Phoenix, 1998).

**Richard Jenkins** was trained as a social anthropologist at Belfast and Cambridge and is currently Professor of Sociology at the University of Sheffield. He has done field research in Belfast, the West Midlands, Wales and Denmark, and is particularly interested in social identity, ethnicity and nationalism, and disability. Among his recent publications are *Pierre Bourdieu* (1992), *Social Identity* (1996), *Rethinking Ethnicity* (1997), and *Questions of Competence* (1998).

**Siân Jones** is a Lecturer in the Department of Art History and Archaeology at the University of Manchester. Her publications include *The Archaeology of Ethnicity: Constructing Identities in the Past and Present* (1997) and a number of articles that explore questions of ethnicity and race within archaeology.

**Caroline Knowles** is a Lecturer in the Department of Sociology and Social Policy at the University of Southampton. Previously she was Associate Professor at Concordia University, Montreal. Author of *Race, Discourse and Labourism* (1992), *Family Boundaries: the Invention of Normality and Dangerousness* (1996), joint editor of *Resituating Identities: The Politics of Race, Ethnicity and Culture* (1996) and author of various articles on race and ethnicity.

**Maria Lauret** teaches American Literature in the School of English and American Studies at the University of Sussex. Before that she was a lecturer in English at the University of Southampton. Her current research interests are race and ethnicity in American literature and culture, the autobiographical writing of women activists, and bilingualism and migration. As well as completing a book on *Alice Walker* (1999), she is currently preparing articles on the fiction of Terry MacMillan and Bharati Mukherjee and on Eva Hoffman's autobiography. Her recent publications include *Liberating Literature: Feminist Fiction in America* and ' "I've got a right to sing the blues": Alice Walker's aesthetic' in Richard King and Helen Taylor (eds) *Dixie Debates: Perspectives on Southern Cultures* (1996).

**David Mason** is Professor of Sociology at the University of Plymouth. He has published widely on conceptual aspects of the study of race and ethnicity and on employment and equal opportunities issues. His publications include *Theories of Race and Ethnic Relations* (1986) jointly edited with John Rex and *Race and Ethnicity In Modern Britain* (1995). He is currently working with colleagues on a volume exploring the recruitment and retention of minority ethnic groups into nursing and midwifery training. He is joint editor of *Sociology*, the journal of the British Sociological Association.

**Panikos Panayi** is a Reader in History at De Montfort University in Leicester and a fellow of the Institut für Migrationsforschung und Interkulturelle Studien at the University of Osnabrück in Germany. His main area of research has consisted of the history of ethnic minorities, particularly within Britain, but also Germany, Europe and internationally. His major publications include *The Enemy in Our Midst: Germans in Britain During the First World War* (1991), *Immigration, Ethnicity and Racism in Britain, 1815–1945* (1994), and *German Immigrants in Britain During the Nineteenth Century* (1995). His current work includes a documentary history of immigration into postwar Britain and a history of race in Germany since 1800. He is also the editor of a series of books entitled *Themes in Modern German History*.

**Ann Phoenix** works in the Department of Psychology at Birkbeck College, University of London. She held the Ribbius Peletier Visiting Professor at the University for Humanist Studies, Utrecht, Netherlands, 1997–98. Her research interests include motherhood and the social identities of young people, particularly those associated with gender, race, social class and adoption. Her publications include *Young Mothers?* (1991); *Motherhood: Meanings, Practices and Ideologies* (jointly edited with Anne Wollett and Eva Lloyd, 1991); *Black, White or Mixed Race?* (with Barbara Tizard, 1993); and *Crossfires: Nationalism, Racism and Gender in Europe* (jointly edited with Helma Lutz and Nira Yuval-Davis, 1995).

**John Solomos** is Professor of Sociology in the Faculty of Humanities and Social Science at South Bank University. Before that he was Professor of Sociology and Social Policy at the University of Southampton, and he has previously worked at the Centre for Research in Ethnic Relations, University of Warwick and Birkbeck College, University of London. Among his publications are *Black Youth, Racism and the State* (1988), *Race and Racism in Britain* (1993), *Race, Politics and Social Change* (with Les Back, 1995) and *Racism and Society* (with Les Back, 1996).

**Rupert Taylor** is a Senior Lecturer in the Department of Political Science at the University of the Witwatersrand, Johannesburg. His fields of interest include: 'race', ethnicity and nationalism in South Africa; political violence in South Africa; and the Northern Ireland conflict. He is currently directing a major research project on 'Peace and Conflict Resolution Organisations in the South African Transition'. Publications include articles in *The Economic and Social Review*, *Telos*, *The Round Table*, *Race and Class*, *Transformation* and *South African Sociological Review*.

# Acknowledgements

This project has grown out of our collaboration in editing the journal *Ethnic and Racial Studies*, and specifically the special issue on 'Teaching Race and Ethnicity: Disciplinary Perspectives' (Volume 19, 4, 1996). This edited collection has developed from that special issue, with all the chapters substantively revised and four new ones added. As with all aspects of producing the journal we, and the authors, have benefited greatly from the editorial advice of Guida Crowley, Managing Editor of *Ethnic and Racial Studies*. Producing an edited volume such as this one means relying on the support and indulgence of all the contributors and we have been fortunate in working with this group of authors. We are also grateful to all our authors for keeping to their deadlines and producing chapters that address some of the key questions and dilemmas that are faced by those teaching and researching in this field. We have also relied on the help and advice of our publishers, Mari Shullaw and Geraldine Williams, who have borne unforeseen delays with patience and a sense of humour.

The figures first appeared in *The Archaeology of Ethnicity: Constructing Identities in the Past and Present*, Siân Jones (1997), Routledge.

# Introduction

*Martin Bulmer and John Solomos*

*Ethnic and Racial Studies Today* is a collection of essays that, taken together, seek to provide a rounded approach to the study of ethnicity and race in the contemporary intellectual environment. This is an ever changing field and we have aimed to provide an overview of more recent trends and developments, whilst not ignoring the need to locate the present in a historical framework. Whilst we do not see this volume as a complete overview of this field it can be seen as an intellectual intervention in the key disciplines and fields of research that have helped to transform the study of race and ethnicity in recent times. By bringing together the views of both more established and younger scholars we have attempted to give voice to a diverse range of views and perspectives, and this should become clear as you follow the arguments to be found in specific chapters.

We hope that by bringing these essays together in one accessible volume we can help to guide both the specialist and the non-specialist reader through the variety of theoretical and empirical studies that have emerged in recent times. The growth of research and scholarship about issues of race and ethnicity has been obvious and much commented upon in recent years Stephen Howe, for example, has argued somewhat provocatively that 'issues of race, ethnicity and gender have become the central preoccupations of debate, to a considerable degree displacing preoccupation with class and economics' (Howe, 1992: 36). Writing from the perspective of literary theory, Appiah and Gates have gone even further by commenting that race, class and gender have become 'the holy trinity of literary criticism' (1995: 1). Comments such as this highlight the perception that the study of race and ethnicity has moved from the margins of academic life to the very core of the curriculum that we teach in disciplines as diverse as sociology, geography, anthropology, political science, literary theory, history and beyond. The development of new courses at both undergraduate and postgraduate levels has proceeded apace and this has resulted in an increased number of student-centred texts being produced (Solomos and Back, 1996; Cornell and Hartmann, 1998). In addition, a growing number of research students is specialising in issues such as race, ethnicity and nationalism and there has been a noticeable expansion in the number of monographs, textbooks and journals published by mainstream publishers.

## The salience of race and ethnicity

It is ironic that it has taken until nearly the end of the twentieth century for race, ethnicity and nationalism to receive this degree of academic attention. W. E. B. Du Bois predicted in 1902 that the problem of the twentieth century would be the problem of the colour line. The salience of race and ethnicity was, indeed, apparent in many contexts as the century moved forward. Western colonialism with its domination of non-European peoples, nationalist movements which arose against colonial rule, the dynamics of race relations in the United States and South Africa, the mass-migration of non-European peoples to industrial societies across the world, all pointed to the centrality of race and ethnicity as major social phenomena. Such societies and forms of social relations were studied by some sociologists, social anthropologists and a smaller number of historians, but many, though not all these scholars, were at the margins of their disciplines. Over the years, some notable influential textbooks appeared, for example by Cox (1948), Hughes *et al.* (1952), Frazier (1957), Smith (1965), Banton (1967), Barth (1969), Blalock (1967), Mason (1967), van den Berghe (1967), Rex (1970) and Wilson (1973). In sociology, however, 'race' has only comparatively recently come to be regarded as a central category in sociological theory (cf Stone, 1977). What is perhaps most distinctive about the present conjuncture is not only this much wider recognition of the theoretical centrality of race and ethnicity, but the spread of this recognition well beyond the traditional triumvirate of sociology, social anthropology and history into many other disciplines.

It needs to be remembered that this expansion in research and teaching has taken place at a time when there has been a noticeable growth of research on these issues. Scholars from a variety of disciplines and perspectives have begun to address race and ethnic issues as key facets of contemporary societies in different parts of the globe. In countries as diverse in their social and political make-up as the United States, France, Germany, Britain, Australia and beyond, we have seen the growth of specialised research centres and groups, and a growth in the number of individual scholars who have chosen to concentrate their research efforts on the changing morphology of racial and ethnic relations. This growing interest in questions of race and ethnicity has been the main factor behind the recent proliferation of new journals which seek in one way or another to explore the impact of these questions from a variety of theoretical and empirical perspectives.

## Changing agendas and perspectives

It is against this background that we decided to produce *Ethnic and Racial Studies Today*.[1] In particular, we wanted to focus on questions about why and how the study of race and ethnicity has changed in a range of disciplines and how these changes relate to new research agendas and social and political transformations in contemporary societies. We felt that this focus was justified because, despite the rapid expansion of courses about race and ethnicity in recent years, there has been relatively little reflexivity and discussion about both the content of what is taught and the pedagogic strategies which are used in different disciplines. With these key concerns in mind we asked our contributors to provide us with a critical analysis of (i) the main trends and changes in their own disciplines and (ii) an account of what issues are likely to come to prominence in the future. In addition, we asked them to reflect on the role of dialogue and exchange of ideas between disciplines and the emergence of new theories and perspectives which challenge established boundaries and discourses about race and ethnicity.

Our feeling was that the time was right to reflect back on important developments over the past few decades as well as look forward to the new issues that we are likely to face in the future. The papers produced in response to our invitations fully confirm our original sense that the time was ripe to address this question. As should be clear from the individual chapters there has, indeed, been intense debate in various disciplines over the past two decades or so. One measure of the intensity of these debates is the attempts to develop critical perspectives that broaden the boundaries of race and ethnic studies. These critical approaches have been influenced by theoretical perspectives ranging from neo-Marxism, feminism, cultural studies, post-modernism, post-colonial theory and other perspectives. The proliferation of new critical perspectives has radically transformed the whole field of race and ethnic studies in ways which make it difficult to see it as a single recognisable field. But these very new approaches can also be seen as providing some of the impetus for new research agendas and new approaches to teaching.

It is not surprising therefore that ideas about race, racism and ethnicity have become the subject of intense debate and controversy. It seems that almost everybody is talking about the role of racial and ethnic categorisation in the construction of social and political identities. Yet it is paradoxically the case that there is still much confusion about what it is that we mean by the use of concepts such as race and racism, as evidenced by the range of terminological debates that have tended to dominate much discussion in recent years (Goldberg, 1993; Miles, 1993; Solomos and Back, 1996). It is perhaps partly the result of this focus on terminology that much of the academic debate in this field has remained somewhat abstract and unsatisfactory.

Another focus of attention has been the questions of citizenship and of what are the boundaries of a society. Legal, political and social definitions of citizenship have varied in different societies, very often excluding wholly, or in part, members of certain racial and ethnic groups. In the recent past, T. H. Marshall's original formulation of citizenship in terms of social class (1950) has been reapplied to the issue of racial and ethnic diversity, to ask what has been the fate of those who do not enjoy full citizenship in the present. What is the citizenship status of migrants and the descendants of migrants (see Soysal, 1994)? What is the structure of ethnic relations in 'civil society' in states formerly under the near-total dominance of the state, such as those of Eastern Europe or South Africa (see Adam and Moodley, 1993; Gellner, 1994)? What is the basis of racial, ethnic and cultural cleavage and conflict in societies as various as Sri Lanka, Fiji, Guyana, Belgium, Canada and Northern Ireland, and their implications for the rights of members of different groups? What are the implications of the greater recognition in the recent past of the rights of various minority groups (such as aboriginal peoples in Australia and Canada, or religious minorities variously) for inclusion in the society? What is the significance of shifts such as Spanish becoming a second language in the formerly monolingual United States? What is the structural situation of what some have termed a black 'underclass' within industrial societies (see Wilson, 1996)?

The rapid expansion of teaching and research on racial and ethnic questions draws strongly upon the evident resurgence of conflicts which are based in one way or another on racial, ethnic or national identities. They take different forms in different parts of the world, whether the former Soviet Union, former Yugoslavia, the Middle East, and so on. For example, the impact of racist and nationalist political movements within Western and Eastern Europe during the 1990s is a clear example of this pattern. Processes such as this have, in turn, stimulated the interest of students and researchers, particularly when faced with the need to explain the causes and impact of 'new' forms of racial and ethnic conflict, the resurgence of racist ideas and movements and related phenomena. Whatever the external factors, however, it is also clear that internal processes within academic life have also pushed racial and ethnic issues on to the core curriculum. These include pressures arising from intellectual debates and trends, the demands of a changing student body and the challenge of new areas of research. One facet of these pressures has been the argument that there is a need to transform the university curriculum so that it covers issues that go beyond Eurocentric perspectives and reflect the increasingly diverse and multicultural composition of the student body. The so-called 'multicultural wars' in the United States over the past decade or so are one aspect of this debate within academic institutions about the boundaries and content of what is taught within universities (Ferguson *et al.*, 1990; Carby, 1992; Gates, 1992a).

A key concern of these approaches has been the need to show that race and ethnicity are not 'natural' categories, even though both concepts are often represented as if they were (Appiah, 1989). Their boundaries are not fixed, nor is their membership uncontested. Racial and ethnic groups, like nations, are imagined communities. They are ideological entities, made and changed in struggle. They are discursive formations, signalling a language through which differences are accorded social significance, may be named and explained. But what is of importance for us, as social researchers studying race and ethnicity, is that such ideas also carry with them material consequences for those who are included within, or excluded from, them.

It has to be noted as well that, although these debates have taken place within the academy, they have also been shaped by wider political considerations. They are seen not just in terms of the content of what is taught in universities but in terms of power relations within society. The discussion about multiculturalism and feminism has highlighted the linkages that often exist between trends within the academy and political conflicts in society. As Charles Taylor notes in his chapter on what he calls 'the politics of recognition', contemporary debates about multiculturalism and feminism involve a critique of political power relations as well as scholarship:

> Not only contemporary feminism but also race relations and discussions of multiculturalism are undergirded by the premise that the withholding of recognition can be a form of oppression.
> (Taylor *et al.*, 1992: 36)

Given the often highly politicised and controversial nature of debates about race and ethnicity it is not surprising that contemporary debates are often couched in terms of political and policy concerns. A key preoccupation in some recent discussions has been to highlight the political and ethical dilemmas which are intimately involved in research on race and ethnicity. These wider political considerations need to be borne in mind in looking at the transformations in scholarship and teaching which are highlighted in the individual chapters included in this volume. Indeed, it would be impossible to provide a coherent explanation for the expansion of race and ethnicity as a field of teaching and research without an awareness of some of these broader trends.

## New contexts and agendas

Part of the dilemma that is faced by all of us who teach and carry out research on racial and ethnic questions is that it is intrinsically difficult to remain completely aloof from the everyday political and policy debates which are part of this field. That is to say, no matter how much we aim to address these questions from a perspective which is academically justifiable and methodologically sound we are inevitably faced with questions about both why we focus our teaching on some issues and not on others, why we carry out research in the first place and what benefits result from our teaching and research. This is not to say, of course, that such questions do not arise in relation to other fields, but merely to emphasise that teaching on race and ethnicity cannot easily be divorced from direct encounters with political and ethical dilemmas.

At the core of these dilemmas is the role of race and ethnic categorisation in shaping social and political relations in society. Another way to make this point is to say that at the heart of contemporary discourses about race and ethnicity there lie questions about social and political inequality, what it means to 'belong' or to be excluded from particular collectivities. Take, for example, the question of 'citizenship rights' in societies that are becoming increasingly multicultural. Within both popular and academic discourse there is growing evidence of concern about how questions of citizenship need to be reconceptualized in the context of multicultural societies. Indeed, in contemporary European societies this can be seen as one of the questions with which governments of various kinds are trying to come to terms. Some important elements of this debate are the issue of the political rights of minorities, including the issue of representation in both local and national politics, and the position of minority religious and cultural rights in societies which are becoming more diverse. Underlying all these concerns is the much more thorny issue of what, if anything, can be done to protect the rights of minorities, and develop extensive notions of citizenship and democracy that include those minorities that are excluded on racial and ethnic criteria.

In attempting to rethink the question of how we teach race and ethnicity it is necessary to remember therefore that at the present time we are confronted both by questions about academic scholarship as well as by much broader questions. Namely: how can courses on race and ethnicity reflect the changing forms of racial and ethnic relations in contemporary societies? What do we aim to achieve through our teaching? How can we develop ways of addressing race and ethnic issues in ways which challenge rather than confirm common-sense images? In substance much of the recent discussion about race and ethnicity comes back to such questions, though as will become clear from the accounts in this volume it is by no means the case that all of them have been adequately resolved.

It also needs to be emphasised that the higher profile of race and ethnic issues in the curriculum has by no means been universally welcomed. Part of the confusion which has arisen in recent years is that there has been a tendency to see the greater emphasis on race and ethnic issues as part of some wider trend towards what is called 'political correctness'. Many of the most strident critics of 'political correctness' see the very aim of including multicultural and feminist perspectives in the curriculum as both misguided and a danger to the maintenance of academic standards and values (D'Souza, 1991). Such criticisms, however, tell us little about the diversity of issues which are actually covered in courses concerned with questions about race, racism and ethnicity.

In fashioning this volume we have inevitably been selective and we have not covered the whole spectrum of subjects within the social sciences and humanities where race and ethnicity are taught as key components of the curriculum. Indeed, a notable feature of the changes that we have seen over the past decade or so in this field is that questions about race and ethnicity are now covered in a much wider range of disciplines and fields of study. We are aware, however, that the teaching of race and ethnic issues has undergone tremendous changes in a range of disciplines that we were not able to cover in this volume. It is a noticeable feature of recent academic debates, for example, that much interesting theoretical and empirical work is being carried out in fields such as cultural studies, literary theory, archaeology and modern languages among others. Indeed it is quite clear that many of the dilemmas and problems raised in this volume have preoccupied scholars and researchers in a whole range of humanities and social science disciplines (Bhattacharyya, 1996).

An additional issue that has to be taken into account is that at the heart of some of the most interesting research on issues such as race, ethnicity and gender is a conscious attempt to cross boundaries in the academy and use multidisciplinary insights in developing new research agendas. This is a phenomenon that has become more marked in recent years, as scholarship on diverse aspects of such issues as race, ethnicity and gender has used a consciously multidisciplinary approach. This is something which needs to be welcomed and which is likely to lead to much fruitful research collaboration in the future.

## Situating the key arguments

The substantive essays in this collection explore the changing context of teaching about race and ethnicity from a variety of disciplinary and conceptual perspectives. More importantly, however, they illustrate the lively nature of trends and developments over the past decade or so and the dilemmas which face us as researchers and teachers. At a broad level, of course, it is evident that there have been quite noticeable transformations in how race and ethnicity are researched and taught in all the disciplines covered in this volume. It has also become clear, particularly over the past decade, that researchers and teachers are making use of theoretical and empirical research outside of their own immediate disciplinary specialisms. It is partly in order to illustrate the changes that have taken place over the past two decades that we seek in this collection both to reflect past trends as well as to suggest the likely routes of future developments.

As a number of the chapters in this volume make clear it is also the case that there are crucial theoretical and political differences about both how race and ethnicity are researched and how they are taught. This point is perhaps best illustrated by David Mason's lucid account of the changing agendas within sociology about what it is that is taught under the broad rubric of race and ethnicity (Chapter 1). Mason's account emphasises the importance of a sociological perspective for any rounded analysis of both the origins and contemporary forms of racial and ethnic relations, but he also seeks to highlight the changing boundaries of sociological analysis in this field. Perhaps the central theme that comes across in his analysis is the extraordinary diversity of theories and perspectives about the role of race and ethnicity within contemporary societies and the increasingly important influence of perspectives which emphasise gender and difference. He argues, for example, that in recent years sociological texts have been heavily influenced by approaches emanating from other fields, including politics and cultural studies.

Chapter 2 by Linda Martín Alcoff explores issues that tie up with many of the concerns evident in Mason's chapter. In a challenging account of recent philosophical debates she reflects on the seeming irony arising from the fact that race is seen as having 'no semantic respectability, biological basis, or philosophical legitimacy' while at the same time 'race, or racialised identities have as much political, sociological and economic salience as they ever had'. Engaging with the work of Anthony Appiah and Paul Gilroy, among others, she argues forcefully that it is precisely because race is such a slippery concept that it serves as a means for converting contingent attributes, such as skin colour, into essential bases for identities. But this is not to deny that race remains, at the level of everyday experience and social representation, a potent political and social category around which individuals and groups organise their identity and construct a politics. As such, race is socially constructed; and blackness and whiteness are not categories of essence but defined by historical and political struggles over their meaning.

Chapter 3 by Caroline Knowles explores a particular facet of this process, by looking at the uses of historiography in the construction of narratives of race and nation in the context of Canadian history. Taking her cue from Foucault's writings on the development of the human sciences Knowles explores both the specific narratives of history with which she is concerned and the broader question of how ideas about race are the product of particular processes which give them specific meanings. Weaving together historical evidence and sociological theorising she seeks to show that ideas about race are crucially about the representation of difference. From this perspective categories such as race and ethnicity are best conceived as political identities, that are used by both dominant and subordinate groups for the purposes of legitimising and furthering their own social identities and interests. In this context, Knowles argues, it is important to remember that identities based on race and ethnicity are not simply imposed but are the end-product of complex interactions between a variety of political and social processes.

Panikos Panayi's account in Chapter 4 of trends and developments in historical writings adopts a comparative perspective and explores the changing terms of historiographical research on immigration and race in Britain and the USA. Panayi, writing as one of a group of younger British historians who have done much to transform the study of immigration and race, explores an astonishing range of material from scholars on both sides of the Atlantic and outlines the changing contours of historical writing as well as situating the key preoccupations of some of the most influential researchers. Two key themes emerge from Panayi's account. First, the relative richness of historical research in the USA as compared to Britain. Second, he points to the broadening out of research agendas that has occurred in recent times as the number of studies in this field has grown.

Chapter 5 by Gargi Bhattacharyya provides interesting insights into the changing terms of debate about race and ethnicity within cultural studies. This is a field that has been an important site for much of the more innovative and challenging thinking about race and ethnicity in recent times. A whole new generation of scholars has begun to carve out their own particular understandings of how popular culture and literature frame our understanding of racialised groups and cultures. Bhattacharyya starts her account of her experiences of teaching race in cultural studies by suggesting that far from being a uniform discipline 'cultural studies' actually refers to 'a disparate morass of social science and humanities practice'. This is by no means a description with which everybody will be comfortable. But Bhattacharyya's provocative account has the advantage that it signals from the beginning the importance of representation in the construction of race as a social category. For her race and ethnicity are discursive formations, signalling a language through which differences are accorded social as well as academic significance. But she also suggests that there is a need for researchers in this field to understand the political importance of 'race-studying', particularly in the present volatile environment.

The need to place understandings of ethnicity and race within particular cultural contexts is also a theme that is taken up from the perspective of anthropology by Richard Jenkins (Chapter 6). Taking his cue from the influential writings of Barth and Geertz he seeks to show that anthropological accounts of ethnicity have much to offer students as well as those concerned with the salience of ethnic, racial and national identities in the wider social and political environment. Pointing to the need 'to relativise notions about ethnicity and to resist the naturalisation of ethnic identity and nationalist ideology', he seeks to demonstrate the role of anthropology in providing a challenge to fixed and unchanging notions of culture and identity, whether codified in terms of race or ethnicity.

In Chapter 7 Karen Henwood and Ann Phoenix explore some of the usages of race in research and scholarship in psychology and the impact that these usages have had on debates about how to teach issues such as IQ, prejudice and discrimination, and related questions. Given the recent controversy about the question of race and IQ in the aftermath of Richard Herrnstein and Charles Murray's *The Bell Curve* we perhaps need no reminding of the controversial nature of debates about race in psychology (Herrnstein and Murray, 1994). What Henwood and Phoenix seek to do, however, is to look beyond public controversies and outline the complex positionings of both teachers and students in relation to courses about race and racism within psychology. In doing so they provide an account of the complexities of teaching such issues as IQ to black and white students, in a context which makes them both politically controversial as well as likely to cause offence and anger among some students.

The political constructions of race and ethnicity are the focus of Chapter 8 by Rupert Taylor. Focusing on the encounter between political science as a discipline and questions about race and ethnicity in the period since the late 1960s, he offers an overview of the ways in which political scientists working from a variety of perspectives have sought to give questions about race and ethnicity a more central role in the discipline. Given the relative importance of recent political accounts of contemporary race relations, a phenomenon also noted by Mason, this chapter provides a clear demonstration of the centrality of politics in the development of racial and ethnic identities.

Maria Lauret's account in Chapter 9 of the impact of race and ethnicity in the field of English studies links up with a number of the other chapters in this volume, particularly Bhattacharyya's, by highlighting the role of feminism and cultural studies in transforming research and teaching in this field. Beginning her account by locating the study of English within the colonial and post-colonial moments Lauret suggests that the recent engagement of the discipline with questions of race and ethnicity has produced at best a limited, and in places, ambiguous, impact. She highlights in particular the continued domination of certain taken-for-granted assumptions about the boundaries of English as a field of study.

The crossovers and dialogues between and within disciplines is perhaps one of the key concerns of a number of the chapters in this volume. This is best illustrated in Alastair Bonnett's critical account in Chapter 10 of the achievements and limitations of recent developments in the study of race and ethnicity within geography, suggesting that most of the really influential studies of race and ethnicity within geography are the product of a dialogue with theoretical and empirical perspectives emanating from cultural studies and sociology. Pitching his argument around the provocative suggestion that geographers of race need to abandon the 'geographical perspective', Bonnett, nevertheless, seeks to demonstrate the importance of a spatial dimension to the construction of racial and ethnic identities.

Finally Chapter 11 by Siân Jones provides an account of a field that is somewhat outside of the mainstream of race and ethnic studies, namely archaeology. Yet as she argues this is in many ways a field of study that has been from the beginning concerned with the attribution of racial and ethnic labels to archaeological remains. She explores the history of archaeological modes of classification from the nineteenth century in some detail and shows that the origin of many of the ideas in the discipline about 'racial' and 'ethnic' diversity can be traced back to the formative stages of the development of archaeology as a field of study. Jones also highlights the complex ways in which questions of 'origin' and 'territory' have become deeply politicised issues in the present environment.

## Whither the study of race and ethnicity?

The accounts of the changing face of research and scholarship that are outlined in this volume provide us with a range of views of what has happened, and not happened, in recent years, and profile some of the trends that are likely to have a direct impact on how we research and teach race and ethnic issues in the near future. The heterogeneity of approaches is evident, and it is likely that the proliferation of intellectual frameworks for analysis will continue. There is no prospect of integrating the different approaches through a single discipline, though there will continue to be a variety of linked groupings of scholars who will share a common approach to the subject either within particular disciplines, or across disciplines. There will continue to be a variety of competing approaches. We may hope that as well as generating perspectives which allow different theoretical approaches to be systematically compared and evaluated, students will be encouraged to apply these approaches empirically and test their explanatory power vis-à-vis rival approaches in particular real world situations.

Perhaps one of the key conclusions that may be drawn from the arguments outlined at greater length in specific chapters in this volume is that we need to attend more to the question of what it is that we do when we teach or research questions of race and ethnicity. All of the chapters in this volume raise important questions for all of us who are actively engaged in research and teaching about race and ethnicity. They help to highlight some of the processes that have helped to firmly establish race and ethnic issues as important issues for scholarly exploration in the social sciences and humanities. But they also suggest important limitations, both in terms of theory and empirical research, that need to be understood and explored. We hope that in bringing them together in this volume we shall encourage more discussion and debate about both the content and the boundaries of 'race' and 'ethnicity'.

## Note

1 This volume grows out of a special issue of *Ethnic and Racial Studies* on 'Teaching Race and Ethnicity: Disciplinary Perspectives' (Volume 19, 4, 1996). In addition to the revised versions of the papers in this special issue we have added new chapters by Linda Martín Alcoff, Maria Lauret, Gargi Bhattacharyya and Siân Jones.

# 1 The continuing significance of race?

## Teaching ethnic and racial studies in sociology

*David Mason*

Writing about the teaching of race[1] and ethnicity in sociology is no easy task. In part this is because accurate and up-to-date information about trends in teaching and curricula practice, even in one's own country, is difficult to come by. As a result, it has been necessary to draw such conclusions as are possible from published sources and in particular from the contents both of specialist texts and general introductions to sociology as a subject.

More generally the task is greatly complicated by the interpenetration of sociology with the contributions of other subjects such as psychology. As we shall see, this multi-disciplinary approach has been especially evident in the United States from an early stage. In particular, there has been a continuing emphasis in many of the major texts on the analysis and dynamics of individual prejudice, a focus almost absent from British discussions. In Britain, by contrast, early developments tended to be framed, with a few notable exceptions, within a more sociologically imperialist climate. However, as we shall see, while the multi-disciplinary thrust of US texts has been maintained, in Britain increasing interdisciplinarity has emerged from the developing theoretical climate of the late 1980s and early 1990s. At the time of writing it is difficult to distinguish books claiming a sociological treatment from those whose focus is more centrally on political processes (Solomos, 1993) or those drawing on cultural studies (Gilroy, 1987; Brah, 1996).[2]

## Early trends

In 1968, the American sociologist Peter I. Rose published a volume entitled *The Subject is Race*. It reported on a study, undertaken in 1966, of the teaching of issues of race and ethnicity in institutions of higher education in the United States of America. The book's purpose was conceived more widely than simply to report on the teaching of race and ethnicity in the contemporary United States. Rather it was Rose's intention to investigate in more general terms the interface between curricula developments and wider political and social processes, using race as a case study.

Nevertheless, Rose's study provides a useful starting point for the present discussion. At one level it provides a prototype for analyses of patterns of teaching in the field. At another, it constitutes something of a baseline against which to interpret the changes which have taken place since it was undertaken and in terms of which to make cross-national comparisons.

For the purposes of the present chapter, Rose's analysis exhibits a number of features which provide enduring counterpoints with the features which have characterised British curricula in the field. In addition, it provides an interesting case study in the influence of external socio-political forces on the academy. As we shall see, these influences have been of considerable significance in structuring the teaching of race and ethnicity in Britain and the United States, as indeed elsewhere.

Rose argued that US studies of race had their origins in the Chicago School, with its analyses of migration and the rapid growth of urban societies. Partly as a result, cultural differences appear to have been given considerable prominence in the courses surveyed by Rose (1968: 3). Nevertheless, a significant factor in prioritising the study of race and the development of courses at undergraduate level was, he argued, the so-called 'Negro revolution' of the post-Second-World-War period and, in particular, the Civil Rights movement. Course content, then, reflected recent upheavals in American society and, indeed, more than 50 per cent of the staff teaching such courses were said to be personally involved in contemporary political struggles (ibid.: 120–1). Despite these influences however, Rose's analysis also drew attention to a considerable degree of time lapse in the design of courses. Thus many institutions were, in 1966, still teaching courses on lines designed by Park, Wirth and Burgess at Chicago some twenty-five years earlier (ibid.: 9). Moreover, notwithstanding the significance of contemporary events in stimulating courses, one in three had not changed in the five years preceding the survey (ibid.: 98).

A number of other features of the character and content of courses revealed by Rose's survey are relevant to the theme of this chapter. The most frequent titles for courses were 'American Minorities' and 'Race and Ethnic Relations', or close variants on these (ibid.: 95). These titles appear to reflect a number of characteristics of the American situation. In particular, they indicate a consciousness of diversity which to some degree flowed from the experience of building a nation from a diverse mix of immigrant groups and which was manifested sociologically in the work of the Chicago School. Related to this is a consciousness, expressed albeit clumsily in the distinction between race and ethnicity, of the crucial differences between the experience of what Blauner was later to call voluntary and forced migration (Blauner, 1972). Indeed, the heritage of slavery was an issue of particular concern, as it had been for the Chicago School (Rose, 1968: 4–5). Finally, these titles seem to reflect both the somewhat earlier discovery (or rediscovery) of ethnicity in the United States when compared with Britain and a recognition that minority cultures themselves contributed to the construction and maintenance of diversity – though this could all too easily spill over into a victim-blaming form of explanation (see the discussion in Rainwater and Yancey, 1967). In this connection we should note that, despite the plurality expressed in these titles, the majority of courses focused on what was characterised as 'the Negro community'. Most also focused primarily, if not exclusively, on the United States (Rose, 1968: 95).

The study revealed that few courses were entitled 'The Psychology of Prejudice' as they might have been had they reflected the concerns of the 1940s and 1950s (ibid.: 95). Nevertheless, Rose described the courses as for the most part quite eclectic in content. Among the topics still prominent were 'the physical anthropology of race' and 'prejudice and racial attitudes' (ibid.: 124–6). Among the most widely used texts were Gordon Allport's *The Nature of Prejudice* and George Simpson and J. Milton Yinger's *Racial and Cultural Minorities*, the latter appearing as the key text in 24 per cent of cases (ibid.: 139ff.).

At about the time that Rose was conducting his survey, in the UK Michael Banton was completing work on his influential book *Race Relations* (1967). Banton's was one of the first British books that might legitimately be described as a text on race and ethnicity. Although written by a sociologist, it was distinguished by its attempt at a wide-ranging approach to its subject matter, taking in historical, anthropological, psychological and sociological perspectives. It was, moreover, comparative, including chapters on 'race relations' in a range of societies including the Americas, South Africa and Great Britain. These features were shared by the M.Sc. in Race Relations which Banton founded at the University of Bristol in 1970.

Banton's book, then, shared features with, but also differed from, many of the courses in the United States described by Rose. It was characterised by a degree of eclecticism (in the positive sense of that term) and by a willingness to consider the contributions of disciplines other than sociology. Its breadth of coverage was not, however, uncritical. Thus, for example, its treatment of physical anthropology was concerned as much as anything else to demonstrate the scientific invalidity of the concept of race.[3] In contrast with many of the courses described by Rose, however, it was self-consciously comparative in its focus. It did not, on the other hand, make systematic attempts to describe minority cultures or social structures in any great detail.

The publication of Banton's text was part of an upsurge of interest in issues of race in British sociology. Of particular importance was the 1969 British Sociological Association Annual Conference which was focused around the theme. The conference witnessed lively debates both about the status of 'race relations' as a field of study and about the appropriate way of conceptualising racism. Many of the key contributions were subsequently published in a volume edited by Sami Zubaida (1970) which was itself to acquire textbook status on many of the new courses at advanced undergraduate and postgraduate level in British sociology departments. One of the contributions to the volume was subsequently expanded by its author, John Rex, into a full-length volume which was to come to compete with Banton's, notably in more theoretically oriented courses (Rex, 1970). Moreover, many of the central themes of the debates initiated at the conference were to reappear from time to time, in different guises, over the ensuing quarter century and are still being played out at the time of writing, even though fashions in both theorising and teaching have undergone a number of transformations.

A further indication of the significance of this period for the development of the subject is that, in 1970, the journal *Race* carried a report of a meeting held in London to conduct informal discussions concerning the appropriate way to teach issues of race (Downing, 1970). The shape of the debate was almost certainly influenced by the pattern of participation and it would be unwise to conclude too much from the report about the state of opinion among teachers of sociology more generally. Indeed, the tone of the piece suggests that at least some key potential contributors were either not present or their views not reported. Nevertheless, the report contains some interesting insights into the perspectives of the participants, most of whom it was reported were sociologists. Indeed, a central issue appears to have been the question of what constituted the appropriate content of a course on the *sociology* of race relations.

A key point of agreement was that sociology courses should *not* be geared to the production of workers in the field. It appears that there was a strongly held view that to accept this role would mean accepting the definitions of the situation provided by organisations in the field of social policy such as the Community Relations Commission (the forerunner of the Commission for Racial Equality) (Downing, 1970: 100–1). In particular, there was a strong consensus, reflecting the political debates of the period, that the starting point of sociological concerns should most certainly not be the alleged problem of immigration[4] (1970: 101). Nevertheless, there was also an acknowledgement that many students were motivated to study the subject by their desire to be involved in the struggle for racial equality. It appears there were differences of view on the degree to which this should be encouraged as well as on the role of research in the same project (ibid.: 100).

At a theoretical level, there seems to have been a degree of consensus about the need to alert students to the significance of the 'imperial factor in world history'. Yet participants also appear to have placed different emphases on the relative importance of class and imperialism, with some arguing that the intersection of class and imperialism could be conceptualised by focusing on the centrality of unfree labour. As at the BSA conference referred to above, the question of whether or not a special theory was required continued to loom large (ibid.: 101).

A discussion of some importance, given subsequent developments, seems to have been the issue of whether or not 'race relations' was an appropriate title. In arguments that prefigured a subsequently emerging orthodoxy, some of those present suggested that this label was in danger of legitimating the concept of race and hence racism. Others argued that, whatever title was adopted, it was essential to focus upon the role of white institutional racism as the key dynamic factor.

At the end of the 1960s, then, there appears to have been a number of interesting points of contrast between the situation in the US and the UK so far as the teaching of race and ethnicity in sociology was concerned. If the evidence of the 1969 BSA conference and the subsequent London meeting are to be believed, there was a greater tendency towards a socio-logical exclusivism in Britain than appears to have been the case in the United States. In part this almost certainly reflects the political context in which the subject came to prominence in Britain. Developing later, it was clearly stimulated by the growth of immigration from the countries of the former British empire in the 1950s and 1960s. Sociologists were, however, concerned not to take on the political agenda of those who saw such immi-gration as a problem. They were keen to ensure that the focus was on the structural determinants of migration and the political context of devel-oping agitation for restrictions. In rejecting explanations rooted either in individual prejudice or in the characteristics of migrants themselves, they were assisted by developments in the United States.[5] There the Civil Rights movement and the emergence of Black Power had brought to prominence explanations of racial oppression which were rooted in the structural char-acteristics of American society. Nowhere was this better summed up than in the idea of institutional racism (Carmichael and Hamilton, 1968). Whatever difficulties there were with this concept (see Mason, 1982; Williams, 1985), it had the effect of ensuring that the focus was firmly on white institutions and practices rather than individual beliefs. More gener-ally, despite clear differences between Britain and the United States in the precise focus of sociological approaches to race and ethnicity, it is clear that the practice of borrowing, some would argue uncritically, concepts and theoretical perspectives from the United States has remained a common feature of the British scene. This was to some extent reinforced in the 1970s and 1980s by the tendency of black people in Britain to seek to learn lessons from their US counterparts (for a discussion of these issues see Small, 1994, especially pp. 4–6).

## Continuities and transformations

My purpose in focusing upon the situation in the late 1960s and early 1970s in Britain and the United States, as revealed by contemporary documents, has been to suggest that these early developments established a pattern on which subsequent trends have been built. They indicate how both contemporary political concerns and national differences play a key role in structuring the curriculum. Moreover, as we shall see, they also indicate that the inertia of the academy, at least so far as course content is concerned, was not confined to the time and place of Rose's early study.

## Political context

We noted above the importance of political influences both on the situation surveyed by Rose and on the development of the teaching of race and ethnicity in Britain. Further aspects of this political influencing of the curriculum will be addressed below. For the moment, it will suffice to note that both continuities and shifts of emphasis have been associated with, if not directly traceable to, the wider social and political context in both the United States and Britain.

In the United States, the continuing and sharpening struggle for racial equality had the effect of ensuring that the teaching of race and ethnicity became both more widespread and central to the curriculum. It also saw the shifts in the organisation of teaching towards curricula more explicitly responsive to growing minority self-assertiveness (as in the growth of ethnic studies or black studies programmes) and towards new theoretical perspectives such as those associated with Afrocentrism.

In Britain, a key socio-political event structuring developments in the academic study of race was the election of a Conservative government in 1979, with an agenda which explicitly questioned all policies and programmes centred on collectively defined entities. At the same time, the growing political assertiveness of members of minority ethnic groups, and the urban disorders of the first half of 1980s, influenced the shape of much academic work, some of which came to assume a key place in the sociological curriculum (see the discussion in Jewson and Mason, 1994). A study conducted under the auspices of the Council for National Academic Awards (CNAA) in 1986, for example, concluded that the two most widely used books in undergraduate courses on 'race relations' were Charles Husband's *'Race' in Britain* (1982) and The Centre for Contemporary Cultural Studies, *The Empire Strikes Back* (1982) (Council for National Academic Awards, 1988: 40–1). Both of these volumes can be said to exhibit a broadly radical and critical approach to the issues, with the CCCS volume being framed within a broadly Marxist perspective of a kind which exerted considerable influence in British sociology in the late 1970s and early 1980s.[6] The prominence of these volumes, particularly given that the second is both theoretically difficult and written in a less than accessible style, may well further attest to the significance of current political fashions relative to pedagogical considerations in the selection of course material. In this connection, we may also note that works by

Robert Miles and John Rex also featured prominently on reading lists, further reinforcing the impression that issues of class and the division of labour were of key significance in the teaching of race and ethnicity in British sociology during the mid-1980s. Interestingly, the CNAA study also reports that relatively few reading lists appear to have featured books by Michael Banton, despite his key role in the development of the specialism within British sociology and his founding of one of the first Masters-level courses on 'race relations' to be located in a British department of sociology (ibid.: 40–1).

## The concept of race

A feature shared by both of the key texts referred to in the CNAA study above was their problematisation of the concept of race. Early sociological discussions in the British literature, including the work of Banton and Rex discussed above, had emphasised the sociological status of 'race' as a category in terms of which people were said to organise aspects of their social conduct. There were, from this perspective, no biological races. Nevertheless, on the principle that if people define a situation as real it is real in its consequences, it was argued that sociologists had to study the 'real' relationships between socially defined 'races'. Similar positions were taken in the US literature by authors such as van den Berghe (1967) and Simpson and Yinger (1965).

By the early 1980s in Britain a new orthodoxy was emerging. This was that not only was there no validity to the biological concept of race but that, in addition, the continued use of the term by sociologists served only to legitimise an ideological construct which obscured the real bases of racialised oppression. This view was most clearly and consistently argued by the British author Robert Miles (1982 – compare his 1993). While not everyone else was able to display the degree of theoretical rigour and intellectual consistency manifested by Miles, it was none the less the case that, in Britain in the 1980s, no sociologist working on these issues and no student learning about them could be unaware of Miles's critique. Almost every monograph, article or textbook now found it necessary to make extensive use of inverted commas whenever the word 'race' appeared.

A key feature of Miles's argument was that the patterns of oppression usually captured by the term 'race relations' (a designation for which he reserved particular scorn) were, in fact, at root variants on classically class-based forms of exploitation. For Miles, then, only an analysis rooted in Marxist theory could begin to uncover the realities of racialised forms of class exploitation. An interesting feature of the development and popularisation of this critique was that it coincided with a marked polarisation of ideology and debate in the political life of Britain in the 1980s (see Jewson and Mason, 1994). Much, though not all, of this debate was conducted, at least on the left, in the language of class even when the interests of other collectivities were being promoted. Given the traditional salience of class in British sociology, it is perhaps no surprise that Miles's perspective was one which attracted a good deal of support. Nevertheless, many of those who were, in principle, convinced by Miles's argument about the status of the term 'race' had difficulty in following through the logic of his account because they were unable wholeheartedly to embrace the Marxist theory which gave it its ultimate power. The result was the proliferation of inverted commas referred to above.

Other forces were already at work. On the one hand, increasingly assertive minority ethnic communities were beginning, both intellectually and on the streets, to challenge the dominance of class-based politics in Britain. Furthermore, a string of Conservative Party general election victories had begun to sap the confidence of the left in the power of its own analyses. It is perhaps no surprise, in these circumstances, that just as the new orthodoxy on the use of the term 'race' appeared to have established itself, so a fresh range of arguments began to emerge which challenged the dominance of class-based accounts and argued instead for a need to take the concept of 'race' seriously (see Gilroy, 1987; Anthias and Yuval-Davis, 1992). These positions do not simply reinstate old-style conceptions of sociological race. Indeed, they share with Miles a concern to understand the dynamics of racism. Nevertheless they do entail a challenge to traditional treatments of class in British sociology and they appear, in part, to reflect important changes in the wider political and theoretical climate. I shall return to some of these issues in due course.

Despite the emergent orthodoxy referred to above and the apparently universal acceptance among British sociologists that there are no races in a biological sense, it would be wrong to suggest that the idea of race in this sense has entirely disappeared. One of the most widely used texts in advanced courses on both sides of the Atlantic has been John Rex and David Mason's *Theories of Race and Ethnicity* (1986). This volume contains a trenchant defence of a biological conception of race by the late M. G. Smith (1986), as well as a critique of his position by Mason. It may be of some interest to note that Smith was, at the time he wrote the chapter, working in the United States. Here, if the evidence of textbooks is to be believed, the critique of race which achieved such prominence in mid-1980s Britain was much less influential. Indeed, there is evidence of a much greater willingness to take biological conceptions seriously.

For example, as late as the 1985 edition[7] of *Racial and Cultural Minorities*, George Simpson and Milton Yinger still found it necessary to discuss biological approaches to race as if they had at least a potential validity. 'Our conclusion is that the possibility of devising a scientific typology of races based either on morphological or genetical characteristics, or a combination of both, is slight' (pp. 30–3). Nevertheless they concede that: 'Obviously racial differences exist' and go on to refer to phenotypical variation (p. 33).

A key reason for this difference of emphasis probably lies in the greater visibility of 'race' as a political and administrative category in the United States. In this connection it clearly denotes phenotypical difference and may well help to reinforce popular biological conceptions which the authors even of sociological texts feel the need to address. The result, Bash has argued, is a 'propensity to "see" race relations where there are none to be *seen*' (1979: 190). Commenting on the lack of clarity about what 'race' means to those who study 'race relations' (ibid.: 194), he asks how a non-social concept got so deeply entangled in sociology. His answer is the power of ideological and political determination (ibid.: 195).

It is in this context that, as late as 1980, a sociology text by Paul Horton and Chester Hunt was referring to 'Mongoloid', 'Caucasoid' and 'Negroid' races in a way which was absent from British texts. Nor was this just a matter of reproducing commonsense labels. Thus the authors argued that the 'racial placement of some groups is uncertain because their physical characteristics overlap' (1980: 352). Moreover, it was asserted that 'a further complication arises from the fact that the races have been busily interbreeding for thousands of years so nearly all racial groups are considerably intermixed' (ibid.: 352). Even as late as 1994, we find a text on *Race and Ethnicity in America* noting that race is a concept popularly associated with physical difference, a view largely endorsed (with qualifications) by the discussion which follows (McLemore, 1994). In the light of examples such as this, it is easy to see why Yehudi Webster has argued that race is embedded in American sociology texts as *the* dynamic of American history (1992: 29).

### Race and ethnicity

A corollary of the apparently greater willingness in US texts to take race seriously is a clearer attempt to distinguish between race and ethnicity. More often than not, the association of race with physical difference leads the term implicitly to be used to refer to divisions between black and white, while ethnicity is much more likely to be used to refer to differences among and between Americans of Asian and European origin. Hispanic and Native Americans often appear to have an ambiguous status in this implicit nomenclature (see, for example, Alba, 1985).[8]

By contrast, there is a tendency in the British literature – particularly that aimed at students – to use the terms race and ethnicity interchangeably. Even where an attempt is made conceptually to distinguish the terms, much substantive discussion effectively uses the concepts to refer to similar processes and groupings. See for example the chapter on race and ethnicity in Worsley (1987) and section 5.4 in Abercrombie *et al.* (1994).

This difference of emphasis almost certainly reflects usage outside the academy and is a consequence of the different political histories of the two societies. Thus in a country whose population was so self-evidently a product of large-scale and recent migrations, differences of ethnic background remain important features of the identities of almost all Americans. Moreover, their significance is constantly reinforced and reproduced by the operation of the political system which rewards effective collective organisation (Mason, 1990). By contrast, the concept of ethnicity found its way into British political and academic discourse largely in response to dissatisfaction with the concept of race and with the assimilationist assumptions of a focus on immigration (Mason, 1992; 1995).

Moreover, there has been a marked tendency in recent years to elevate the conflation of the concepts of race and ethnicity into a theoretical principle by invoking the concept of racialisation. This notion seeks to identify the processes by which ethnic and other differences are naturalised. It is, thus, associated with the emphasis, born testimony to by the titles of an increasing number of texts, to identify 'racism' as the key analytic category. (For examples of texts which address these issues see Skellington, 1992 and Solomos, 1993. For critiques, from rather different standpoints, of the conceptual inflation of the concept of racism see Mason, 1994 and Miles, 1989). This kind of emphasis has, until recently, been relatively absent from American texts, although it is increasingly prominent in some recent volumes (see Goldberg, 1990; 1994; Webster, 1992)

## The visibility of race and ethnicity in the general sociological curriculum

If at the time of Rose's classic study, the teaching of race and ethnicity was yet to become fully embedded in US sociology courses, the same can no longer be said to be true. For historical, political and administrative reasons, issues of race and ethnicity now have such a high profile that Webster (1992) can portray them as evidence of 'the racialising of America'.

A recognition of the centrality of issues of race and ethnicity to the modern world has been much slower to develop in British sociology. For example, the 1986 CNAA survey referred to above found that, although gender appeared in and permeated all courses, this was not true of race which often received a perfunctory treatment by contrast (1988: 39). Even where it appeared in courses and texts, moreover, there was a tendency for the subject to be compartmentalised in a way which was becoming ever less true of issues of gender. Thus Worsley's 1987 edition of what was an influential and widely used undergraduate text in British sociology contained a chapter on race and ethnicity but close inspection reveals relatively few references to racism and exclusion in other parts of the book. Similarly, in another widely used text, *Contemporary British Society* by Nicholas Abercrombie *et al.*, there is also a tendency for issues of race and ethnicity to be treated in isolation (1994). Even by 1991, only 31 of the 60 British universities replying to a survey of sociology curricula, conducted by sociologists at the University of East Anglia, returned details of courses classified under the heading 'race relations'.

Finally we should note that there are marked differences of emphasis to be found in US and British texts where race and ethnicity are discussed. In Britain, where these issues appear, the focus tends to be on macro issues of discrimination and exclusion. By contrast, in US texts, there is evidence of the two features which are much less common in their contemporary British counterparts. One is a continuing interest in issues of individual prejudice. The second is a much greater tendency to focus on minority communities themselves. Thus, Simpson and Yinger (1985) contains detailed sections on characteristics of minorities, addressing such issues as family patterns which tend in Britain to be dealt with in specialist monographs. In Britain, moreover, most specialist volumes, such as those reporting on the studies carried out by the Policy Studies Institute (Brown, 1984; Jones, 1993; Modood *et al.*, 1997), *and* texts on race and ethnicity (Mason, 1995; Skellington, 1992), tend to confine themselves to statistical and case study analyses of discrimination and disadvantage.

## Trends and developments

### America and the rediscovery of (under)class

Paradoxically, given what has been said about the centrality of race to American sociology, and about the relative decline of class in British sociology, some developments in America seem almost to have been pushing in the opposite direction. The growth of a substantial (if still limited, see Small, 1994) black middle class has led to the development of attempts to question the pre-eminence of race as a determinant of social placement. The earliest, and most famous of these attempts, which has been subject to considerable critique, was probably Wilson's *The Declining Significance of Race* (1978).

Interestingly, there have more recently been attempts on the right of American politics to develop arguments drawing on similar observations about patterns of mobility.[9] Thus recent Republican Party assaults on affirmative action have often been formulated in terms of the requirement to address those in need without adopting group-centred programmes of redress. The concept of class connotes a political agenda not readily embraced in these circles. Instead, the focus of such arguments (at the level of rhetoric at least) is on addressing, individually conceptualised, depressed socio-economic status. Characteristically, however, this focus has been re-collectivised by invoking the notion of *under*class. In the work of Murray (see for example, 1984) and others this model effectively blames the dispossessed for their own situations through notions such as that of dependency culture. While in a US context, the concept of underclass is almost inevitably read as one which embraces the minorities clustered stubbornly at the bottom of the socio-economic ladder, it is interesting that in Britain it has not usually had this political resonance. Instead, the notion of an underclass has more frequently been used – on both right and left – to characterise the situations and conduct of the long-term unemployed of all groups – with the young white single mother as likely as anyone to be demonised.

Lest it be assumed that these developments foreshadow the beginning of the end for a race-centred interpretation of US society, we should note that, in addition to the taken-for-granted association of the 'underclass' with minority status, explicit attempts have resurfaced to explain underclass status in explicitly biological terms. Thus Herrnstein and Murray (1994) have sought to prove a genetic basis for what they claim to be a hierarchy of intellect and talent whose alleged immutability has echoes of old-style race science (Stepan, 1982). Against this background, theoretical attempts in the work of writers such as Bash, Goldberg and Webster to question the significance of race, replacing this notion with a focus on the process of racialisation which parallels similar trends in British sociology, are important counters to some of the continuities in the US literature discussed above.

## Resurgent nationalism and the rediscovery of European ethnicity

We noted earlier, the tendency in the British literature aimed at students to conflate notions of race and ethnicity. This parallels a general tendency in British studies over a long period to prioritise the study of racialised exclusion over that of ethnic difference. Hand in hand with this was a tendency to emphasise the commonalities of the exclusionary process and to downplay differences in the experiences of groups. Nowhere was this better exemplified than in the debate over the appropriate use of the concept 'black' (see the discussion in Mason, 1992; Modood, 1988; 1992). By contrast with the US literature, little attention was paid in mainstream texts to the variations in the experiences of different groups and still less to the details of variations in culture and identity (Ballard, 1992).

The emergence of a challenge to this state of affairs had a number of origins. One of these lay outside Britain's shores in continental Europe and led to a rediscovery of the kind of comparative dynamic characteristic of some of the early British texts. The fall of the Berlin Wall in 1989, and the subsequent collapse of the Soviet empire had profound consequences. Rapid increases in levels and patterns of intra-European migration went together with a resurgent nationalism as some in Western Europe, such as the citizens of the former GDR, sought to reclaim a lost identity and others, alarmed by the pace of events, sought refuge in chauvinistic exclusion.

The resultant reawakening of a concern with issues of nationalism also owed much to more global events, such as the reassertion of national sentiment in the countries of the former Soviet Union and the ethnic conflict in the former Yugoslavia. That these events also coincided with the nearing of the fiftieth anniversary of the liberation of Nazi concentration camps may also be of some significance, not least because of the evidence of a resurgent racism in many of the countries of Western Europe (but see Miles, 1994 on this).

In Britain, further impetus was provided by a developing debate about closer European union, in which nationalist sentiments were on prominent display. This followed a period in the 1980s when the Conservative Party in government had pursued an explicit policy of promoting a renewed sense of national pride and distinctiveness (see the discussion in Jewson and Mason, 1994). At the same time, the sense of exclusion to which this had given rise among Britain's minority ethnic citizens found voice in the development of a body of work at the interstices of sociology and cultural studies which sought to deconstruct the implicit messages of British nationalism (see, for example, Gilroy, 1987. See also, Haseler, 1996).

For a variety of reasons, then, issues of ethnicity and race are increasingly being studied and taught alongside those of nationalism. The formation of the Association for the Study of Ethnicity and Nationalism in the early 1990s, bringing together sociologists, political scientists, historians and others, marks an important aspect of the increasing interdisciplinarity which was noted at the outset of this chapter. At both undergraduate and postgraduate levels, moreover, increasing numbers of courses in British universities are focusing on these issues (see for example, ASEN, 1994–5: 49–50).

## The rediscovery of migration

Issues of migration had an early significance in teaching about race and ethnicity on both sides of the Atlantic. In the case of the United States, the pioneering work of the Chicago School placed much emphasis on the comparative migration experiences of members of different groups (Lal, 1990) while these issues were subsequently taken up in a more radical discussion by Robert Blauner (1972). In Britain, much of the early literature in the field placed great emphasis on the migrant origins of Britain's minority ethnic citizens, a fact which reflected both the state of theoretical development of the subject (Banton, 1967) but also the assimilationist thrust of much public policy (Mason, 1995).

In the late 1970s there was a growing interest in Britain in the commonalities of experience of the UK and other Western European societies. By the time of the 1987 CNAA survey, books focusing specifically on migration issues had become prominent in sociology curricula (see especially Castles and Kosack, 1973 and Castles, 1984). These volumes, like the work of Miles (1982), were written largely from a Marxist perspective and formed part of an attempt to prioritise class processes as the dynamic of what others saw as 'race relations'. While this strand of class-based theorising has lost some of its momentum in recent years, the events of the early 1990s described above, and particularly the growth of intra- and extra-territorial migration, helped to give migration issues a renewed prominence.

This growth of interest in migration in Europe has been paralleled by a more general recognition of the significance of migration in a modern world (Castles and Miller, 1993; Cohen, 1987) increasingly conceptualised by sociologists in terms of the concept of globalisation. An important strand in this increasingly global perspective has been a developing body of literature dealing with notions of diaspora. This concept seeks to understand how processes of, both forced and voluntary, migration and settlement are linked to continuities and transformations in culture and identity (Brah, 1996; Gilroy, 1993a and b).

## Gender and the problem of essentialised categories

The 1986 CNAA study discussed above found that gender issues had become well established and routine features of the sociological curriculum. Even though the same was not true of race and ethnicity, it is noteworthy that where these issues were addressed, gender issues were also present, a fact reflected by the prominence of Amrit Wilson's *Finding a Voice* (1978) (CNAA, 1988: 40). Nevertheless, the success of the 1974 British Sociological Association Annual Conference in pushing gender and women's issues more squarely onto the research and teaching agenda, was not matched by the development of a widespread corresponding sensitivity to the interpenetration of gender by ethnicity. Indeed a significant turning point was the development of a vigorous debate in the pages of *Feminist Review* from 1984 onwards (see, for example, Amos and Parmar, 1984).[10]

To some extent, the growth of sensitivity to the intersection of gender and ethnicity reflects the successes of feminism both inside and outside the academy, as well as a growth in the numbers of black women scholars. At another level it also reflects the impetus given by post-modernism and post-structuralism to the questioning of essentialised categories of all kinds. A burgeoning emphasis on the significance of difference, and on issues of identity, has given rise both to a greater sensitivity to the gendering of ethnic boundaries and to an increasing number of courses and texts where these issues are prioritised. Among the most influential texts are probably Anthias and Yuval-Davis (1992), a volume which has its origins in pioneering courses at the University of Greenwich (ASEN 1994–5), Bradley (1996) and Andersen and Hill Collins (1995). Important recent additions to this developing literature include Brah (1996). Despite this, it is by no means clear that in mainstream texts on gender, issues of race and ethnicity have yet acquired the degree of prominence for which these authors would argue (see, for example, the relatively limited coverage in such texts as Abbott and Wallace, 1990 and Lupton *et al.*, 1992).

## *Fractured identities, fragmented categories*

In understanding these developments, it is important to note that they are congruent with, and take much impetus from, the emergence of the post-modernist and post-structuralist thrust of much contemporary sociological theory. By emphasising difference, diversity and identity, such theorisations make it much easier to recognise the conditional and situational character of people's identities and to take cognisance of the ways in which ethnicity, gender, class and age (to name but a few key aspects of identity) may interact in complex and changing ways to structure people's images of themselves and others. It is no accident that these complex interrelationships are of increasing importance in books designed as texts for use in sociology courses (see, for example, Anthias and Yuval-Davis, 1992; Bradley, 1996; Rattansi and Westwood, 1994).

These trends have been given further emphasis in Britain by the emergence of evidence which suggests that the structural locations, for example in the labour market, of different minority ethnic groups are increasingly diverging (see Modood *et al.*, 1997). These data have begun to call into question some of the grosser taken-for-granted categories hitherto used by sociologists in researching and teaching about race and ethnic stratification.

## Conclusion

We have, then, in many ways come full circle. The recent British sociology of race and ethnicity shows clear signs of influences drawn from sources as diverse as political science and cultural studies. The theoretical vehicle for this development has been the decline of structuralism (especially Marxist structuralism) and the rise of post-modernist conceptualisations. The result has been the rediscovery of patterns of difference, and variations in identity, which were always present but frequently hidden behind the fog of abstruse and inflexible theorisations.

The strength of these developments, and as we have seen their influence can be discerned in texts appearing on both sides of the Atlantic, is that they offer the opportunity to be more responsive than has sometimes been the case to the self-definitions of the subjects of our studies. The danger is that the real strength of the sociological imagination could in the process be lost. This is the recognition that all aspects of social life are relational. The choices of each and every one of us are constrained by the prior decisions both of ourselves and others. At the same time the power to define the conditions under which such choices are made is not evenly distributed. It is this which makes currently fashionable stress on racism and processes of racialisation of central importance to the continued contribution of sociology to the understanding of one of the central dynamics of the modern world. Whatever reservations we may have about the detail of particular theorisations (Mason, 1994), this stress helps us avoid the danger that the retreat from class analysis will be merely to the world of style. Difference is important and it is critical that we teach our students to appreciate and analyse it. It is equally critical that we teach them that as well as liberating it can also be oppressive and that all choice implies constraint. Among those constraints are the patterns of resource distribution and access which structure people's power chances and which have traditionally been the focus of much mainstream sociology.

Central to the choices and constraints which structure the life chances of people in the modern world are those associated with race and ethnicity. A sociological curriculum which enables students to understand that world must place these issues, alongside those of class and gender, at the centre rather than, as so often in the past, on the periphery of its concerns.

## Notes

1  I use the term race here in the varied senses in which it appears in the course and texts which are my focus. It is, however, important to make it clear that my own theoretical perspective on the concept is one which sees it as expressive of a particular kind of social relationship in which racism is intrinsically embedded (see the discussion in Mason, 1994).

2  In a 1991 survey of sociology curricula in British universities conducted by sociologists at the University of East Anglia, these books by Gilroy and Solomos were among the most commonly cited in returns for courses grouped under the heading 'race relations'. The other most prominent volumes were Bhat *et al.* (1988) and Miles (1989).

3  This was also true of the M.Sc. which included a course on physical anthropology but which was taught in an unwaveringly critical way.

4  A key influence on the growth of interest in issues of race and ethnicity was the developing political controversy surrounding the emergence of a substantial and growing population of people who had migrated to Britain from the countries of the former British Empire and whose skin colour was not white (see Mason, 1995: chapter 3).

5  This is not to say that assimilationist assumptions, in various guises, were banished either from political and popular discussions of 'race relations' or from the academy (see the discussion in Mason, 1995).

6  The prominence of the CCCS volume indicates the growing influence of cultural studies on sociological debates – an influence which has been continued by the growing popularity of the work of Gilroy (e.g. 1987) and the growing influence of post-modernist accounts (see below).

7  The volume was reprinted in each of the following two years.

8  The term minority is often used in a US context as a generic surrogate for both terms. For a discussion of some of the issues associated with this and related terms see Mason (1992).

9  I am not suggesting any causal relationship here.

10 We should not, of course, overlook such pioneering work as that of Angela Davis (1982).

# 2 Philosophy and racial identity

*Linda Martín Alcoff*

In the 1993 film, *Map of the Human Heart*, an Inuit man asks a white engineer who has come to northern Canada to map the region, 'Why are you making maps?' Without hesitating, the white man responds 'They will be very accurate.' Map-making and race-making have a strong historical as well as conceptual relationship. The ordering and labelling of natural terrain, the classifying of natural types, and the typologies of 'natural races' emerged simultaneously in what Foucault called the Classical episteme. Arguing via Foucault, both Cornel West and David Theo Goldberg have attempted genealogies of modern racism, meaning here not contemporary racism so much as the racism of modernism, that link the Western fetishistic practices of classification, the forming of tables, and the consequent primacy of the visible with the creation of metaphysical and moral hierarchies between racialised categories of human beings (West, 1982; Goldberg, 1993). Given this genesis, the concept of race and of racial difference emerges as that which is visible, classifiable and morally salient. West argues that the application of natural history techniques to the study of the human species yields a comparative analysis 'based on visible, especially physical, characteristics...[which] permit one to discern identity and difference, equality and inequality, beauty and ugliness among animals and human bodies' (West, 1982: 55). Goldberg argues that the universal sameness that was so important for the Liberal self required a careful containment and taxonomy of difference. Where rights require sameness, difference must be either trivialised or contained in the Other across a firm and clearly visible border.

The result of these classification practices juxtaposed with liberal ideology is a paradox wherein 'Race is irrelevant, but all is race' (Goldberg, 1993: 6). Visible difference is the route to classification and therefore knowledge, and yet visible difference threatens the security of claims to know by challenging universal applicability and invoking the spectre of relativism. Classification systems can contain this threat and impede relativism by enclosing the entirety of difference within a taxonomy organised by a single logic. In this way the continuing hegemony of liberal discourse is ensured. But the resultant juxtaposition between universalist legitimation narratives that deny or trivialise difference and careful delineations of supposedly morally relevant phenotypic human difference is one of the greatest antinomies of modern discourse.

We have finally come to recognise and acknowledge this paradox, but we have not yet solved or moved beyond it. Today the naturalistic classification systems which would reify human variability into moral categories, the Eurocentric teleologies which would excuse if not justify colonialism, and the phallogocentric binaries which would obscure relations of domination by presenting them as 'separate spheres', have been largely exposed as specious. And the realm of the visible, or what is taken as self-evidently visible (which is how the ideology of racism naturalises racial designation), is recognised as the product of a specific form of perceptual practice, rather than the natural result of human sight. Thus Foucault claims that:

> the object [of discourse] does not await in limbo the order that will free it and enable it to become embodied in a visible and prolix objectivity; it does not preexist itself, held back by some obstacle at the first edges of light. It exists under the positive conditions of a complex group of relations.
>
> (Foucault, 1982: 45)

His central thesis in *The Birth of the Clinic* is that the gaze, though hailed as pure and pre-conceptual, can only function successfully when connected to a system of understanding which dictates its use and interprets its results:

> What defines the act of medical knowledge in its concrete form is not...the encounter between doctor and patient, nor is it the confrontation between a body of knowledge and a perception; it is the systematic intersection of two series of information...whose intersection reveals, in its isolable dependence, the *individual* fact.
>
> (Foucault, 1975: 30)

On this account, which is hardly unique to Foucault, visibility itself cannot serve as the explanatory cause of the development of racial taxonomies. The apparent obviousness of racial difference – the emphasis on hair type, nose shape, and skin colour – is a produced obviousness.

The visibility of racial identity is a peculiarly variegated phenomenon with little acknowledgment of this by dominant discourses. Those of us with hybrid identities surely have a better sense of this, as our public identity is variously interpellated across geographical borders or even just neighbourhoods. When the mythic bloodlines which are thought to determine identity fail to match the visible markers used by identity discourses to signify race, one often encounters these odd responses by acquaintances announcing with arrogant certainty 'But you don't look like...' or then retreating to a measured acknowledgment 'Now that you mention it, I can sort of see...'. To feel one's face studied with great seriousness, not for its (hoped for) character lines, or its distinctiveness, but for its telltale racial trace, can be a peculiarly unsettling experience, fully justifying all Sartre's horror of the Look (Piper, 1992).

Anti-essentialisms have corroded the sense of visible difference as the 'sign' of a deeper, more fundamental difference, a difference in behavioral disposition, in moral and rational capacity, or in cultural achievement. Moreover, there is a newly emerging scientific consensus that race is a myth, that the term corresponds to no significant biological category, and that no existing racial classifications correlate in useful ways to gene frequencies, clinal variations or any significant human biological differ-ence. For semantic realists such as Anthony Appiah, the only philosophically respectable position one can take in the face of this evidence is that the concept of race cannot be used correctly, that there is no philosophically defensible way to realign the term race with a referent, even one which would invoke historical experience or culture rather than biology (Appiah, 1992: 32, 45).

So today race has no semantic respectability, biological basis or philo-sophical legitimacy. However, at the same time, and in a striking parallel to the earlier Liberal attitude toward the relevance and irrelevance of race, in the very midst of our contemporary scepticism toward race stands the compelling social reality that race, or racialised identities, have as much political, sociological and economic salience as they ever had. Race tends toward opening up or shutting down job prospects, career possibilities, available places to live, potential friends and lovers, reactions from police, credence from jurors and presumptions by one's students. Race may not correlate with clinal variations, but it persistently correlates with statisti-cally overwhelming significance in wage levels, unemployment levels, poverty levels and the likelihood of incarceration. As of 1992, black and Latino men working full time in the US earned an average of 68 per cent of what white men earned, while black and Latina women earned 59 per cent. As of 1995, Latino and black unemployment rates were more than double that of whites.

But these sociological facts are not thought to entail philosophical significance. For those still working within a Liberal framework, the devastating sociological reality of race is but an artificial overlay on more basic elements whose specificity can be legitimately set aside toward the aim of a general analysis. For post-modernists, race is a contingent construction, the epiphenomenon of essentialist discourses and thus ulti-mately without any more explanatory power or epistemological relevance than on the Liberal view. Thus, for all our critical innovations in under-standing the vagaries of racist domination and the conceptual apparatus that yields racism, we remain stuck in the modernist antinomy that race is (fundamentally) irrelevant, even though all is race. It will be my contention that we will not be able to progress beyond this unworkable dilemma until we acknowledge the philosophical salience of racial identity, a project that must begin with understanding what racial identity is.

## Race as ontology

Refusing the reality of racial categories as elements within our current social ontology only exacerbates racism, because it helps to conceal the myriad effects that racialising practices have had and continue to have on social life, including philosophy. In claiming that race is an ontological category, I don't mean to say that we should *begin* treating it as such, but that we must begin acknowledging the fact that race has been 'real' for a long time. And I am not putting this forward as a strategic essentialism: the claim that race is philosophically salient is not merely a strategic claim, but a truth claim. There is a visual registry operating in social relations which is socially constructed, historically evolving and culturally variegated but none the less powerfully determinant over individual experiences and choices. And, for that reason, it also powerfully mediates subjectivity. Consider the following passage from Richard Rodriguez:

> I used to stare at the Indian in the mirror. The wide nostrils, the thick lips. Starring Paul Muni as Benito Juarez. Such a long face – such a long nose – scuplted by indifferent, blunt thumbs, and of such common clay. No one in my family had a face as dark or as Indian as mine. My face could not portray the ambition I brought to it.
>
> (Rodriguez, 1992: 1)

This mediation through the visible, working on both the inside and the outside, both on the way we read ourselves and the way others read us, is what is unique to racialised identities as against ethnic and cultural identities. The processes by which racial identities are produced work through the shapes and shades of human morphology, and subordinate other markers such as dress, customs and practices. And the visual registry thus produced has been correlated with rational capacity, epistemic reliability, moral condition and of course aesthetic status. Yet as a result of the theoretical critique of race, this visual registry has largely not been brought into theoretical play, in either cultural studies or in philosophy (Dominguez, 1995).

This visual registry cannot be fully or adequately described except in ontological terms, because the difference that racialising identities has made is an ontologising difference, that is, a difference at the most basic level concerning knowledge and subjectivity, being and thinking. If we say that race is not an ontological category, and that it is a mere artificial overlay on top of more basic and more real categories, we risk losing sight of how significant the effects of racial identities have been, and how those effects have permeated every philosophical idea. Ontology itself might then be able to avoid a much needed self-critique. Metaphysics and epistemology could proceed with their habitual disregard for issues of race, and political philosophy could continue to introduce racial topics only in the stages of applied theory.

Obviously, when I say that race is an ontological category I am using ontology here to refer to basic categories of reality which are within history, at least partly produced by social practices, and which are culturally various. Race itself signifies differently and is lived differently between different discursive and cultural locations. This usage of ontology is controversial, and I cannot take the space here to fully justify it, but I will make one point. The problem with the social constructionist, anti-essentialism view that we should give up the language game of ontology altogether is that we are then left with a reduced ability to offer *deep* descriptions of reality, descriptions which can differentiate between more and less significant and persisting features of reality. The weakness of a strict social constructionist approach is that it tends toward flattening out all descriptive categories as having equal (non-)metaphysical status. Thus, for example, male/female is put on the same plane as masculine/feminine, and the importance of the biological division of reproduction is made analogous to gendered dress codes. In order to avoid this, without lapsing back into essentialism, the traditional ontological project of ascertaining basic categories can be reconfigured as the attempt to ascertain those elements of reality which, although mutable, currently intersect and determine a wide variety of discourses and practices, and thus are more fundamental not because of their ahistorical or transcendental status but because of their central intersectional position.

The fact that race has lost its scientific credibility does not entail, then, that it has lost its ontological status, since on this usage ontology does not imply a reference in a transcendental reality. Race does not need to refer to a natural kind or a piece of reality in a metaphysical realist sense if it is to have any ontological meaning. What is race, then? Race is a particular, historically and culturally located form of human categorisation involving visual determinants marked on the body through the interplay of perceptual practices and bodily appearance. Race has not had one meaning or a single essential criterion, but its meanings have always been mediated through visual appearance, however complicated.

The criteria determining racial identity have included ancestry, experience, outside perception, internal perception, coded visibility, habits and practices – all these and more are variously invoked for both individuals and groups. The criteria which will be primarily operative vary by culture, neighbourhood, historical moment, so that some people place ancestry as all determining, while others make subjective identification the key.

What is a philosopher to do in the face of this variation? We could take ordinary language, the way in which people speak of race, and use it to sift through these criteria to show which are most consistent with the way we speak. This approach could certainly be useful in pointing out contradictions between the way we speak and what we believe, and in showing the presuppositions we are implicitly committed to by the way we speak, but it cannot show us what the 'truth' of racial identity is. Phenomenological description of the experience of racial designations would also be useful in achieving a better understanding of the lived reality of race, but this again is not decisive in establishing the 'underlying essence' of race.

My view is that the meaning of race will shift as one moves through the terrain and interplay of different discourses, where here discourses signify practices and institutions as well as systems of knowledge (a usage well exemplified in Wittgenstein's concept of a language game, which involves linguistic practices connected with and embodied in actions). The 'answer' to the question of what racial identity really is will depend on what language game we are playing, although the relativism of this situation can be mitigated by showing overlaps between language games, and by offering immanent critiques that reveal internal contradictions, such as a language game that claims to be non-racist but in reality is.

Philosophy is a prime example of the latter. It has committed both crimes of omission – the neglect of race – and crimes of commission – correlating race with epistemic reliability (Kant) and potential for self-government (Mill). But given this, we still have yet to understand either what racial identity is or how we should articulate its relationship to philosophy. In order to answer these questions, we must first address several others, not only the scepticism toward race, but also the post-modern critique of identity and of the visible, and the political debate over identity politics. It is these debates, more so than the scientific status of race, that will determine the future of philosophical treatments of racial identity. I will summarise some of the relevant issues in these debates, and then try to address them in the context of race.

The principal argument against identity politics has been that it assumes an essentialist, coherent identity that is efficacious over one's political orientation, epistemological standpoint and justificatory status. And so it might be thought that making racial identity epistemologically salient, e.g., could lead to a reductionist form of evaluation that puts identity considerations over argument, i.e. holding that which is pious is so because the gods love it rather than that the gods love it because it is pious.

Also relevant is the critique of the tyranny of the visible, as in Rorty's denigration of the visual metaphor for metaphysical realism, to Martin Jay's discussion of the anti-ocularcentric thrust of critical theory, to Jameson's blunt claim that 'the visual is essentially pornographic...' One thing that this view has in its favour is that it would make sense of the non-reciprocal visibility of dominant and non-dominant racial identities: where the invisibility of whiteness renders it an unassailable norm, while the visibility of non-whiteness marks it as a target and a denigrated particularity.

And both the concepts of identity and of race are often charged with assuming a unity and homogeneity that do not in fact obtain. Iris Young, building on Derrida and Adorno, criticises the idea that identity is a coherent unity which can serve as the origin of thought and practice, and which can be neatly separated from external things such as others or discourses (Young, 1990: 303–5). This description is metaphysically incorrect, for reasons with which we are all familiar, having to do with the fundamental disunity of the self, its lack of complete self-knowledge, and its constitution by and through processes of narrativisation which are only partially accessible to the subject herself (Ricoeur, 1990). On the basis of these arguments, Young would have us make a parallel case against group identity, and reject identity concepts altogether.

Racial identities are increasingly recognised as particularly disunified (since their group-status is even more obviously arbitrary or conventional than nation or culture), split within by class, gender, sexuality, etc., and, as Danielson and Engle point out in their collection *After Identity*, without clear borders or a unifying internal essence (Danielson and Engle, 1995: xiii–xix). Moreover, Freud argued that the effort to overcome disunity through collective identification or group solidarity may itself be the sign of a pathological condition caused by 'the inability of the ego to regain autonomy following the loss of an object of desire' (Steinberg, 1995). Thus, the conclusion of these critiques is that racial identity is a dangerous illusion.

Now, I take all of these worries about racial identity very seriously. My original entry into this area of work was motivated by a concern to understand and in some sense validate hybrid identity or hybrid positionality against purist, essentialist accounts. And the motivation for this was the felt alienation of having a mestizo identity (normative in Latin America and the Caribbean) but living in a purist culture (the US), where racial categories are assumed to be mutually exclusive. In my nuclear family, which is anything but nuclear, I have a cholito Panamanian father (mixed Spanish, Indian, African), a white Anglo mother, and through my father's multiple liaisons, a range of siblings from black to brown to tan to freckled, spanning five countries and three continents at last count. This personal genealogy has not motivated me to try to repair dissonance into a coherent unity, but rather to understand the formation and position of the self precisely within an unresolvable heterogeneity.

If I did not have any sympathy for the anti-essentialist, my concern with the persistent paradox of the relevance of race would not be felt so strongly. It is because the arguments against racial identity have merit that the paradox is a paradox and not simply an error. But in the face of these anti-race arguments, we need a better position than one which merely relies on the withering away of racial categorisation. And we need one that can do two things the anti-essentialist positions cannot do: (1) take into account the full force of race as a lived experience, understanding this not as mere epiphenomenon but as constitutive of reality, and (2) acknowledge and account for the epistemological and theoretical importance racial perspective has had on, for example, the undermining of modernist tele-ologies (e.g. Du Bois's use of slavery to undermine US supremacist claims, and the Frankfurt School's critique of Western rationality from the perspective of the Holocaust). These facts suggest that we need to understand racial identity as having both metaphysical and epistemological implications.

## Race as identity

Racial identifications have been causally associated with Classical Liberalism and philosophical modernism. Given the fact that the practices of racialising identity developed within the greatest period of colonialism and genocide the world has ever known, anti-racists have been understandably sceptical about the possibility of racial identity coexisting alongside equality and justice. Furthermore, the liberal conceptualisations of justice and enlightenment presupposed a decrease if not an end to the social relevance of racial particularity, and this can be traced out in the history of integrationist thought in the US, as Gary Peller has so usefully shown:

> A commitment to a form of universalism, and an association of universalism with truth and particularism with ignorance, forms the infrastructure of American integrationist consciousness.... Integrationist beliefs are organised around the familiar Enlightenment story of progress consisting of the movement from mere belief and superstition to knowledge and reason, from the particular and there-fore parochial to the universal and therefore enlightened.
>
> (Peller, 1995: 74)

Where truth and justice require universalism, racial identity cannot be accorded salience without endangering progress. Racial identity threatens to return us to feudal hierarchy, a system in which identity determined one's life, which was precisely the system against which liberal enlighten-ment was organised and developed. As a result, anti-racism is assumed to require being an anti-racial ideology (at least in so far as race has political or non-trivial salience).

Furthermore, an anti-racism that pursues universalism against particu-larism also 'confirms our sense of the possibility of true and authentic relations that transcend racial status and other forms of cultural distance and difference' (Peller, 1995: 76). It thus legitimates our perhaps natural hope for significant human relationships against ones that are necessarily deformed or atrophied by structurally produced separations. For whites or others who benefit in the present from a history of oppression, the appeal of universal racelessness may also lie in its ability to deface their/our race-based connections with that unpleasant past; in other words, it may entitle whites to believe they/we don't need to acknowledge the salience of white identity and thus to avoid the moral discomfort that that identity cannot help but present.

But there is an argumentative complicity, whether intentional or not doesn't matter of course, between the suspicion against the visible, against identity, and certainly against the intersection of these which would occur in a racialised conception of identity, and the continuing inattention to race matters in philosophy and political theory. As many people have pointed out, one of the persistent problems with the discourses in the US around multiculturalism and cultural studies is that race, racism and racial hierarchies are relatively ignored. Explorations of culture and ethnicity can all too easily avoid any account of white supremacy and focus instead on the recognition of difference, flattening out differences in a way that makes them appear equal. Race, on the other hand, is difficult to focus on for very long without it working to discredit the imagined landscapes of pluralist difference that cultural studies so often presuppose. And main-stream political language in both Britain and the US codes racial talk as cultural talk, so racist claims can be cloaked as claims about cultural difference.

Interestingly in this context, Lewis Gordon's recent book, *Bad Faith and Antiblack Racism*, argues that, in an antiblack world, blackness signifies absence, the absence of identity in the full sense of a self, a perspective, or a standpoint with its own self-referential point of view (Gordon, 1995: chapter 14). In other words, what is denied black people is the ability to wield the Look, to be a source of value and meaning. The infamous three-fifths formulation from the US constitution might be explicated as a concept of black personhood as having a consciousness without judgment, or a limited capacity for affective sensibility and cognitive distinctions. Antiblack racism denied visible black people the standpoint of a subject as capable of judging and knowing and reciprocating in an intersubjective relationship between persons.

Charles Mills argues in his essay 'Non-Cartesian sums: philosophy and the African-American experience' that the concept of 'sub-personhood,' or *Untermensch*, is a central way to understand 'the defining feature of the African-American experience under conditions of white supremacy (both slavery and its aftermath)' (Mills, 1994: 228). By this concept, which Mills develops through a contrast drawn between the Cartesian sum and Ralph Ellison's invisible man, Mills elucidates the comprehensive ramifications that white racism had on 'every sphere of black life – juridical standing, moral status, personal/racial identity, epistemic reliability, existential plight, political inclusion, social metaphysics, sexual relations, aesthetic worth' (ibid.).

To be a sub-person is not to be a non-person, or an object without any moral status whatsoever. Rather, Mills explains:

> the peculiar status of a sub-person is that it is an entity which, because of phenotype, seems (from, of course, the perspective of the cate-goriser) human in some respects but not in others. It is a human (or, if this seems normatively loaded, a humanoid) who, though adult, is not fully a person...[and] whose moral status was tugged in different directions by the dehumanising requirements of slavery on the one hand and the (grudging and sporadic) white recognition of the objec-tive properties blacks possessed on the other, generating an insidious array of cognitive and moral schizophrenias in both blacks and whites.
>
> (ibid.)

On the basis of this, Mills suggests that the racial identity of philosophers affects the 'array of concepts found useful, the set of paradigmatic dilemmas, the range of concerns' with which they each must grapple. He also suggests that the perspective one takes on specific theories and posi-tions will be affected by one's identity, as in the following passage:

> The impatience, or indifference, that I have sometimes detected in black students [taking an ethics course] derives in part, I suggest, from their sense that there is something strange, for example, in spending a whole course describing the logic of different moral ideals without ever talking about how *all of them* were systematically violated for blacks.
>
> (ibid.: 226)

The result is an understanding that black lived experience 'is not subsumed under these philosophical abstractions, despite their putative generality' (ibid.: 225).

As a further example of Mills's claim, consider the following passage from Hannah Arendt:

> In America, the student movement has been seriously radicalised wherever police and police brutality intervened in essentially nonvio-lent demonstrations: occupations of administration buildings, sit-ins, et cetera. Serious violence entered the scene only with the appearance of the Black Power movement on the campuses. Negro students, the majority of them admitted without academic qualifications, regarded and organised themselves as an interest group, the representatives of the black community. Their interest was to lower academic standards. They were more cautious than the white rebels, but it was clear from

the beginning (even before the incidents at Cornell University and City College in New York) that violence with them was not a matter of theory and rhetoric. Moreover, while the student rebelling in Western countries can nowhere count on popular support outside the universities, and as a rule encounters open hostility the moment it uses violent means, there stands a large minority of the Negro community behind the verbal or actual violence of the black students. Black violence in America can indeed be understood in analogy to the labor violence in America a generation ago; and although...only Staughton Lynd has drawn the analogy between labor riots and student rebellion explicitly, it seems that the academic establishment, in its curious tendency to yield more to Negro demands, even if they are clearly silly and outrageous, than to the disinterested and usually highly moral claims of the white rebels, also thinks in these terms and feels more comfortable when confronted with interests plus violence than when it is a matter of nonviolent 'participatory democracy'.

(Arendt, 1969: 18–19)

The ambivalence Mills points to can be discerned in this account. On the one hand, black students are clearly persons, having a self-interested perspective which they pursue through collective action, and capable of greater collectivity across campus and community divisions than the white students. On the other hand, this perspective is less intelligent, hence its desire to lower standards, and (probably as a result) it is too self-interested, too particular, and thus unable to achieve the moral approbation of the purportedly disinterested white rebels. Arendt clearly pits morality against self-interestedness, the universal against the particular, once again. But the result is a curious replay of the liberal antinomy between having a racialised self and having a less developed self, between being a person with a perspective and being a non-person precisely because of that perspective: having 'demands' but demands which are silly, outrageous and pursued through what she clearly considers unnecessary violence.

There is no question that Arendt's white racial identity affected her ability to assess black student actions, or that her response to the possibility of black-organised violence was affected by her identification with its targets. This is so obvious as to be uninteresting. But does this judgment entail the reductionist evaluations imputed to adherents of identity politics? Are we forced into holding that Arendt's views can be reduced to a consideration of Arendt's race? Or if we want to avoid such a position, are we forced to conclude that her race was irrelevant to the above account? It seems clear to me that racial identity is a crucial category of analysis to have at our disposal in order to understand Arendt's reactions to and assessment of black students. Yet I believe we can retain this category without essentialising racial identity or reducing philosophical analysis to racial identification. I will develop this case through a reading of Paul

Gilroy's *The Black Atlantic: Modernity and Double Consciousness* (1993a).

This book has a twin purpose. On the one hand, Gilroy's purpose is to reconfigure and reconceptualise the concept of black identity so important to cultural studies, black studies and Afrocentric theory, in such a way that he can avoid the metaphysical criticisms of prior concepts of identity and he can develop a more adequate accounting of the cultural formations and political practices created under diaspora conditions than Afrocentric theories can explain. As Gilroy tells the story, there is an identifiable cultural formation organised by the black diaspora and existing in multiple sites which he groups together under the term black Atlantic. Given the internal cultural, linguistic and geographic heterogeneity of this group, to call it a 'culture' would be actually misleading and more evocative of homogenisation than the term black. Moreover, the racial designation more accurately signifies the principal organising logic of this group, which was and is the historical experience of an institution of slavery that operated through phenotype. This experience has yielded an ongoing process of identity formation that cannot be traced back to an African essence or distilled into its pure type, but that is persistently involved in the proliferation of ever new hybrid identities. Thus, Gilroy's analysis is both centred around identity and insistent on the fundamental hybridity and openness of identity (Gilroy, 1993a: xi). Against those that would emphasise the enduring manifestation of roots in black culture, and against the association of black liberation with a return in some sense to those roots, Gilroy uses the imagery of the diaspora precisely to articulate a mobile and mediated identity, internally heterogeneous, and whose very survival and ability to flourish has been predicated on its character as always open to new mutation:

> In opposition to...nationalist or ethnically absolute approaches, I want to develop the suggestion that cultural historians could take the Atlantic as one single, complex unit of analysis in their discussions of the modern world and use it to produce an explicitly transnational and intercultural perspective.
>
> (Gilroy, 1993a: 15)

His choice of the word 'produce' rather than 'discover' is clearly intentional.

The second major purpose of this book is to show how this perspective has been and can be brought to bear on an account of modernity generally. Along the lines of Mills's argument above, Gilroy claims that a critique of modernity which is entirely immanent is insufficient. That is, a critique which uses the Enlightenment's concepts of reason and liberation to critique its practices and its self-understandings will not go deeply enough. In his readings of Du Bois, Richard Wright and others Gilroy claims to be able to trace:

the formation of a vernacular variety of unhappy consciousness which demands that we rethink the meanings of rationality, autonomy, reflection, subjectivity, and power in the light of an extended meditation both on the condition of the slaves and on the suggestion that racial terror is not merely compatible with occidental rationality but cheerfully complicit with it.

(Gilroy, 1993a: 56)

Thus, it is through 'the slaves' perspective' that a more thoroughgoing critique of the Enlightenment can advance. This perspective begins from a more sceptical position on 'the democratic potential of modernity' than for example Jürgen Habermas is said to have. It would insist that Columbus accompany Luther and Copernicus as the standard bearers of modernity, with all the repercussions that must then follow concerning how we assess that standard. Locke's *Second Treatise* could no longer be taught without a mention of his contribution to writing the Carolina slave constitution (Mills, 1994: 226). Gilroy uses Frederick Douglass's slave memoirs to suggest a revision of Hegel's Lord and Bondsman narrative, wherein it is the slave that 'actively prefers the possibility of death' rather than the master. Douglass's version reveals the prior structure of enslavement which mandates the slave's survival in bondage over the possibility of his death, and locates the slave's first moment of agency in his determination to violently counter the violence which has already been inscribed in the social relation. This retelling of the narrative more correctly locates the origin of institutional violence as prior to the slave's enslavement, and thus raises 'queries about the assumption of symmetrical intersubjectivity' which grounds so many modernist accounts of self-formation.

Gilroy's point is not to draw a sharp border between slave and non-slave perspectives, and at one point he even aligns Habermas with 'a good many ex-slaves' in his commitment to 'making bourgeois civil society live up to its political and philosophical promise' (Gilroy, 1993a: 49). But although there is much intermixture and overlap between perspectives, they are not all coextensive, and one can shift the horizons of visibility by occupying the centre as opposed to the periphery of a black Atlantic perspective. This understanding of identity in terms of perspective suggests a definition of identity as a social location, a location within a social structure and marked vis-à-vis other locations which gives the identity its specificity rather than its internal characteristics (Alcoff, 1988).

Gilroy is not arguing here that the perspective engendered by identity has a singularly determinate effect on thought. He rejects Patricia Hill Collins's 'collapse' of being and thinking 'so that they form a functional unity that can be uncritically celebrated' (Gilroy, 1993a: 52). And he suggests, rightly, that a determinist view of the impact of identity on thought would inhibit the scope of critical reflection on that thought. Moreover, he argues that such an account of knowledge would 'simply end up substituting the standpoint of black women for its forerunner rooted in the lives of white men', simply replacing white men with black women in the myth of 'stable, ideal subjects' (Gilroy, 1993a: 53).[1] And as a myth, postulating a convenient but specious concept of the self, such an account cannot last very long.

However, despite his hybrid, postmodern-influenced, problematised notion of identity, for Gilroy identity, and in this book it is racial identity he is exploring, remains the central term of his analysis. He repeatedly criticises those whose critique of racial essentialism leaves them 'insufficiently alive to the lingering power of specifically racialised forms of power and subordination' or those who have been 'slow in perceiving the centrality of ideas of race and culture' to the investigation of modernity (Gilroy, 1993a: 32, 49). And he repudiates theories of the self which would, like Marshall Berman's, try to conceptualise it at a more abstract, more putatively universal level, below the effect of racial configurations.

*The Black Atlantic* does a masterful job arguing against purist, nationalist paradigms by showing how these cannot account for what is essentially an 'intercultural and transnational formation' (Gilroy, 1993a: ix). It makes the unifying theme not an internal core or original historical moment or homogeneous cultural elements but the 'well-developed sense of the complicity of racialised reason and white supremacist terror' which provides a perspective informing literary, musical and philosophical creativity (ibid.: x). In this way, hybridisation and identity can coexist, at least as long as global white supremacy continues to structure intersubjective relations through racialised identities.

Gilroy's book also serves as an empirical rejoinder to the metaphysical arguments of post-modernism, which set a priori limits on the plasticity of identity concepts.[2] Gilroy's argument comes out of specific analyses of cultural products, rather than accounts of the limits of language, and demonstrates the usefulness of a unifying concept like the Black Atlantic to understand and appreciate a wide range of forms.

There are others besides Gilroy who are making similar moves. Kobena Mercer's recent collection of essays exhibits the same reluctance to either embrace nationalist or Afrocentric treatments of black identity or to dispense with identity as irrelevant (Mercer, 1994). And like Gilroy, Mercer negotiates between these conceptions through a diasporic aesthetic, which relies on analogous positionality and historical experience rather than a deep self or unified politics to establish identity. Roberto Fernandez Retamar's 'Caliban' is another example: proposing Caliban, a figure from English literature, as the symbol of Latin American identity. Fernandez Retamar's account thus exemplifies what Trinh Minh-ha calls the fearless affirmation of the hyphen, as well as a conception of identity primarily in positional terms:

To assume our condition as Caliban implies rethinking our history from the *other* side, from the viewpoint of the *other* protagonist.

[Quoting Marti:] 'We must stand with Guaicaipuro, Paramaconi [heroes of Venezuela, probably of Carib origin], and not with the flames that burned them, nor with the ropes that bound them, nor with the steel that beheaded them, nor with the dogs that devoured them.'

(Retamar, 1989: 16, 19)

I would argue that the concept of identity found in these works as in Gilroy, Mills and Gordon is a concept not organised around a claim to sameness, which is what invites much of the criticisms of identity concepts. Rather, as in Gordon's diagnosis of racism as positing an absence, what the claim of identity here is organised against is the assumption of lack. In this context identity is put forward not as sameness opposed to difference but as substance opposed to absence. It is also opposed to notions of the self which formulate it primarily as an abstract form without content, a decontextualised ability to reason without any interested positionality. Examples here would be the Cartesian sum, a self as a thinking, abstract process or ability, and the early Sartrian model of the self as the ability to negate.

Against such contentless models works such as Gilroy's could be understood as consistent with a more substantive understanding of the self which can sustain particular identities in a way I just have time here to sketch. From Bourdieu one might take the concept of the self as a sedimentation of dispositions and practices developed through a personal history, and understand that history in terms of an experience which is always carried forth even if interpreted anew (as in the later Sartre). Racial identifications will affect the particular manifestation of both these elements (practices, experience), but in order to more fully account for race we must also include the element of visibility, as an embodied manifestation that invites and elicits determinate though contextually variable meanings.

On this kind of account, race can be understood to figure in identity formation not as a metaphysical necessity but as a necessity within a given historical context. And from here one might go on to develop a phenomenology of racial identity as, for example, a differentiation or distribution of felt connectedness to others. This will necessarily be a complex issue, undetermined solely by phenotype. The felt connectedness to visibly similar others may produce either flight or empathic identification or other possible dispositions.

Gilroy's description of the black Atlantic identity has the power to incorporate this openness and constant mixture with the connecting elements of a post-slavery diasporic perspective, such that phenotypic race is never sufficient yet never completely absent. This provides us with a metaphysically more accurate, and politically less problematic formulation of racial identity, not based on purity or the continuity of original essence, and one not closed to new incarnations.

I began this chapter with the example of a non sequitur exchange, where an Inuit questioned the point of map making and a white man responded with a reassurance of accuracy. The assumption in some of the anti-identity dismissals of race seems to take the form of an inverse of this exchange, such that a denial of the possibility of accuracy is somehow taken to entail a denial of the possibility of maps. My argument would be that this response is no less of a non sequitur than the one before.

## Notes

1 He calls Hill Collins's account of knowledge 'experience centered' meaning to differentiate it from theoretical critique, but I would take issue with this characterisation. One could have an experience centred account of knowledge, or at least one that emphasises the importance of experience, without either a transparent view of experience or an anti-theoretical disposition. The complex history of twentieth-century radical empiricism as well as the phenomenological tradition are counterexamples to this assumption.

2 For a similar argument against setting a priori limits on the plasticity of social practices, see Judy Butler's review essay 'Poststructuralism and postmarxism' in *Diacritics* Winter 1993, 3–11. Here she is critiquing Ernesto Laclau's 'description of the logical features by which any social practice proceeds' on the grounds that it postulates 'a logic to which social practices are subject but which is itself subject to no social practice' (p. 9). I would make a related claim that we cannot determine in advance, outside of social practice, the 'logic' of identity concepts, or their inevitable political effects.

# 3 The symbolic empire and the history of racial inequality

*Caroline Knowles*

## Historiography and political projects

History as Stanley (1993: 41) points out does not consist of slices of a past revealed, but of competing written versions of the past – historiography. This chapter explores the ways in which accounts of racial inequalities draw upon historiography. Historiography organises a selected series of ambiguous events into a narrative form. In this sense, historiography continuously reinvents and narrates the past (Portelli, 1991) creating new relationships between past and present as Freeman (1993: 30) claims in discussing memory. Historiographies of race and ethnicity comprise a diverse set of textual accounts which, for analytic purposes, are divided in terms of their relationship to the present and their analytic focus. All histories are selective responses to the present (Foucault, 1977: 308) but a working distinction can be established between the two kinds of histories. The first are histories deployed by cultural and social scientists where there is an explicit relationship to the present and the political project of uncovering and objecting to racial inequalities. The object of these histories is to expose racial inequalities in a narrative which marks the continuities between past and present. The second are histories construed by historians where the relationship to the present and to a set of political objectives is more obscured and implicit. The object of these histories is a reinterpretation of the past. The difference between the two is a matter of emphasis and political commitment: it is about whether the past is the analytic focus or an analytic device deployed in some broader argument.

It is the explicitly present and more directly politically motivated historical analyses of cultural and social scientists which this chapter subjects to critical commentary. The explicitly politically directed histories concerned with present racial inequalities, construed by cultural and social scientists such as the Centre for Contemporary Cultural Studies (1982), Kiernan (1984) and Winthrop Jordan (1984) in Britain and Khan (1991), Bolaria and Li (1989), bell hooks (1982, 1992) and Angela Davis (1982) in North America, have made important contributions to the theorisation of race and to anti-racist politics. These histories were popular in the 1970s and

1980s on both sides of the Atlantic and their impact on black studies in the United States can still be seen. These histories of cultural and social scientists approximate to what Canguilhem calls 'sanctioned history'; history in which the past is read through the grid of the present, and in which the present functions as the standard of reason. Cultural and social scientists primarily work through secondary sources, drawing on the work of historians, for whom politics and the present are implicit. The work of these historians, such as Ken Post and Richard Hill, is subjected to scholarly criticism elsewhere (see Cambridge and Feuchtwang, 1990). Not included in this analysis, although they are connected, are the many analyses of colonialism as discourse inspired by Said's *Orientalism* (1978) which are focused more on literary criticism and cultural theory than examining contemporary race politics.

This chapter is a critical commentary offered in support of the theorisation of race and anti-racist politics pursued by cultural and social scientists. But it argues that the theorisation of the race concept which emerges from these accounts is too generalised to inform an effective anti-racist politics. First, I look at a theoretical and critical exploration of how present accounts of race and ethnicity are analytically and politically constrained by simplistic histories.

Slavery, colonialism and early (often nineteenth-century) race[1] theory provide the historical material most often used in reinventing the history of racial inequality in Britain and North America: a history in which Asians form a subordinate part of the category 'black' (Modood, 1994). Slavery, colonialism and race theory are processes, each of which has a vast conceptual hinterland; a multiplicity of associations with race and ethnicity which are, as this chapter will argue, rarely explored. As a result of this lack of exploration, there is no analysis of what race means in these processes. Although accounts of these complex processes vary in richness of detail, many are highly schematic, stylised and caricatured. Ambiguity and complexity are frequently substituted by a stark simplicity which operates as a defence against the dilution of a central message concerning racial oppression. Consequently a simplified past and present emerges from these accounts in which slavery and colonialism carry a heavy burden of representation.

This past and present is united by its successive examples of black oppression, which is the analytic focus of such accounts. Slavery and so on are symbolic of past oppression and inequities, invoked to sustain an account of the present and to assert a continuity between past and present. History in this way is employed as a narrative device in which the forms of racial inequality are less important than its general essence – black oppression. The oppression of black people in white-dominated societies is established as an ongoing set of processes which are deeply embedded in a Western sense of nationhood, identity and self, and the experience of oppression itself becomes significant in organising black identities. hooks (1982: 15–49) for example poignantly recalls the sexism of the black female slave experience and its part in constructing the contemporary experience of African American women (ibid.: 51–85). Jordan's (1984: 50) account of early English impressions of Africans in describing the 'Apes of Africa' impart a sense of the barbarity of English superiority involved in English-ness. Histories of racial inequality are hence a symbolic, narrative device in securing two analytically and politically constrained identities – one black the other white, rooted in a differential relationship to oppression. The construction of unitary and racially demarcated identities is theoretically and politically problematic. The fragmentation of black identities at the level of cultural expression (Hall, 1992: 254) has so far failed to address the political rationale for unitary identities – the need for black self-defence through anti-racist struggles. Racism and anti-racism are both forms of social and cultural production construed in political discourses and one requires the other. Assertion of racial disadvantage and marginalisation requires counter-assertion and self-defence.

Self-defence has two dimensions; a gathering of the potential forces to be mobilised in resistance to racism and a discourse on victimhood. If the forms of contemporary resistance are as generalised as the forms of oppression and identities which are deployed as narrative devices in historiography then the politics of black self-defence will be hampered by a lack of specific targets for political reform. White oppression is essentially elusive and deeply embedded in the everyday. The advantage of a discourse claiming victims is the part it can play in mobilising a collective memory and a version of white history, so that written versions of the past register rather than overlook the forms of human barbarity implicated in slavery and colonialism. But embedded in the politics of victim-hood is also an appeal for restitution, a debt owed by society to the oppressed; a statement of entitlement. This is highly contentious, at least in African American politics. Steele (1990: 15) for example argues that victim-hood does not actually benefit victims and that the politics of entitlement has encouraged African Americans to invest in victimisation and poverty in a manner which is both immobilising and disabling. An important moral claim about victims and entitlement can also become an easy way for whites to indulge their racial guilt in a few handouts to alleviate the worst excesses of black poverty and marginalisation – the approach of the Reagan/Bush administrations to racial inequality.

A key problem with simplistic histories of blackness and whiteness is that they rarely discuss what these concepts mean and how their meanings have changed. In focusing on the *fact* of black oppression and not its mechanisms an opportunity to understand the meanings of blackness and, indeed, the meanings of whiteness – a neglected dimension of race analysis except as part of a general account of 'oppression' – is missed. It is important to understand whiteness and the mechanisms deployed in its defence because these issues connect with some important themes in contemporary North American (and British) politics concerning the legacy of the racial sins of colonialism and slavery. The United States, for example, has seen some aggressive demands for a statute of limitations on historical guilt and the apparent minority privileges they have sustained in the striking down of equity and affirmative action programmes in some states. This raises some important questions about the contemporary meaning attached to whiteness in the context of bids to reformulate it in more positive terms. Gallagher (1995: 177, 180) argues that the 'white man's burden' has been resurrected at the end of the twentieth century, only now it is claiming the status of victim in a search for what Blauner (1972: 278–9) calls a 'useable past'. As whiteness, along with other racial categories, is constantly constructed and reconstructed there are bids to sanitise it through selective acts of historical forgetting. Simplistic and generalised accounts of white oppression can more easily be turned back on themselves so that oppressors become victims. More thorough, and hence more convincing, accounts of the meaning and defence of whiteness through black oppression are less easily overturned and re-appropriated for other political purposes. The rhetoric of black self-defence has produced its own forms of white resistance and these need to be properly understood and countered.

So, to summarise the theoretical background, histories requiring victims and resistances at this general level are highly problematic though they speak volumes about the failure of white-dominated societies to seriously address racism as a political problem. In mobilising historical processes like colonialism in symbolic form as narrative devices we miss the conceptual field attached to empire which has a rich hinterland of racial thinking and racial imagery which can be used to embellish a theory of race and to sustain less general and more highly targeted political projects. These histories also fail to specify the relationship between past and present except in the most general formulation of a racial oppression spanning historical epochs.

In order to provide an example of Stanley's 'competing versions of the past' this argument is pursued in more detail with the help of an example of this kind of general formulation of historiography, Khan's (1991) 'Influences shaping relations between the East Indians and the Anglo-Canadians in Canada: 1903–1947' published in the *Journal of Ethnic Studies*.

## The symbolic empire

Khan uses the notion of empire to argue that the disenfranchisement and exclusion of East Indian immigrants to Canada (primarily British Columbia) in the first years of this century centrally concerns Canadian visions of itself as the heir to the (British) empire. This in turn exacted certain requirements (whiteness) in terms of immigration. Empire is presented as the key to a Canadian identity and a Canadian interpretation of the significance of East Indians as immigrants to Canada. This analysis is offered to support an (implied) account of present Canadian race politics.

Empire in the sense in which it is deployed in this kind of argument is a narrative device. Of course the (British) empire no longer exists, but it narrates a past invoking in symbolic form, a present of white supremacy and black subjugation in which blackness and whiteness become disembodied essences: skin symbols of a text that has been stripped away. The symbolic empire sustains two important but limited political points. Whites share a history of racial violence which they have attempted to obscure in their own inventions of empire, slavery and so on. And there must be a space for black self-defence, as part of a more broadly based political programme, in white-dominated societies.

As an analytic device the symbolic empire is problematic. First, it assumes that black and white were centrally significant distinctions in the conceptualisation of empire. Empire subjects in British political discourses were conceptualised as administrative units as Indians, Nigerians and so on, sometimes grouped together but not primarily categorised by skin colour. Empire subjects were by no means conceptualised as an undifferentiated mass, but distinguished on the basis of their capacity for nationhood. Similarly, Canadian political discourses in the early part of this century conceptualised and specifically excluded immigrants on the basis of source countries. Classification by skin colour is a feature of post-immigration race-relations issues in 'host' white countries and a feature in discourses on resistance to racial exclusion.

Second, the symbolic empire conceals what needs to be revealed if we wanted to develop a theory and politics of race. Empire is a concept which organises, and is organised by, other concepts; it is a part of a conceptual field. If we examine the conceptual field of empire we find a richly textured discourse about race, nation and peoples. We also find forms of connection and political community, such as nationhood in the making. Most importantly it is possible to map the range of meanings which were attached to key concepts. Empire has some definite conditions of production and administrative arrangements in which concepts are embedded, produced and organised. The symbolic empire on the other hand has no form and the meanings of key concepts are asserted rather than investigated.

Third, in the symbolic empire all ambiguity and sense of contestation are removed. There is no sense of history as competing accounts of the past. Empire was never an object of unitary analysis in Canadian or in British political discourses. Canadian notions of (British) empire are, at the very minimum, fractured by Quebec's version of history and the nation-building project (Berger, 1969).[2] Similarly, there was a growing voice of

opposition to empire in Britain earlier this century among liberal and
social democratic supporters of colonial freedom.

Finally, to conceptualise India as part of a symbolic empire in the first
half of this century (as Khan, does) is to overlook the specific history of
that country. By 1900 India was only formally still a part of the British
empire. Its transitional status as a 'nation in waiting' was vigorously
pursued by civil disobedience and by constitutional negotiations and was
clearly understood both in Britain and in Canada (Jacobs, 1922: 4,642;
*Queens Quarterly*, 1927–8, 1930, 1933; *Times*, 19 June 1931: 10).[3] By
1920 Britain was clinging to India by brutal military and policing action
alone (see, for example, the All India Congress Committee, 18 July 1930).
The Indian empire was over despite the fact that full independence did not
come until 1947.

## Nationhood

When empire is investigated as a concept constructed in political
discourses[4] and through political and administrative actions, the symbolic
empire is displaced by an emerging Indian nationhood. India became the
first non-white country to achieve independent nationhood from the
British empire. The terms on which it did this powerfully contextualised
India, generating a discourse on the capacity of Indians for political association which re-emerged when they became immigrants to Britain in the
1960s (Knowles, 1992) and which took a particular form in Canada in the
early part of this century. The Canadian contextualisation of East Indians
may be seen as a defence of a particular vision of the nation-building
project in Canada. This argument is pursued using two vignettes. One
discusses the imperial vision of Indian nationhood in the 1930s. The other
the conceptualisation of East Indians in Canadian political discourse in the
1920s in defence of a white Canada. The two are clearly connected though
not in any straightforward way.[5]

### Indian nationhood

The colonial vision of Indian nationhood dominated the formal construction of the Indian nation-state. This was a matter of hegemony, and not
consensus, in British politics and contrasts markedly with Indian visions
(there were many) of nationhood. In so far as the formal construction
of the Indian nation-state left its archaeology in political discourses, it
is evident that Britain imposed certain conceptions of readiness for
nationhood, democracy and citizenship. Indians emerged from this
contextualised in political debates as lacking in citizenship capacity, a
status they carried with them to the countries to which they migrated.
Indian nationhood, at least in the imperial imagination, was a matter of
'readiness' and the extent to which a democratic political framework could

be assembled. Readiness for nationhood was largely formulated in a social democratic political framework[6] and could only occur under specific conditions. From the 1920s India was part of the British Labour Party's fantasy of commonwealth as an expression of human solidarity and international co-operation (Knowles, 1992).

Readiness for nationhood was partly a matter of race. 'British and other European races' were distinguished from 'native communities' (Labour Party, 1933: 3) for whom nationhood was a distant prospect; and race was a matter of culture, industry and civilisation. Readiness was also a matter of constitutional viability. This included the stipulation that India form a single 'peoplehood' at the level of the nation state, despite the fact that India had never been a single political unit even under imperial rule. Readiness for nationhood was jeopardised by India's social heterogeneity which complicated the business of forging a 'peoplehood'. Readiness was also jeopardised by India's social structure seen as partially modern but containing remnants of feudal and theocratic orders. Finally, readiness was a matter of demonstrating a capacity for civil order as a precondition for political community, and India was seen as volatile and conflict torn because of the emerging political forces created by the imperial-driven prospect of a communal award (e.g. *The Times*, 19 June 1931: 10).

Democracy was a key concept in the political debates surrounding Indian independence. Throughout its dealings with India Britain held up an ideal form of democracy which it later failed to implement. For example, despite parallels drawn with Canada (*Times of India*, 13 January 1931: 1), federal India took the Canadian system of a territorial federation plus a system of sectional representation organised by religious affiliation, caste, gender, economic status and so on. Also Britain only selectively enfranchised sections of the Indian population carefully distinguishing those who were 'capable' of citizenship from the 'incapable'. The 'incapable' comprised the peasantry and untouchables; in fact most of the population. When independence was finally awarded in 1947 the vast majority of the Indian population were not enfranchised, and those who were had a partial form of citizenship as workers, as women and so on.

Imperial conceptions of nationhood delayed Indian independence by half a century. The boundary between empire and nationhood had until 1947 been organised by skin colour. As India was poised to join Canada, Australia, New Zealand and South Africa, the 'white club' of the commonwealth, it was importantly contextualised as an unstable, poorly developed and hopelessly plural society. The political arrangements for Indian nationhood invoked an explicit imperial commentary on the capacity of the Indian people for 'proper' political association. An old debate concerning race and 'mind' was given a new configuration in a discourse about the capacity for nationhood. As Britain pronounced the masses of India incapable of 'proper' political participation India moved from subjecthood to second-class nationhood and this, arguably, did as much damage as a couple of centuries of imperialism.

## Canadian nationhood

Bauman's (1992) observation that modern nation states are the product of nationalist discourses and the hegemonising actions of the elite in which identities and counter identities are conceived and sustained and in which we-ness is constructed through they-ness, aptly describes the nation-building project in Canada and its relationship to East Indians. Indian-ness and East Indian-ness are contextualised by the different political discourses, administrative actions and projects in which they were invoked. Indian-ness was construed as an act of colonial tutelage in which British constructions of India were about construing a form of (makeshift) nationhood in the discharging of (imagined) colonial responsibilities. Concurrently, Canadian nation-building, a process the Canadian government controlled through immigration, was in full swing. Canadian constructions of East Indians emerged not out of fantasies of empire as Khan suggests, but in defence of its own nation-building project which required the exclusion of East Indians and other 'Orientals'. In Bauman's terms the we-ness of Canadian nationhood was construed in the exclusion of the they-ness of East Indians and Orientals.

There were many versions of Canadian nationhood (Berger, 1970) in the first half of this century of which (a relationship to British) imperialism was only one form. French and English Canada had radically divergent notions of history and national identity, with the Quebec nation-building project challenging what Bodeman (1984) refers to as Anglo Canadian social mythology, and with Anglo/French charter groups usurping the land and social organisations of native Canadians. The hegemonic Anglo vision of Canadian nationhood is the one discussed here, because it had a force in immigration policy which controlled the composition of the nation, and not because it was uncontested.

The nation-building project has many dimensions which usefully contextualise the need for the expansion of the population. The generation of an appropriate and productive work-force both agricultural and artisan, a transport infrastructure and the development of Canada as a world economic force were all part of securing Canadian prosperity (Tolmie, 1926). Within this context the calibre of nation-building material was important and the quality of immigrant populations was a recurring theme in twenties federal parliamentary debates. Although quality was predominantly a matter of ethnic origins and racial characteristics, it was not exclusively so. Debates concerning the advisability of bringing young Dr Barnardos children from Britain to be trained on the farms as Canadian citizens raised questions concerning the need to select out the 'dishonest, untruthful or mentally backward' so as to transport only those who could be given a 'certificate of character' (Hocken, 1926). Clearly there were eugenic concerns about the fitness of the white races where this involved selecting the offspring of 'failed' families.

The immigrant/alien distinction, however, was central in identifying nation-building material and in construing the character of the nation which immigrants were to join. The twenties were seen as an important period in nation-building. With more careful immigration control to the south Canada was in a position to 'choose, to select, to reject' (Guthrie, 1924). Canada's favoured sources of immigration, as the statistics for the early part of this century shows, was Northern Europe and the United States (except blacks, see Williams, D., 1989). The transporting of Barnardos children, the assisted passages schemes and the state-assisted settlement of the United Empire Loyalists all support this project of building Canada out of white people even though this included the less preferred Central and Southern Europeans. In an explicit reference to East Indians an MP petitioned – 'Let us see that we pump into this country a proper class of immigrants...from Europe' (Jacobs, 1922: 2,514) and 'get people of the right type who will stick to the country until they become good Canadian citizens' (Tolmie, 1926).

The agricultural imagery of homesteading and the ownership of land was important in structuring both an image of Canada and the immigrants deemed suitable for nation-building. 'In this dominion of Canada every man [sic] can have some stake here: if he will practice thrift and make a few sacrifices in his young manhood he can have land of his own and a house of his own' (Hocken, 1924: 1,057). Canadians were still settlers who had hewn a livelihood out of the untamed forests and grassland and the work and sobriety required of land ownership was seen as a discipline against disruptive behaviour and political agitation. Rural life was the training ground for Canadian citizenship. The farm was where young immigrants would acquire 'moral education...lead a good life...(and) become good citizens' (ibid.: 4,006). The farm was the moral centre of Canadian life and it was defended in a political debate which reiterated the 'absolute' importance of continued oriental exclusion. Whiteness in the form of Canadian citizenship hence acquired an edifice of meaning in the political debates surrounding immigration. Nation-building through immigration control was not just the latest technique of a general white oppression continuing from colonialism: it gave a specific and racially exclusionary meaning to being Canadian which tied it to agricultural enterprise.

Aliens on the other hand were specifically excluded as potential nation-building material. Whilst immigrants join (on whatever conditions) a host population, aliens invade it and displace others whose claims have, by implication, a greater priority. Aliens (the Chinese, Japanese and East Indians often referred to as Hindus or Hindoos) were primarily admitted as a cheap disposable contract labour force under bonds posted by the companies like the British Empire Steel Corporation and referred to as 'the prohibited classes' and as 'undesirables' (Woodsworth, 1924). Immigration restrictions were also successfully directed at black populations of West Indians and African Americans. In the period 1897–1930 it is claimed that less than 1 per cent of Canadian immigrants were of African descent (Williams, D., 1989).

The exclusion of aliens was effected through immigration legislation targeted at specific sources and through the removal of normal citizenship rights. The 'Single Continuous Journey' provision (1908) added to the (1906) Immigration Act effectively excluded those travelling from India to Canada by virtue of the ways in which shipping lines were organised. The Chinese were also explicitly excluded by the Chinese Immigration Act (1923) and neither were repealed until 1947 (Taylor, 1991). East Indians without Anglo Saxon parents were disenfranchised (1907) in British Columbia leading them to lose their federal vote too (Khan, 1991: 102). East Indians did not become enfranchised Canadian citizens until 1947, the same year India got formal independence from the British empire.

Aliens are construed in political discourses as displacing Canadian interests. Their effects on Canadian jobs, their ownership of property, the size of their populations and effects on education are carefully documented in the Province of British Columbia (1927) *Report on Oriental Activities*. This report suggests that there was a concerted attempt by that province, which contained nearly all the alien population of Canada,[7] to drive aliens out of the key economic activities of mining, lumbering, the saw mills and fishing, placing fishing in the hands of 'White British subjects and Canadian Indians' (p. 3). The trade union lobby especially staunchly defended Canadian workers against cheap alien labour which depressed living standards. Aliens were excluded from public works and held strictly controlled trade licences through which they earned their living. Fears of displacement were clearly expressed in parliament – 'We in British Columbia want no more Hindoo, Chinamen and Japs running our stores. They are running white people out' (McBride, 1923: 4,648) – and on the streets in the form of anti-oriental riots in Vancouver in the early years of this century (Ward, 1990).

Aliens in general and East Indians specifically were conceptualised as the bearers of lower standards of civilisation, as a 'heathen debased class of people' oblivious to the higher cultural forms of white settlers with whom they could never assimilate. 'They are shack dwellers, men who do not make any effort whatever to improve the country, and they live under conditions we could not tolerate for a moment' (Dickie, 1923: 4,661). Civilisation was one of the markers which made them un-assimilable into Canadian nationhood. Assimilation was partly a matter of conscious choice. 'They do not know our language nor do they know our customs, and what is more they do not want to know them' (Neill, 1923: 4,645). But it was also a matter of suitability and capacity (Misrow, 1915: 33).

East Indian aliens were incapable of citizenship or full political membership of the Canadian nation. This was made explicit in their
disenfranchisement and connects with British assessments. Britain had
objected to the disenfranchisement of East Indians in British dominions at
the imperial conference in 1918. It was swiftly pointed out that East
Indians did not have citizenship in other (white) commonwealth countries
either; worse still 'there was not even the faintest pretence at suffrage in
India so how absurd to enfranchise them in Canada' (Neill, 1923: 4644).
The fear in British Columbia was that enfranchised East Indians, who were
only capable of sectional political will, would use their political muscle to
get immigration restrictions removed and hence flood the west coast of
Canada with their relatives. This is ultimately a commentary on 'the
Eastern mind'. As one MP put it – 'they (Hindoos) have the mentality of
children without childhood's innocence' (Dickie, 1923: 4,661).

The Canadian nation and its potential members are affirmed in the
construction of aliens. Immigrants are all that aliens are not. Immigrants
contribute to rather than detract from Canadian prosperity and development. Immigrants are civilised, capable of citizenship and assimilable.
Alien is a political category against which 'Canadian' and 'immigrant' are
construed. The visibility of aliens was a marker of important differences
the most significant of which was 'mind'. The logic of unassimilability was
that Canadian nationhood was being defended from the impact of lesser
standards of peoplehood. The discourses around aliens was about the
affirmation of a Canadian identity and the material from which it
construed itself. The distinction between alien and immigrant was conceptualised in racial terms. British constructions of the Indian nation and
Canadian constructions of a nation-in-process to be defended against inap-
propriate (alien) populations both highlight the significance of political
capacity in different ways. Ultimately political capacity was about a state
of 'mind' and 'mind' was conceptualised as a property of racial memberships.

Racial difference and race competition are key concepts in the Canadian
context. Much of the Canadian attempt to mark and exclude aliens
revolves around the conception that races were naturally occurring categories of the population, interbreeding 'stocks' with a habitat or 'place'
decreed by a natural order, and especially by the environment. Climatic
tolerance was especially privileged and ruled out those accustomed to a
'tropical climate' with 'manners and customs so unlike those of our own
people' (Misrow, 1915: 33 citing the immigration regulations used to
exclude East Indians). Horticultural metaphors are employed to discuss
racial 'rooting' and 'transplanting' to support arguments about which
people *belonged* in Canada and which people were *alien* (Humphrey,
1923: 4,648). The problem with aliens was that they had been 'transplanted' to, but did not 'grow' naturally in, the country of which they were
ignorant' (Neill, 1923: 4,645). Some people took more easily to Canadian

soil – and those people were the assimilable who could be rendered invisible within a white majority. Racial mixing was seen as inherently problematic, provoking disorder. Race was used in the Canadian context to invoke distinctions between populations which should not co-exist in the same political community or share a membership of nationhood. Statements about belonging were accompanied by warnings of the effects of defying what was seen as a 'natural' order by introducing race mixing and race competition. At this time the multiracial society could not be other than a recipe for social disintegration because Canadian multiracialism was only capable of incorporating a collectivity of Europeans until the 1960s.

Notions of racial stock, racial capacity, race competition and racial difference are key concepts in British and Canadian discourses and this chapter has made an attempt to unpick some of the concepts mobilised in the use of these terms so as to move analytically beyond the generalised notions of race deployed in accounts of the symbolic empire.

## Racial inequality in the present

If all histories are really accounts of the present then the present invoked by the symbolic empire is a present in which visible minorities in Canadian society are excluded and marginalised. In replacing the symbolic by the discursive empire, which turns out to be a series of discourses on Canadian and Indian nationhood a number of things are apparent. It is apparent that Indian nationhood was construed in second-rate terms and that Canadian nationhood was defended against precisely the kinds of immigrants whose capacity for citizenship was in question. In the sense in which both Britain and Canada contributed to the conceptualisation of (East) Indian-ness, India was indeed an empire project. But what does this discursive empire (which turns out to be two nationhoods in process) offer to an account of racial equality in the present? Khan's (1991: 10) suggestions of understanding a 'history of the concept of race' hints at the very important themes of exclusion and marginalisation which do comment on the present state of race and ethnic relations in Canadian society. This general admonition to 'understand' does not however release us from the necessity to comment on what precise forms this might take, a project from which Khan opts out.

Immigration is an obvious candidate for analysis of exclusionary and marginalising practices. Immigration is still the major nation-building tool in Canada and nation-building remained an explicitly white enterprise until well into the sixties (Satzewich, 1989; Ward, 1990) when it was officially (at the level of stated policy) deracialised and organised to meet labour needs on the basis of a points system. By 1991 Britain had slipped from first to eighth position as a source country for Canadian nation-building material, superseded by Hong Kong, Poland, China, India, the

Philippines, Lebanon and Vietnam (Statistics Canada, *Year Book*, 1992), the result of a shifting emphasis placed on investor immigrants and refugees. It appears as if racially organised exclusion and marginalisation no longer occur. However, in order to be sure that immigration has been de-racialised it would be necessary to compare entry numbers with applicants. We would also need to be sure that immigration practices and procedures (and not just policies) are conducted in a way which does not privilege one source country over another (Taylor, 1991). Immigration remains an important issue not just because it still controls the nation-building process but because it is a system of 'signs' to former immigrants now settled in Canada about exclusion and marginalisation. Immigration policy indicates how they are regarded, their value in, and their significance to, Canadian society. In popular discourse, if not officially, one's status as an immigrant is significant in the mediation of entitlement to society's resources.

The federal government has made it clear that it is seeking the legislative means to more effectively manage immigration levels set by parliament, and that there is an explicit intention to cut the number of refugees to Canada by 40 per cent (*Globe and Mail*, 17 June 1992) by giving immigration officers at points of entry the power to decide if a refugee claim is valid. This sustains the idea that refugee and immigrant populations (many of which are now visible minorities) need more careful management and regulation and are by implication undesirable additions to the nation. Overall, immigration is a significant regulatory mechanism which invokes a discourse on rights and nationhood, but whilst it is no longer permitted to make distinctions based on race it still carries some significant implications for visible populations.

To find examples of marginalisation and exclusion of visible populations in Canada we must also look beyond immigration to internal and informal systems of racially organised exclusions around the distribution of jobs, housing, wages, education and other social resources. The lack of proper ethnic monitoring in the distribution of these resources makes general comments about the structural position of visible populations difficult to sustain. However anyone interested in the microanalysis of racism is not short of case studies of teachers and health care workers who have been subjected to racial abuse, of human rights abuses involving psychiatry (Knowles, 1996) and of the violent and discordant relationship between law enforcement agencies and black populations in major Canadian cities. Khan's reliance on the past to make a case about the present is in part a reaction to the difficulty of speaking about race in a country where there is a determined race blindness, an aggressive official multiculturalism and a concern with political correctness.

## Conclusions

The discursive empire of two nations in process is no more 'real' than the symbolic empire which it replaces. Reality is not the point. The point is which is the more enabling analytic device for a commentary on race and racism past and present. This chapter has shown that the symbolic empire is limited. The discursive empire of nations emerging on the other hand allows us to see how notions of race have an entire conceptual field and a set of political and administrative actions in which they are deployed and acquire meaning. In place of generalised notions of black oppression past and present we have a more precise notion of the form oppression took and takes, how notions of racial difference were invoked and administered. This provides us with some concrete targets for political intervention around immigration practices and around issues of distribution.

## Acknowledgements

Thanks to Noel Dyck and David Mofford for their comments on this chapter, and also to Francine Robillard for help with manuscript preparation.

## Notes

1  Phenotype and biology alone did not organise the racial mapping of peoplehood in the nineteenth century but were contested by comparative philology (see Leopold, 1974). Racial mapping was organised in relation to political and administrative actions and these cannot be predicted from some general account of nineteenth-century race theory.

2  See, for example, Henry Borassa's *Great Britain and Canada* (1902) and John Ewart's *Kingdom of Canada* (1908) discussed in Berger (1969 and 1970).

3  Indian independence was guaranteed in the Montagu Chelmsford Declaration (1917) and the Government of India Act (1919). The fact-finding missions by British politicians and trade unionists culminating in the reports of the Indian Statutory Commission (1930), the Royal Commission on Indian Labour (1931) and the Round Table Conferences (India Office, 1930–1) held in London with (imperially selected) representatives of Indian opinion were all attempts to develop a constitution which could give political expression to the complexities of Indian nationhood.

4  Political discourse provides some important clues as to how (East) Indians were dealt with as a population in administrative and political terms. Clearly political discourses are also a limited investigative tool and tell us little about popular discourses and nothing about the ways in which (East) Indians conceptualised themselves.

5  Clearly there was a relationship between Britain, Canada and India mediated through the administrative apparatus of empire. This chapter demonstrates certain similarities in British and Canadian discourses concerning (East) India at the level of conceptualising what it meant to be (East) Indian and the prioritisation of citizenship capacity as indexical of other capacities.

6  The British Labour Party was highly involved in negotiating Indian independence and a second-class citizenship for Indians. It was the Labour Party (as

the colonial government between 1929 and 1931) which ran the Round Table Conference negotiations, participated in the key royal commissions which established the conditions in which independence would be granted, and which finally awarded independence in 1947.

7 MPs from British Columbia took a harder line on East Indian immigration than those in the rest of Canada, as this was where most of Canada's East Indian population, estimated at 1,200 (Jacobs, 1922), lived.

# 4 The historiography of immigrants and ethnic minorities
## Britain compared with the USA

*Panikos Panayi*

History is written by those with power. The mere act of producing a historical study indicates that a group has gained power. For any group, the production of history is as fundamental as literature or music. The most important 'groups' for the writing of history since its development as an academic subject during the nineteenth and twentieth centuries have been national. American historians write mostly about their own history as do their British counterparts. In comparison, few people attempt to deal with thematic projects: comparative history is the exception. The reasons for this are twofold. First, linguistic problems, as empirical research forms the basis of writing for a trained historian. Just as important, however, is the all-embracing control exercised by nationalism over all modern human activity. We cannot expect history to be excluded from this control.

Like all else in nationalism, the standard histories of individual countries, especially in Europe, have tended to be exclusive of minority groups, be they on a class, gender or ethnic basis. The birth of history as an academic discipline in the nineteenth century meant the production, especially in Europe, of glorified national histories. Only with time, especially under the influence of academic Marxism after the Second World War, did this situation change. Initially, the working classes moved to the forefront with the development of social history, followed by the study of women and minorities, partly because these groups gained positions in the academic historical profession, therefore writing the history of the groups of which they formed a part.

Clearly the picture varies from one state to another, as ethnic minorities are studied earlier in countries where they are central. The notable example here is the USA, although even in Britain important work on Irish and Jewish immigrants within the country was produced in the second half of the nineteenth century. However, one major tendency in historical writing of minorities is to create ghettos; so that, for instance, historians of immigrants in Britain tend to be ghettoised in their profession and viewed as a minority by the mainstream, in the same way as the subjects which they study.

This situation may be inevitable given the continued domination of the historical profession by native-born, middle-class males who can trace their ancestry in their country of residence through several generations, a position which exists in Britain, much of Europe and the USA. The move into the mainstream of immigrant and ethnic history, particularly in Europe, cannot fully take place until people with foreign origins obtain academic positions as easily as natives.

Clearly there are variations between different states in the above processes. The centrality of race in the development of the USA means that the history of minorities has been written both by historians of solid white middle-class stock, and by those who proudly display their ethnic origins. The picture contrasts with Britain, which, until the influx of postwar immigrants, regarded itself as ethnically homogeneous, a position which did not change until the 1960s. Historians in Britain turned their attention to immigrants after social scientists, who had begun to produce studies of newcomers, especially from the West Indies, as soon as their presence became noticeable in British cities during the 1950s (Banton, 1955; Glass, 1960).

At this stage, we have to re-emphasise the centrality of history to group identity, pointing to the development of concepts of multiracialism in the USA at an earlier stage than within Britain. In the latter the perceived idea among the right that the population has a common ancestry acts against the move of immigrant and ethnic history into the mainstream. History differs from social science because of its centrality to group identity. The heritage of a nation-state needs to be protected because the acceptance of outsiders as part of a country's ancestry represents an important indication that it has become pluralistic and multiracial. In both Britain and the USA this process is perceived to have happened to a greater or lesser extent although at different stages and to varying degrees.

## Britain

In Britain the study of immigrants and ethnic minorities has only recently begun to move into the mainstream. Nineteenth-century historical writing was characterised by the production of glorified histories of England in the Whig tradition whose central argument focused upon a progression away from the arbitrary power of medieval monarchy moving ever on towards a liberal paradise. Two central characteristics of such writing consisted of its belief in progress and its tendency to ignore the position of the working classes, whose fate improved only gradually as a result of the democratisation process consequent upon industrialisation.

In opposition to such writing, a distinct working-class history began to develop during the first half of the twentieth century, especially under the influence of scholars such as G. D. H. Cole (1947) and J. L. and L. B. Hammond (1919). A major turning point came with the publication of E. P. Thompson's *The Making of the English Working Classes* in 1963, after which numerous less ambitious books appeared on individual aspects of working-class life and particular geographical locations. At the same time the development of social and economic history in British universities allowed the creation of a large number of lectureships, often taken up by scholars writing about the working classes, a process which continued until the 1980s. This development was also fundamentally influenced by the working-class origins of many of the individuals taking up the new posts, who had made their way up the educational ladder through the grammar school system implemented by the 1944 Education Act. Essentially, by writing about the working classes they were reconstructing the history of their parents and grandparents.

Few of the historians appointed during the 1960s and 1970s ventured into the field of immigrant history because they remained as concerned about their own new subjects, which excluded immigrants, as the people who had written before them. Nevertheless, this could not remain the situation for long, primarily because of the transformation of Britain caused by the postwar immigration of newcomers from the empire and commonwealth. Social scientists such as Banton (1955) and Glass (1960) immediately focused upon the newcomers, meaning that the concern with race would eventually seep through to historians, whose methodology and areas of concern change less quickly than those of sociologists and political scientists.

The growing obsession of British society and politics from the 1950s with the impact of immigrants, leading to a series of immigration acts and to the passage of race relations legislation, created the idea of a multiracial society in which careers were open to all, irrespective of ethnic and social origin. This development has had two effects. First, it has forced a small number of British historians to turn to the impact of immigration and racism during the nineteenth and twentieth centuries. Second, it has allowed an equally small number of historians of immigrant origin to enter the historical profession, who write history close to their experience in the same way as historians of working-class origin did.

However, at this stage we need to recognise that the growth of the study of minorities in British history does not simply consist of a reaction to contemporary events during the postwar period. Two groups in particular, the Irish and the Jews, have a lengthy historiography stretching back to the second half of the nineteenth century and remaining distinct from the mainstream Whig interpretation of history.

Beginning with the Irish, the starting-point in their historiography is with John Denvir's informative *The Irish in Britain* (1892), which gives an account of contemporary Irish settlements throughout England, Wales and Scotland, as well as providing much detail about their historical development. The next contribution of equal academic merit, which did not appear until the 1940s, was J. E. Handley's meticulously researched two-volume social history of the Irish in Scotland (1943; 1947), which has yet to be superseded. Two decades later there followed J. A. Jackson's *The Irish in Britain* (1963), an important survey focusing upon the nineteenth and twentieth centuries.

By this point the postwar influx of Irish immigrants to Britain had swollen to over 900,000 or 2 per cent of the population (Holmes, 1988: 216). Consequently, an increase in the study of their nineteenth-century predecessors followed. This has resulted in the production of numerous books focusing upon particular urban environments, including Lees on London (1979), Finnegan on York (1982) and Fielding on Manchester (1988). In addition, several nationwide collections of essays and books have appeared (Swift and Gilley, 1985; 1989; Davis, 1991) together with countless articles on numerous themes. Furthermore, Irish Studies Centres have also been established at the Universities of Liverpool and North London, which focus heavily upon the Irish in Britain.

Anglo-Jewry has an even fuller historiography than the Irish in Britain. We can take 1851 as the starting-point because that year witnessed the publication of Moses Margoliouth's monumental three-volume *History of the Jews in Great Britain*, tracing the history of Jewish settlement from pre-Roman times to the Victorian era (Margoliouth, 1851). The period until the outbreak of the First World War saw the appearance of further but more limited studies (for example, Mills, 1863; Hyamson, 1908) as well as the establishment of the Jewish Historical Society of England which published its *Transactions*.

Consequently, the groundwork was laid for Cecil Roth, the father of twentieth-century Anglo-Jewish history, who began his productive career in the interwar years and continued to write on numerous general and specific aspects of the Jews in England after the war (1941; 1950). The only other figure who could really compare with Roth was V. D. Lipman, who produced a series of books and articles, most notably his *Social History of the Jews in England* (1954).

The 1960s and early 1970s represent a major breakthrough in the historiography of Jews in Britain, with the publication of three major social histories of the late-nineteenth-century influx from Eastern Europe (Gartner, 1960; Garrard, 1971; Gainer, 1972). Since then, Jewish history has witnessed the production of numerous studies, focusing especially upon anti-Semitism, ethnicity and relations between different groups within Anglo-Jewry. The leading figures in the field now are four British Jews, Geoffrey Alderman, David Cesarani, David S. Katz and Tony Kushner, each of whom has written on a variety of areas (Alderman, 1983; 1992; Cesarani, 1990; 1994; Katz, 1982; 1994; Kushner, 1989; 1992), together with an American, Todd M. Endelman (1979; 1990). We should also mention Colin Holmes (1979) and Bill Williams (1976), among others. Bill Rubinstein (1996), an American Jew with a Chair in History at Aberystwyth, has most recently produced one of the longest books on Anglo-Jewry, which, however, distances itself from the above-mentioned figures. More than any other area of ethnic history in Britain, Jewish history is written by members of the group (although Holmes and Williams are notable exceptions).

Few other groups in Britain have a historiography as long and detailed as that of the Jews and Irish. Exceptions with regard to longevity include Huguenots, whose *Transactions* date back to 1885. Similarly, Gypsies have a journal devoted to but not written by them: the *Journal of the Gypsy Lore Society*. Germans, meanwhile, like the Irish and Jews, have a historiography stretching back to the late nineteenth century, beginning essentially with Karl Heinrich Schaible's *Geschichte der Deutschen in England* (1885). The works of the next two authors who approach the subject of Germans in Britain, Ian Colvin (1915) and C. R. Hennings (1923) are unreliable because in both cases the First World War colours the perspectives of the writers. Only from the 1970s has the history of Germans in Britain begun to attract close attention, with a focus primarily upon refugees from Nazism but also, in more recent years, on the nineteenth and early twentieth centuries (Mosse *et al.*, 1991; Panayi, 1991; 1995; 1996). The recent historiography of Germans has involved both Germans and non-Germans and in this case it is difficult to speak of history representing an ethnic identity, although there are exceptions, notably C. C. Aronsfeld (1956; 1962), a Jewish refugee from Nazism writing on German Jews in Britain.

Italians have attracted serious academic attention only in the last decade, with the two leading scholars, Lucio Sponza (1988) and Terri Colpi, proudly displaying their Italian origins, the former being an immigrant himself and the latter describing herself as 'a third-generation Italian Scot' (Colpi, 1991: 5). Both have devoted much attention in their work towards the persecution of Italians. In addition, several smaller-scale studies have appeared on Italians (Rea, 1988; Hughes, 1991).

The final immigrant group in Britain to consider consists of non-Europeans, whose historiography began after the Seond World War, under the impact of Commonwealth immigration. However, the writing of their history points to the charade of British multiracialism. A frank assessment would have to direct attention to the fact that the writing of black history especially has been carried out primarily by white middle-class intellectuals, both British and American.

The reasons for this are legion. First, we have to point to the structural racism of British society, which discriminates against Afro-Caribbeans at every turn, hindering social mobility. We should therefore not be surprised at the existence of racism in the historical profession. The black history which is produced by black people tends to be on a local scale. We can mention the Black Cultural Archives in Brixton. However, the existence of such groups may be a reaction against the exclusiveness of the historical profession.

We can also mention the production of general books on immigrants in

Britain. These are essentially four in number. The first, from 1897, is William Cunningham's *Alien Immigrants in Britain*, which covers the period from the Norman invasion until the late eighteenth century. The next major general book does not appear until 1984 when Jim Walvin's superficial *Passage to Britain* was published. The most important landmark in the historiography of immigrants in Britain is Colin Holmes's *John Bull's Island: Immigration and British Society, 1871–1971* (1988), a 448-page study, representing the culmination of more than a decade's work and an essential starting-point for anyone either teaching or researching the theme of immigrants in Britain. The only other general work on the history of immigrants in Britain is my own *Immigration, Ethnicity and Racism in Britain, 1815–1945* (1994), an altogether different work from Holmes's book, primarily aimed at students and summarising the main arguments in 134 pages, followed by twenty-three pages of documents. It contains incisive arguments, in contrast to *John Bull's Island*, whose strength lies in the depth of its empirical research.

By the middle of the 1990s historians had begun to turn their attention to the process of immigration in the early postwar period, using government files at the Public Records Office and following on from the work of pioneering sociologists Bob Carter, Clive Harris and Shirley Joshi (1987). The books by Ian Spencer (1997) and Kathleen Paul (1997) represent deep digging by empirical historians and will no doubt be followed by further similar studies as postwar British history comes under the microscope with the release of new documents.

The state of British immigration history at the present time can only be considered as healthy. While the study of minorities may not have moved fully into the mainstream of historical research and teaching, it is now relatively straightforward to publish in the area, with both specialist and larger publishers, depending on the scope of the subject. There are also two important journals, *Ethnic and Racial Studies* and, more importantly for historians, *Immigrants and Minorities*. The latter is edited by Colin Holmes and two of his former research students, David Mayall and Donald MacRaid, and aims at publishing historical pieces.

Despite the increasing acceptance of immigrant history by British academic historians, it still faces hostility. As recently as 1986 the late Professor Sir Geoffrey Elton, Regius Professor at Cambridge and one of Britain's leading historians, as well as a Jewish refugee from Nazism,[1] could declare: 'Schools need more English history, more kings and bishops.... The non-existent history of ethnic entities and women leads to incoherent syllabuses' (Kushner and Lunn, 1990).

Nor is the historiography of immigrants in Britain complete; gaps exist. In the first place there has been a concentration, as there has been in historical writing in general, upon the nineteenth and twentieth centuries. Second, even in the modern period, some important minorities have been virtually ignored, notably Americans and French people. Thematically there has been an over-concentration upon hostility towards newcomers caused both by the Anglocentric approach of historians such as Holmes, and by the sad fact that English government and society do not value foreign languages. This second factor also partly explains the lack of attention to the process and mechanics of immigration, as an examination of sources in the areas of origin of newcomers is essential for this field. Thus, despite the numerous studies of late-nineteenth-century Jewish newcomers to Britain, we have no explanation of any merit as to why they came. Much work has been carried out on the social structure of newcomers. Ethnicity, meanwhile, has not necessarily been approached under this heading and there has been a reluctance to borrow ideas from social scientists. Anglocentrism also prevents an examination of ethnicity, as the newcomers tend to be viewed as victims of British society. In many cases, however, especially before state extension in the twentieth century, immigrants could get on with their own lives in their own ethnic communities.

## USA

The contrast between Britain and the USA is significant. In comparison to a society with an endless history which until the past thirty years has viewed itself as ethnically homogeneous, we are faced with a country which has regarded itself as a nation-state since the eighteenth century and which by the end of the nineteenth had begun to accept concepts of multiculturalism, if only because of the sheer weight of numbers involved in late-nineteenth-century immigration. In addition, the existence of Native Americans, already present before Europeans, together with the importation of African slaves, means that race has played as fundamental a role in US history as class has in Britain.

Consequently, minorities have received far more attention in the USA. Historians of America cannot ignore the history of slavery and the Civil War that followed, neither can they overlook immigrants because as Oscar Handlin wrote in 1951, 'Once I thought to write a history of the immigrants in America. Then I discovered that the immigrants *were* American history' (Handlin, 1973: 3). In addition, the pluralistic nature of American society, allowing ethnic and other groups to develop their own power bases, means that they inevitably produce their own history. Furthermore, the sheer size of the historical profession in the USA means that vast amounts of attention have focused upon every aspect of American life, the history of ethnic groups being no exception.

The specific field of immigration can be divided at least threefold into the study of Europeans, Asians and Latinos. The first have received the most attention over the longest period of time. Frederick C. Luebke (1990) has pointed to Frederick Jackson Turner (1881–1932) as a precursor of American immigrant historiography, but has also demonstrated that he produced relatively little work and that his approach was

Eurocentric. His ideas revolved around the 'frontier thesis' which involved immigrants in their new environment adapting and becoming hardier. However, the real beginnings of the historiography of immigration, especially the focus upon Europeans, starts essentially in the 1940s and 1950s, with three figures playing a leading role: Marcus Lee Hansen, Oscar Handlin and John Higham.

Hansen had already focused upon immigration during the 1920s, reviewing books published on immigrant groups for the *American Historical Review* and producing an important article for the same journal on 'The history of American immigration as a field for research' (1927) in which he pointed particularly to the possibility of work on migration and ethnicity. Two of his books were published posthumously in 1940, *The Immigrant in American History*, which deals with a variety of issues, and *The Atlantic Migration*, a meticulous, monumental and seminal study of the processes which brought people to America from 1607 to 1860 (Hansen, 1940a; 1940b; Vecoli, 1973: 82; Luebke, 1990: 43).

Handlin is probably the most influential writer in the historiography of American immigration, if only because of the sheer weight of his production; he published five books, both general and specific, on the subject between 1941 and 1959, followed by another in 1972. Two general themes emerge from Handlin's work: the importance of the urban environment (1941) and, as a consequence of this, the need for the development of ethnicity among the newcomers because of the shock of living in a new and hostile environment (1973) although his work examined all aspects of the immigrant experience (1959).

If Hansen can be regarded as the father of US migration historiography, and Handlin as the central figure in the history of ethnicity, the same role was played by John Higham for the study of hostility towards immigrants, with the publication of his *Strangers in the Land* (1955). As its subtitle suggests, *Patterns of American Nativism, 1860–1925*, it traces the major elements of hostility towards perceived outgroups, revolving around an Anglo-Saxon outlook.

The study of hostility towards European newcomers has played less of a role in immigrant historiography in the USA than it has in Britain due to both the fact that most attention in the field of racism has focused upon anti-black hostility and to the immigrant origins of most Americans which means that they choose to devote more attention to the mechanics of migration and, more importantly, to ethnicity.

In fact, European scholars have played a large role in migration research. We can point to the work of British researchers such as Charlotte Erickson (1957), Philip M. Taylor (1971) and Maldwyn Jones (1976), as well as that of German scholars such as Wolfgang Kollmann and Peter Marschalck (1973) and Dirk Hoerder (1985). Hoerder's Marxist interpretation, which focuses upon the role of the US economy in nineteenth-century migration, is the most incisive interpretation, although we cannot ignore the population growth which pushed people out of Europe.

Ethnicity has been the main focus of studies by Americans. Something of a reaction took place against the work of Handlin and his concept of the uprooted huddling together, reaching a culmination in Bodnar's *The Transplanted* (1985). Bodnar wrote that 'the immigrants were not clinging together as clusters of aliens or workers but were, in fact, badly fragmented into numerous enclaves arranged by internal status levels, ideology and orientation' (p. xvii). Studies of ethnicity and the urban life of individual minorities have continued apace. These have focused upon both post-1945 newcomers as well as nineteenth-century immigrants. The largest national grouping, the Germans, have received much attention: their most important students have included Carl Wittke (1952; 1957), Frederick C. Luebke (1969; 1990), Kathleen Neils Conzen (1976) and Stanley Nadel (1990). A similar list of scholars could be made for other groupings.

Turning to racism, one group of immigrants which has attracted attention consists of Asian Americans, especially Japanese and Chinese during the second half of the nineteenth and first half of the twentieth centuries. One of the leading scholars here is Roger Daniels (1962) who wrote about anti-Japanese sentiment in California before the First World War and has since produced several books on the internment of Japanese Americans in the Second World War (1975; 1993). However, the historiography of racism towards immigrants is not simply bound up with Asian Americans. We can point, for instance, to studies of anti-Semitism (e.g. Quinley and Glock, 1979; Dinnerstein 1994), Germanophobia (Luebke, 1974), as well as some general studies on US racism (Daniels and Kitano, 1970; Jordan, 1974).

More recently, studies of Asians in America have moved away from a focus simply on racism, although studies of social structure and ethnicity are not a new phenomenon (Daniels and Kitano, 1988). Furthermore, the influx of newcomers from other parts of Asia, including India, Korea and Vietnam, has led to an interest in the new groups (Reimers, 1985; Daniels and Kitano, 1988; Takaki, 1989).

One of the major areas of growth consists of the history of Latinos. This minority is unique in the USA in that it consists of people who are indigenous in the south and south-west of the USA, together with immigrants from Central and Latin America. Until the 1970s, this group had received little attention: the most important book being Carey McWilliams's *North from Mexico: The Spanish-Speaking People of the United States* (1949). More recently, this area has taken off with the production of significant numbers of general surveys and monographs (Garcia, 1981, 1991; Rosenbaum, 1981; San Miguel, 1987), while general studies of immigration now focus heavily upon the group (Daniels and Kitano, 1990; Dinnerstein, Nichols and Reimers, 1990).

US immigration history is a thriving subject. Apart from the sample of books outlined above, we can also mention the *Journal of American Ethnic History* and the *Harvard Encyclopedia of American Ethnic Groups* (Thernstrom, 1980). Furthermore, the above brief survey has not allowed me to comment upon several of the major developments in the historiography of immigrants such as an increasing interest in women and the question of social mobility across generations. A particularly important recent development has been an increasing number of books focusing upon multiculturalism (Fuchs, 1990; Takaki, 1993).

The phenomenon of white middle-class males writing on the history of ethnic groups of which they are not a part also exists in the USA, although in this case affirmative action policies have been implemented in an attempt to lessen the problem. In 1991, however, 88.9 per cent of doctorate recipients in history in the USA were white, while nil per cent were Native American, 4.7 per cent African Americans and 1.8 per cent Latinos. The gender distribution was far more impressive, as 37.5 per cent of Ph.D.s were gained by women (Gardner, 1993), demonstrating that women can enter the professions if they have the right racial and social origins.

The majority of black historians are studying the history of their own community because white society and the white historical profession allows them to do so. In fact, the academic study of black history by US blacks has a tradition dating back to the start of the twentieth century, a time when white scholars paid little attention to the history of blacks. The pioneers of this field included Carter Godwin Woodson, born in Virginia in 1875. He played a leading role in the establishment and running of the Association for the Study of Negro Life and History in 1915. In the following year the group launched the *Journal of Negro History*, of which he was editor. He also wrote several books covering education, migration, religion and historiography. Slightly older than Woodson, and outside his circle, but just as influential, was W. E. B. DuBois (1868–1963), the first black person to receive a doctorate from Harvard, in 1895, on *The Suppression of the African Slavery Trade to the United States of America, 1683–1870*, published in the following year (Thorpe, 1979; Meier and Rudwick, 1986). His subsequent work was as varied as Woodson's and his most important books included *The Souls of Black Folk* (1903) and *Black Reconstruction in America* (1935).

Two major works appeared in the 1940s 'which made dramatic impacts upon the American reading public' partly because of the background against which they were written (the New Deal, resistance to Nazism, and opposition to white European imperialism) (Drimmer, 1968) but also because of their quality. Gunnar Myrdal's (1944) *An American Dilemma* is not only the best book written on American blacks, but also one of the most outstanding social science volumes of the twentieth century, covering virtually every conceivable aspect of the issue it seeks to tackle, and indicating that a *complete* outsider, in this instance in the form of a Swede, may be best placed to write the most perceptive work on a subject. John Hope Franklin, nevertheless, wrote the second major work on blacks during the 1940s in his *From Slavery to Freedom* (1948), which has subsequently passed through several editions. The book is a comprehensive history which begins in Africa.

During the 1950s the expansion of black history quickened. Particular questions attracted much attention, especially aspects of slavery, but also, for instance, segregation and reconstruction (Drimmer, 1968). Notable books from the 1950s included Stanley Elkins's *Slavery* (1959) and Kenneth Stampp's *The Peculiar Institution* (1956). In addition, the 1950s also resulted in the launching of *Phylon*, a new black history journal.

Since the 1950s various new developments have taken place. First, black history has become increasingly popular among progressively minded white intellectuals which has resulted in an increase in the numbers of whites researching in the area, although such an interest is not completely new. The most notable of such scholars have included August Meier and Elliot Rudwick who published a series of books in the field (1970; 1973; 1976) and Gilbert Osofsky (1935–74), also prolific during his lifetime (1966; 1968). In addition, there has been an increasing interest in black history by mainstream US publishers, such as Oxford University Press, and by funding bodies. New subjects of research include the Civil Rights movement (e.g., Garrow, 1986; Sitkoff, 1981). As with the writing of the history of immigrants, that on blacks is also healthy.

Finally, we can say a few words about the historiography of Native Americans. The first point, which applies to this case more than to any of those outlined above, is that it has been dominated by whites. However, there have been attempts to encourage Native Americans to study their own history. For instance, some universities have launched Native American Studies programmes, while the American Indian Historical Society publishes the *Indian Historian*, which carries work by both Native Americans and whites. Furthermore, historians such as Vine Deloria are of Indian origin. Much of the research on Indians has been carried out by anthropologists. The range of topics covered is wide, including specific tribes, general histories of all Native Americans, studies of particular geographical areas of the USA, as well as much work on relations with whites (Washburn, 1971; Berkhofer Jr, 1973; Deloria, 1984; 1985).

## Conclusion

There is no doubt that during the course of the twentieth century, as the British and US historical professions and their fields of interest have grown, so has the amount of attention they have devoted to the history of ethnic groupings within their national boundaries. Equally, there is little doubt, due to the centrality of immigration and ethnicity in American life, that such subjects have attracted more attention in that country.

Apart from the amount of attention that these areas receive on their own, the other indication of the differences in treatment of the two subjects by historians is the way in which they are treated by mainstream scholars. It would be impossible to write a history of the USA without reference to the central issues of slavery and immigration. However, in Britain histories of the country constantly appear without reference, for instance, to Irish and Jewish immigration during the nineteenth century. We can, for example, refer to the *Cambridge Social History of Britain*, a three-volume series which has no essay on immigrants (Thompson, 1990). Similarly, Kenneth Morgan's (1990) history of Britain since 1945 devotes just six out of 516 pages to immigration, which is staggering considering the root and branch impact of newcomers upon postwar Britain. This situation in Britain is aggravated not only by a reluctance to accept the role of immigrants in the country's history, but also by the national myth, which revolves around the concept of Britain as a tolerant state (Panayi, 1993: 1–2).

In the case of both Britain and the USA we have seen that the historiography of ethnic minorities has not been dependent upon mainstream historians but was developed, in many cases, by scholars who formed part of the community about which they wrote, the best examples being the Irish and Jews in Britain and blacks in the USA. In all cases there has been a certain amount of colonising by historians from the dominant ethnic groupings. In other cases, such as blacks in Britain, or Native Americans, whole subject areas have been created by white middle-class intellectuals, who have rescued subjects which would have remained dormant for decades to come. Ultimately, there is no ideal as to who best writes ethnic history, insiders or outsiders. The best general book on immigrants in Britain is written by an Englishman, Colin Holmes. The main scholars of Anglo-Jewry are Jews: Alderman, Cesarani, Katz and Kushner. The real problem lies in the fact that within the historical profession, in both the USA and Britain, the overwhelming majority of those with posts are white European middle-class males. They can write about any subject they wish. However, the same is not true of minorities, especially those with darker skins, who are, at best, confined to their own areas. In Britain black people born within the country are not given history posts in universities. There are countless explanations for this situation, linked with the structural racism in British society which the white middle-class intellectuals who make up the historical profession cannot escape from. One can only look forward to a time when people with dark skins and strange names are allowed to teach something other than their own history (although they should continue to do that) in the same way that whites research in whichever field they wish.

Despite these reservations, countless works are published each year in both Britain and the USA on all aspects of immigration, ethnicity and racism within the two countries. This has become one of the easiest fields in which to publish. While it may mean that much work of low quality results, the best books are of the very highest standard – empirically, methodologically and theoretically. There is little reason to doubt the continued healthy position of this field of historical research.

## Acknowledgements

I am extremely grateful to Tony Kushner and Jim Ralph, who commented on this chapter and, especially, to Jason MacDonald, who both read through it and provided references on the USA. Needless to say, I remain solely responsible for all the opinions expressed.

## Note

1 Another major historian of Britain, Sir Lewis Namier, who died in 1960, was also Jewish. The reasons why some individuals ignore their own group are interesting. On the one hand we might suggest that writing on mainstream history may be a confirmation of the desire to assimilate. On the other hand, such scholars may feel that the history of their own group is too small a subject to study. Or perhaps they simply do not wish to do what is expected of them by historians around them, by not writing about their own group.

# 5 Teaching race in cultural studies

## A ten-step programme of personal development

*Gargi Bhattacharyya*

Throughout this chapter I have refered to the fictional entity 'cultural studies' on the assumption that readers will recognise this short-hand for a disparate morass of social science and humanities practice, with no particular unifying trait.

## Representations

The race course I teach currently begins, as do many courses in my department, with issues of representation. In many ways this is the key twist added by cultural studies, in all kinds of disciplines a turn to the cultural has involved a recognition that the hard business of the material world is shaped by the slippery business of representation – the best-known accounts of this conundrum come from those who live in the tumbling down house of cultural studies. In the arena of race-studying, the interest in representation appears as an extension of the ongoing critique of race science (see Barkan, 1992). Now that we all understand that race is not truly a biological phenomenon and that it is cultural stories which 'race' the body, not physical attributes, all attention has shifted to the workings of these cultural stories. Across a range of disciplines, but most markedly in cultural studies, race has come to be seen as a category primarily constituted through representation, with all of its unpleasant social effects coming after these stories. Now even the most hard-nosed versions of social inquiry, the counters and measurers, also include a consideration of representation. The upshot of all this is that, in many ways, studying and teaching about race across topics and approaches leads back again and again to the issue of representation (see Gilroy, 1987; Barker, 1981; CCCS, 1982). Partly because of this, there doesn't seem to be much writing around on these issues which does not fit in the endlessly elastic field of cultural studies. In the sections which follow I hope the range and concerns of my non-discipline will become more apparent.

*This is the first lesson – all too obvious and well-practised already. In this lesson we learn to pay close attention to stories and pictures, because, somehow, the most ugly events of our flesh-and-blood world can be traced back to the realm of images.*

## Everyday culture

The Centre for Contemporary Cultural Studies famously inaugurates the study of racialised relations in everyday life. When *The Empire Strikes Back* begins:

> There are many reasons why issues raised by the study of 'races' and racisms should be central to the concerns of cultural studies. Yet racist ideologies and racial conflicts have been ignored, both in historical writing and in accounts of the present. If nothing else, this book should be taken as a signal that this marginalisation cannot continue. It has also been conceived as a corrective to the narrowness of the English left whose version of the 'national-popular' continues to deny the role of blacks and black struggles in the making and remaking of the working class.
>
> (CCCS, 1982: 7)

the terrain of study looks very different. On the whole, the work which precedes this moment is concerned with the welfare and integration of immigrant communities (Dummett, 1973), or the perpetuation of colonial relations within the white nation (Rex, 1973; Katzelson, 1973), or the analysis of racism as another contradiction of capital (Miles, 1982). While the development of a cultural study of race and racism retains important concerns from this earlier work – most obviously in continued concerns about the experience and effects of diaspora, the spatial relations of 'race' and the particular role of the urban and the mysterious relation between race and class – the shift into everyday life changes the shape of all these debates.

Now few people care to pursue that elusive metanarrative which will explain (and, we hope, explain away) all our painful social relations in one beautiful sweep of abstraction. Instead we all redirect our gaze to more close-to-home business, hoping to see the secrets of existence in the texture of everyday living. This is a recognition both that the spreadout powers of racism cannot be conceptualised without a detailed attention to context and that we, poor racialised beings, are not constructed wholly through the experience of racism. Turning our attention to more everyday culture is a way of registering this contextualised detail and exploring people's strategies for resisting, surviving and just plain living. In recent cultural studies this has happened most markedly in explorations of the role of popular expressive cultures. This work argues that participation in popular cultural forms such as music is central to self-articulation, restating an argument which has been prevalent across genres of cultural studies. In relation to issues of race and ethnicity, this is extended to argue that this participation in popular culture is especially important to diasporic peoples (who are often those bearing the brunt of racism). This analysis privileges the everyday forms of recorded music, film and video as the most portable and exchangeable expressions of diasporic experience. Work in this area examines both the meanings and expressions which are favoured within examples of these chosen forms and the practices through which these artefacts are consumed, exchanged and communicated (Gilroy, 1987 and 1993a; Back, 1996; Gillespie, 1995).

*This second lesson reminds us that the truth of all our lives is just under our noses, not far away from us, but instead so close to home we can hardly see it.*

## Gender

British academia being the strange shaped place that it is, discussions of race in certain disciplines have come on the tail of more established discussions of gender. There appears to be some recognition that British academia is hopelessly parochial, exclusionary, unable to reconcile old structures of privilege with any kind of new idea – against this background, the small institutional successes of academic feminism through the 1980s made space for more discussion of the other differences of our social lives. Whereas the sociology of race had attempted to describe patterns of disadvantage and theorise the social structures from which these came, the feminism which hits the campus circuit in Britain wants to pay some attention to who is doing the talking, from what position and experience. And that shift in emphasis, whatever its much-discussed shortcomings, opens the door for all sorts of diverse talk (Amos and Parmar, 1984).

It is true that, in earlier encounters at least, much of this talk has been acrimonious. The feminism which found space in British universities often expressed a concern to voice women's experience or, for the more theoretically inclined, to explore the feminine imaginary. Black feminism challenged this assumption that the terms 'woman' and 'femininity' could be employed without examination. The critique of black feminism argued that this discussion of femininity privileged white women's experiences and voices and silenced women who did not conform to this vision of what it was to be a woman. This excluded black women in particular from the terms of the debate and instead instituted a new norm for discussions of gender. Against this, black feminism has attempted to develop an analysis of gender which can encompass the differences among and between women (Mirza, 1997). This acknowledgement of diversity has become the new orthodoxy in feminist inquiry (for a critique of this which gives a scary and not altogether welcome insight into the white psyche, see MacKinnon, 1996).

The development of a distinctive arena of black women's thought and politics within the boundaries of the rich world has been complimented by a growing awareness of the range of women's experiences across the world and a recognition of white women's (and even white feminism's) complicity in the uneven relations of our internationalised world. This work looks at the particular processes of gendering in particular locations – and reads this back against the longer history and global position of that place (Spivak, 1987).

These two themes in feminist writing – the recognition that gender is experienced differently in relation to ethnic identity and that there are uneven power relations among women across the globe – contribute to a renewed concern in all sorts of academic writing, including cultural studies, to address the difficult social relations made through the intersections of class, race and gender. This threesome has become at once a standing joke about sad academic credentialism and a continuing aide-memoire to students of cultural and social life.

*This is the third lesson – that no-one lives through one name alone and that the shape of a body is only one aspect of experience.*

## Institutions

Most accounts (muttered at conference tea-breaks or written in fighting-talk style) have it that cultural studies has forsaken all analysis of institutional processes. Instead, allegedly, this area of study rushes to embrace a concoction of obtuse theorisation and treasured ephemera as the route to truth. In the process all the dull everyday business of life – battles about places to live and learn, the means and quality of life, the ability to live in safety and comfort – were forgotten in favour of the assorted glamours of grand theory and popular expressive culture. Of course, nothing is ever so clear-cut – particularly in the messy inbred world of the university. The move to consider a wider range of representations hoped to develop a more refined institutional analysis, one which could encompass an account of the world around this institutional interaction. More recent work also attempts to rope in the unruly morass of cultural meaning and say something about the relation to social outcomes.

Most obviously, the non-tribe of cultural studies has been concerned to explore and critique the determinants of institutional knowledge. This, again, has been a concern about representation and the social effects of representations made by the powerful. Work in cultural studies has been concerned to chart the role of the media and other popular representations in the formation of popular opinion, and, by implication, policy. In particular, this work has explicated the process by which certain issues and their policy responses become racialised – most famously, in work on crime, welfare and national boundaries (Hall *et al.*, 1978; Cohen and Bains,

1988; Samuel, 1989; Cashmore and McLaughlin, 1991; Morrison, 1993; Gooding-Williams, 1993).

More than this, other work attempts to identify the processes through which institutional knowledges are created – the processes through which race is constituted as a problem requiring policy responses. This work builds on studies of the history of race-thinking, work which examines representational practices in a range of institutional arenas (Gilman, 1986; Stepan, 1982; Kohn, 1995). Alongside this extensive body of work on the formations of institutional knowledges, another strand of work has developed which examines the cultural formations of particular institutional locations. Although some of this work is less clearly located in cultural studies (often coming from more established fields such as sociology or education), the desire to understand the construction of meaning and identity and to base analysis on the experience and testimony of the people involved resonates with the development of cultural studies. This work, often focusing on the key locations of young life such as school, the entry or non-entry to work, or leisure spaces such as clubland, uses the mixed bag of ethnographic practice to chart the ways in which people negotiate structures of power, including the powerful structure of racism (Mirza, 1992; Willis, 1977 and 1978; Thornton and Gelder, 1996). The upshot is that all sorts of work in cultural studies remains concerned to analyse racism in particular, but ethnic particularity also, in its institutional manifestations – both through an understanding of how institutional knowledge and power is made and mobilised and by examining the ways in which people resist and live through these misshapen structures.

*This is the fourth lesson – when we learn to look again at everyday pains and begin to see clearly how this hurt happens.*

## Cities

The idea of the city and the particular cultural formations of the urban have become increasingly central themes in cultural studies generally and accounts of minority communities and cultures of racialisation in particular. The city becomes a sign of social life as we know it, a ready-made case study for a dizzying gamut of social theory (see Keith and Pile, 1993). For our purposes, the city is, in particular, the archetypal place of diverse and shifting populations. Either explicitly or implicitly, cultural studies has taken the city to be the arena in which race as we live it is staged. The city – as opposed to a largely unspoken and problematically nostalgic view of the suburb, province or rural location in which population, and therefore identity, is static – is depicted as the point where different ethnicities meet. This is the encounter which makes race happen, we imagine – conveniently forgetting that we don't believe in essential differences (biological or cultural) any more.

This interest in the city as the space of diverse ethnicities can translate into an interest in the mythic racial neighbourhoods of the multicultural city (Keith and Rogers, 1991). A series of works seeking to give voice to the everyday experience of minority communities also highlights the importance of the ethnic enclave in the articulation of minority identities. Cultural expression here is also seen as the marking of territory, the occupation of various spaces and the range of everyday activities which make up community formation in particular locations – so understanding the lives of any group of people also entails understanding the places in which they live, play, hang out. This work counters popular mythologies of the inner city as disintegrating, dishevelled and downright dangerous, with all of these unhappy attributes coming from the presence of black people – and instead celebrates the neighbourhoods most subject to racist vilification as the sites of community strength and creativity (see Gillespie, 1995 on Southall, Black Audio Film Collective, 1986 on Handsworth).

Alongside this re-evaluation of the worth and vibrancy of black neighbourhoods, cultural studies has asserted that diverse populations are what make cities such good and exciting places. Whereas an older sociology of race has focused on the city as the site of inter-ethnic encounter and described the problems which can arise from this, cultural studies has more often viewed inter-ethnic encounters as sites of productive interchange, events which give rise to new cultural forms encompassing all our new identities (Gilroy, 1993b; Hewitt, 1986). Cities are celebrated as the places where we all practice living with difference and where the ideal of cosmopolis may still overcome the horrors of racist violence.

The more practically minded in cultural studies (a more numerous grouping than is generally acknowledged) translate these ideas about the positive values of multi-ethnic city living into policy-oriented work which feeds local authority decision-making and wider decisions around the ongoing and mysterious business (in Britain at least) of urban regeneration.

*This fifth lesson teaches us that it is important to know about the locations of social events and that territory can be empowering, creative and strength-giving, not simply defensive.*

## Sexuality

Although sex is still not always acknowledged as a relevant area of inquiry in relation to race, there is more and more work which explores the connections between these two dangerous and confusing dynamics.

Most noticeable is the emergence of historical accounts which examine the construction of exotic myths as part of a wider examination of Western subjectivity. This work builds on the insights of *Orientalism* (Said, 1978) in order to show how central an idea of the East as place of sensual abandon is to the construction of a white Western identity of (assumed) reason and control. Readings of a range of documentation, from travel-writing to orientalism proper to government reports, reveal how embedded the idea of a hypersexual devious and deviant racialised other is in Western narratives about the rest of the world (Kabbani, 1989; Pratt, 1992; Harris, 1984; Stannard, 1992).

An increasing interest in the unseemly frequency of tales of sexual titil-lation in racist mythologies past and present has lead to the speculation that racism is itself constructed as a sexual fear. Some writers argue that racism is an anxiety about maintaining the purity and absolute boundary of blood line – the sexualised spectre of the racial other and the scary possibility of sexual contact across racial boundaries represents the continual threat of contamination (R. Young, 1995; L. Young, 1996). The excesses of racist violence are an indication of how unsettling this threat is to the racist imaginary. These ideas have the great benefit of explaining racism as a sickness of the white and powerful psyche. Looking at the role ideas about sex play in the whole nasty mess of racist culture gives us a chance of understanding some of the particular pathologies of racist violence – with this analysis the high levels of sexual degradation, torture and mutilation which have been suffered by the victims of racist attack in a range of settings begin to make some kind of sick sense. We also begin to have some hope of comprehending the twisted logic which can deem certain people to be both most despised and most desired at one and the same time. A range of work inspired by cultural studies builds on these troubling insights to show how deeply embedded the idea of black sexual threat is in the logic of racist violence – from the everlasting myth of the black rapist who poses a constant threat to the purity and safety of white women, justifying an endless stream of attacks against black men, to the more titillating idea of black women built for sex who can therefore never be assaulted.

*This sixth lesson tells us that sex and the fear of sex is at the heart of racist culture and that what people fear they try to destroy.*

## Whiteness

After an eternity of studying minorities in order to discover the roots of their unhappy lot, academic talk including cultural studies has recently realised that understanding white racism can only come through an exami-nation of majority cultures. In large part, this has involved the study of whiteness – in an echo of the many years we have all spent studying black-ness.

Of course, whiteness is a very different object of study from blackness – something which has become painfully apparent as attempts are made to view whiteness as just another ethnicity. However much we argue that everyone has ethnicity, that this is not a code-word for dark skin or minority status, it has proved remarkably difficult to define the cultural traits which constitute dominant white ethnicities. More than this, pinning whiteness down as any kind of ethnicity at all has been a slippery business. Explicit invocations of white identity tend to be limited to the rhetoric of the far right, making whiteness seem synonymous with white supremacism. More everyday versions of white identity and privilege remain mysterious. Discussions of whiteness argue that this is not inci- dental and, on the contrary, a central characteristic of white identity is this invisibility. Richard Dyer famously suggests that whiteness retains its power through the belief that others are raced, while whites are just people (Dyer, 1997; Ware, 1992; Allen, 1994; Pfeil, 1995).

Work around whiteness has tried to address this power through hidden- ness in a number of ways. One strategy has been to make visible the processes by which whiteness becomes an unspoken norm of human expe- rience. This tactic develops most forcefully from the critiques of black feminism, in which black women challenged the ability of white women to speak for all women while in fact taking their own (limited and racially privileged) experience as the norm. The lessons of these fights train a wider section of people to spot the tricks which assume whiteness to be an unspoken norm for all humanity. It is these lessons which give rise in the broad field of cultural studies to work which seeks to document the lived experiences of white identity and to find a language which can reveal these lives to be racialised too. Another complementary strand of work seeks to historicise the development of white identity by charting the tangled process by which certain people emerge into the privilege of whiteness. Both sets of work show white identity to be strategically constructed and ultimately malleable.

This renewed interest in white identities comes alongside an increase in work examining the construction and experience of minority white identi- ties. The development of work in the fields of Irish and Jewish studies has allowed more open discussion of the rifts within the category of whiteness and has enhanced understandings of the dirty business of racism by exploring the uncertain and changeable status of these white-but-not-quite groups of people. The insight that whiteness itself may be a fragmented category is beginning now to feed into further study of other 'white' identi- ties, most notably those of travelling peoples and, in a British context, ideas of Scottishness and Welshness in a space of Anglo privilege.

*The seventh lesson taught here is that race is an experience and name which touches us all, whatever we may think. Understanding the ways in which it touches us differently is the key to revealing its power.*

# Identity

It seems belated to raise the issue of identity so late in my list of key points – but to begin with identity would be misleading. Although many of the themes of recent work in cultural studies in the area of race and ethnicity skirt around the issue of identity, the question of identity is rarely the thing which structures this work. Instead discussions of identity emerge out of this more general study and debate.

Identity is, again, another of those categories which seems to defy clear definition and it is hard to summarise work around this issue. Certainly there was a period when conferences and anthologies rushed to include the term 'identity' in their titles and publicity, and a number of well-known and much-discussed publications anthologised debate in this area (Rutherford, 1990; Hall and du Gay, 1996). Although this debate extended beyond considerations of race alone, the overall impression was that identities were most clearly marked for those who in some way inhabited the margins of society. The powerful (all those infamous straight white class-privileged and able-bodied men) seemed to have hardly any identity at all – except perhaps the fantasy category of villain to our marginal saints. The developing debates around whiteness and the longer running exploration of cultural construction of lived national identities goes some way towards shifting this focus from margin to centre (again).

The organising idea of identity has played a particular and central role in talk around the development of new articulations of ethnicity. It is this idea of identity as the name of the multiple stories we tell about ourselves which shapes discussions of our new ethnicities. It is because we come to understand identity as performed and constructed within particular contexts that we also begin to consider the possibilities of new identities on new terrains. Now we start to think about the new negotiations of identity which come with the experience of diaspora, new social formations and, particularly, in the intersections of changing and diverse gender categories and sexualities (Mercer, 1994; Brah, 1996). The imaginative leap which the concept of identity in this creative sense gives to the study of ethnicity allows us all to move away from ideas of ethnicity as a negative determination – instead of being seen as a fixed (and often painful) legacy which you inherit, ethnic identity comes to be seen as another strategic performance, something which you stage in everyday life according to circumstances, using a variety of repertoires which might include a version of the traditional as well as the influences of the new context (Parker, 1995).

*Here the eighth lesson is to remember that the stories we tell about ourselves are the most complex of all – assuming you know all the meanings at first glance can only limit the scope and possibility of each human tale.*

## Pedagogy

Although pedagogy may seem an unlikely theme at this late stage of our list, concerns around the business of teaching and education typify a certain moment in cultural studies debate. An interest in the politics of teaching has been central in the development of cultural studies – the challenge to older forms of knowledge production has been a challenge to the authority and power granted to certain forms of 'knowledge'. Cultural studies has sought to critique existing structures of power and knowledge – and this has involved not only questioning what counts as knowledge and why, but also thinking again about how this knowledge is imparted and to whom. This whole critique is closely tied to a wider idea of institutionalised education as a form of social control – once teaching and learning has been identified as another branch of the ideological state apparatus, it is hard to sustain an idea of teaching as a vocation of pure and selfless do-gooding. Instead, we all emerge as state agents, paid to maintain the infamous status quo.

This suspicion about our ability to teach anything at all, apart from a docile automaton obedience, translates into a more particular set of concerns around the teaching of 'race'. After fighting to make a place to discuss issues of 'race' and ethnicity in the space of the university, people found that the well-documented critiques of race-awareness training in local authorities and of the development of a 'race relations industry' generally (some of which were written by the teachers of a cultural studies of 'race', see Sivanandan, 1982; Gilroy, 1987) made race-teaching in the university a more uncomfortable affair altogether. Perhaps talking about the construction of race and racism was not an unambiguous gain and we ourselves had become unwitting participants in the race industry? Perhaps teaching race was another way of making black people into objects of study again? There seemed to be no way to avoid replicating the bad power relations of institutional education. Largely, people stopped believing in their ability to teach people not to be racist and tried to settle for more modest gains in understanding.

However, at the same time another body of work (largely US based) continues to propose teaching as a new and radical political practice for black people. This work argues that teaching as a radical gesture, in black communities, builds on older traditions of public interchange and debate and of mentoring within communities. Empowerment here can take place because this teaching refuses the constraints of institutional disciplines – this idea of teaching goes beyond classes and assessments and professional practice to become a transgressive project in which education becomes the practice of freedom (hooks, 1994a; hooks and West, 1991).

Overall there seems to be an agreement among race-teachers that professional responsibility is about balancing the need to further local political agendas through education with the humility of acknowledging our place in the constraints of the international economy of the academy.

*This ninth lesson reminds us that the will to know is a gesture of power and that no knowledge can be clean of the structures which make it. Good education acknowledges this without giving up on the possibility of learning.*

## Politics

Inevitably I have to end with the standing joke of cultural studies – the demand for political relevance. Politics is the first and last excuse for the whole range of bad behaviour which sadly characterises cultural studies. All the serious attempts to make intellectual work accessible and demo-cratic, working hard to register the textures of everyday life in academic writing, all of those honourable endeavours are marred by sporadic anxi-eties and embarrassing soul-searching about the relation to politics. In the end, almost all cultural studies work trips up on the question of whether academic work can be part of the struggle (the work that avoids this ques-tion also usually disavows its allegiance to cultural studies). This anxious and impossible wish to do the right thing by writing and teaching intensi-fies greatly in relation to hot topics such as race.

Rather than repeat the heated debates around the most righteous approach to academic study, I prefer to suggest a few more measured responses to this ongoing anxiety.

Despite the powerful critique of the race industry which has been devel-oped in part through cultural studies, plenty of thoughtful work still seeks to effect change through affecting policy. In particular, the impact of cultural studies has given rise to versions of policy work which try to take account of people's varied and multiple identities and to give voice to everyday experience. Another version of this work champions the benefits of community-based research and tries to tie writing to the needs of the voluntary sector or community activist groups. Although none of these endeavours is straightforward (and certainly do not represent a straightfor-ward route to freedom), they still represent a continuing and honourable attempt within cultural studies to address the politics of race in some responsible fashion.

In the end, the most heartening development for me has been the move away from inflated claims about the central importance of academic work (with all the associated fighting and bad behaviour) towards the more humble project of honestly locating academic work in the scary wider structures of all our social lives, from the continuing corrosion of class privilege and disprivilege in access to education to the diffuse powers of global capital. Knowing your place in the teaching machine seems like the most ethical approach to teaching about race or teaching about anything which we are able to achieve (Spivak, 1993).

*This tenth and last lesson tells us that studying and understanding can contribute to the gains of political work, but in the end, this is only writing.*

# 6 Ethnicity etcetera

## Social anthropological points of view

*Richard Jenkins*

My title poses two implicit questions: one about the nature of ethnicity and one about the nature of social anthropology (which, for stylistic reasons, I will generally abbreviate to anthropology). To address them in reverse order, the disciplinary question has two dimensions: first, the intellectual content of anthropology and second, its relationship to cognate disciplines.[1]

With respect to intellectual content, anthropology is perhaps most simply defined by reference to what anthropologists, in their teaching, research and writing, do. Their primary emphasis is, as it has always been, upon understanding the cultural Other (defined, historically, from a European or North American cultural viewpoint). This, perhaps more than anything else, underpins the anthropological emphasis upon the personal experience of field research. The basic epistemological premise of the discipline is that to understand Others they must be encountered. If the *sine qua non* of history is the engagement with primary sources, the equivalent for anthropology is fieldwork. A comparative, essentially relativist perspective on socio-cultural diversity is also central to anthropology. But perhaps the most important foundational assumption of modern anthropology is that human beings, regardless of cultural differences, have more in common than not. It is this 'psychic unity' which allows sufficient cross-cultural understanding for the interpretive and comparative enterprises to be epistemologically defensible.

With respect to theory, social anthropology has always participated in the field of general social theory (although the theoretical tradition deriving from Weber has had few anthropological adherents). From a past in which a structural functionalism deriving from Durkheim ruled the anthropological roost, the discipline has become theoretically diffuse, if not fragmented: Marxism, transactionalism, culturalist interpretivism, structuralism, post-structuralism, feminism and post-modern critique are all actively represented in the current anthropological firmament.

Substantively, anthropologists have focused upon some dimensions of social life more than others: symbolism, ritual and religion, kinship and the family, morality, custom and law, micro-politics, and ethnic and communal identity are perhaps the most conspicuous and characteristic.

These interests derive partly from the engagement with other cultures, partly from the experience of data gathering within 'face-to-face' communities, and partly from anthropology's nineteenth-century origins in the marriage of romantic exoticism with evolutionism in the context of European and North American colonialism (Kuper, 1988). As a distinctively anthropological portfolio of interests, it is biased in the direction of the *cultural* and the *everyday*:

> Anthropologists...have always derived their intellectual authority from direct experience of life....That is, they knew the exotic Other and their readers did not. Within that framework of bridging the gap between civilised and primitive, they emphasised the salience of the everyday, the ordinary.
>
> (Grimshaw and Hart, 1995: 47–8)

The world is changing rapidly, however, and anthropology with it. The 'primitive' or the 'exotic' can no longer serve as unproblematic touchstones of the anthropological enterprise.

Additional subjects and issues have been taken up by anthropologists in the last two or three decades: *inter alia* these include urbanisation (typically in the 'developing world'), socio-economic change and 'development', health care and illness, nutrition, the impact on indigenous communities of tourism, literacy and processes of literisation, migration, and nationalism. A further important development within the discipline has been a modest shift in its relationship to the exotically Other. This has occurred in three phases. First, as early as the nineteenth century but more commonly from the mid-twentieth century onwards, the metropolitan peripheries offered accessible and relatively exotic alterity, in the shape of residual hunters, fishers and nomads, or peasants. Subsequently, second, the exotic Other migrated to the metropolitan homelands of anthropology to become ethnic minorities; anthropologists followed them home. Third, and perhaps most radically, anthropologists have begun to pay more attention to their own cultural backyards (Jackson, A., 1987; Forman, 1994).

These trends – theoretical and topical diversification, and a widening of cultural and/or geographical scope – reflect anthropology's attempts to negotiate the post-colonial, post-1945 world.[2] They have brought with them, however, problems in disciplinary boundary maintenance. It is, for example, no longer as easy as it was to distinguish anthropology from its closest and most obvious rival, sociology, simply by referring to field and topic. This particular fault line has been further confused as sociology has itself moved in to a fully global arena and engaged with a widening topical agenda. The development of interdisciplinary feminism as a unifying intellectual field of critical discourse has also contributed to the blurring of boundaries as, arguably, has the debate about post-modernism. Nor is sociology the only problematic boundary: social psychology, social geography and social history might also be mentioned here.

In some other respects, however, anthropology has been moving further away from sociology, in particular. As a consequence of the institutional specialisation which has encouraged the growth of separate departments within universities and colleges, the heightened competition for dwindling resources, the partial abandonment of the shared theoretical heritage of structural functionalism, and the perceived threat posed by the modest convergence of the disciplines in terms of field and topic, boundary maintenance on the part of anthropologists has become more assertive than hitherto.[3] The difference between anthropology and sociology seems to matter more than it did twenty or thirty years ago. Despite the fact that personnel and, even more important, ideas do cross disciplinary boundaries – most usually, at least in Britain, from anthropology into sociology – those boundaries remain.

Which brings me to the 'ethnicity etcetera' of the chapter's title. What do anthropologists mean when they talk about ethnicity? Historically speaking, ethnicity, for anthropology as for other disciplines, is a relatively recent term, coming into conventional usage in the 1960s. Within American anthropology in particular, this was in part the result of a gradual shift of analytical framework, from 'race' to 'culture' to 'ethnicity' (Wolf, 1994). It can also be interpreted as a change in the conceptualisation of one of the basic units of anthropological analysis, from the 'tribe' to the 'ethnic group' (Jenkins, 1986: 172–8; 1997: 18–24). More recently the unit of analysis in this respect has widened to reflect an increasing concern with the 'nation' and the processes whereby ethnic groups and categories are incorporated into states (Williams, B. F., 1989; Verdery, 1994). It is now anthropological common sense to consider ethnicity and nationalism in the same analytical breath, although 'race', as we shall see, is more problematic. It is also true to say that the study of ethnicity has become one of the major growth areas within the discipline, 'a lightning rod for anthropologists trying to redefine their theoretical and methodological approaches' (Williams, B. F., 1989: 401).

Being a growth area has encouraged a healthy diversity: the anthropological model of ethnicity is a relatively broad church which allows a wide range of phenomena under its roof. What is more, it remains firmly grounded in empirical research. In this field as in others, anthropologists are most concerned to get on with writing detailed ethnographies of specific contexts. There is little to compare, for example, with the abstraction of some sociological debates about the relationship between 'race', racism and ethnicity (for example: Anthias, 1992; Mason, 1994). At the level of meta-theory, it is perhaps worth noting the small but not insignificant contribution made by the writing of descriptive ethnographic texts about specific localities to a taken-for-granted view of the world as a mosaic of definite cultural *difference*, rather than a seamless web of over-lapping cultural *variation*.

The strong ethnographic tradition notwithstanding, however, there is theory and there are definitions. Perhaps the most general is the notion of ethnicity as the 'social organisation of culture difference' originally proposed by Fredrik Barth's *Ethnic Groups and Boundaries* (1969), the seminal text from which stems much current anthropological conventional wisdom about ethnicity. This definition implies not only cultural differenti-ation, but also contact between the collectivities thus differentiated, it is about 'us' and 'them' (Eriksen, 1993: 10–12). In this collection of essays, Barth and his collaborators ushered in an increasing awareness on the part of many anthropologists that culture is a changing, variable and contin-gent property of interpersonal transactions, rather than an entity 'above' the fray of daily life and somehow producing behaviour. As Barth has recently suggested – with his tongue only partly in his cheek, perhaps – this point of view anticipated in some respects the post-modern constructionist view of culture (Barth, 1994: 12).

Reflecting the ethnographic concern with the lives of concrete subjects and with their 'actually existing' social relationships (Radcliffe-Brown, 1952: 190), one can also point to Geertz's definition of ethnicity as the 'world of personal identity collectively ratified and publicly expressed' and 'socially ratified personal identity' (1973: 268, 309). Thus ethnicity has to mean something – in the sense of making a difference – not only to the people one is studying, but also to the individual persons.

The anthropological 'basic model' of ethnicity can be summarised thus:

- ethnicity is about cultural differentiation;
- although ethnicity is centrally concerned with culture it is also rooted in, and to some extent the outcome of, social interaction;
- ethnicity is no more fixed or unchanging than the culture of which it is a component;
- ethnicity is a social identity which is both collective and individual, externalised in social interaction and internalised in personal self-awareness.

In the discussion which follows I will elaborate upon this and doubtless introduce some important caveats, but as a general model it would be supported by most anthropologists.

It is not my intention to provide a comprehensive overview of anthropo-logical treatments of ethnicity. This would be an impossible task, given space constraints, and there are already available a number of complementary essays in this territory (Cohen, 1978; Williams, B. F., 1989; Eriksen, 1993; Banks, 1995). I will focus instead upon three areas of debate which seem to me of timely significance and which present difficulties and opportunities in the teaching of 'ethnicity etcetera' from an anthropological point of view.

## The primordial versus the instrumental

This is a perennial debate about the nature of ethnic identity to which all students should be introduced: is ethnicity a fundamental, primordial aspect of human existence and self-consciousness, essentially unchanging and unchangeable in the imperative demands it makes upon individuals and the bonds which it creates between the individual and the group? Or is it, to whatever extent, defined situationally, strategically or tactically manipulable, and capable of change at both the individual and collective levels?

This argument takes its place alongside a range of theoretical controversies about the capacity of humans to intervene in their own lives, to determine or to be determined. But the primordial model also has deep roots in the Romantic reaction to Enlightenment rationalism. Finding some of its more respectable voices in the work of Herder and Hegel, this is more than an academic point of view, providing the intellectual charter for much ethnic chauvinism and nationalism. It naturalises ethnic groups and justifies ethnic sentiments. It can also be identified at play in the ongoing debate about the modernity and nature of nationalism (Bauman, 1992; Smith, 1994).

Within anthropology, the name most often identified with a primordial view of ethnicity is Clifford Geertz (1973: 255–310). Drawing upon Shils, Geertz is concerned with the obstacle posed by 'primordial attachments' – deriving mainly from kinship, locality and culture, and encompassing more than ethnicity – to the development of modern civic political sentiments. Against this position one is generally offered an 'instrumentalist' or 'constructionist' perspective. Deriving in the main from Barth – although, as Eriksen reminds us (1993: 54–6), Barth himself has been accused of a form of primordialism by Abner Cohen – this is the model of ethnicity which emphasises its plasticity, the fact that people (and peoples) can and do shift and alter their ethnic ascriptions in the light of circumstance. The pursuit of political advantage or material self-interest are the calculi which are typically held to inform such behaviour.

The debate is, however, not as clear-cut as it seems. Both positions have at least as much in common as not (Bentley, 1987: 25–7). What is more, the protagonists are usually misrepresented. Geertz, for example, recognises the role of culture in defining the primordial 'givens', and that the 'strength of such primordial bonds, and the types of them that are important, differ from person to person, from society to society, and from time to time' (1973: 259). He also recognises that what matters is that ties of blood, language and culture are *seen* by actors to be ineffable and obligatory. Later in the same piece (ibid.: 269–70) he argues that in some senses 'primordial attachments' are stimulated and quickened by the political modernisation of the nation-state (a point which, in all of its essentials, was also made later by Anthony Cohen, 1985: 117).

Barth, for his part, never neglected the power and stability of ethnic identifications: the 'organising and canalising effects of ethnic distinctions' (1969: 10). As much concerned with the persistence of ethnic boundaries as anything else, he argued that under certain, not uncommon, circumstances ethnic change *can* happen, not that it *must*. More important perhaps, Barth's point of view is often presented fossilised in its 1969 version. Since then he has explored the importance of ongoing and historically relatively stable 'streams of tradition' or 'universes of discourse', within the constraints of which ethnic identities are produced and reproduced in practice (Barth, 1984; 1989). Most recently, in a discussion which explicitly refers to the 'privacy of...hearts and minds' (1994: 29), he points to the need to add micro and macro levels of analysis to the median level upon which his original arguments concentrated.

There are other reasons for becoming impatient with this debate. In the evocative words of one teaching text, it offers a contrast between 'ethnicity in the heart' and 'ethnicity in the head' (Banks, 1995: 183–7), which alerts us to the need to acknowledge affect and emotion in our considerations of ethnicity (Epstein, 1978). But there is, it must be said, no necessary contradiction between instrumental manipulation, on the one hand, and sentiment, on the other. They may actually go hand in hand. They may also, of course, conflict, as may many different sentiments and opposing instrumental goals; difficult decisions, of a kind which form the staple of politics, are the result.

On another tack, there is, however, good cause to reject totally any absolutist primordialist view. Too much ethnographic evidence exists of the fluidity and flux of ethnic identification for any other position to be sensible, and the theoretical argument in favour of a constructionist view is too well founded. Nor did Barth 'invent' this understanding of ethnicity. Leach's classic study of Shan and Kachin in highland Burma (1954) is an ethnographic precursor in important respects, and even earlier the American sociologist Everett Hughes (1948) outlined a theoretical model of ethnicity which anticipates Barth by more than twenty years. Many, many other works could be cited to make the point: recently, for example, a range of work about East Africa has offered a similar view (e.g. Schlee, 1989; Spear and Waller, 1993).

However, nor can we deny the longevity and stubbornness, under particular circumstances, of ethnic attachments (Rex, 1991: 11). But to acknowledge this neither necessitates embracing a notion of primordiality nor abandoning a social constructionist point of view. There are a number of important points here. First, it is not stretching the point to regard ethnic differentiation – the social construction of 'us' and 'them', marked in cultural terms – as a ubiquitous feature of human societies. The only possible exception to this might be an imaginary society existing in total isolation. To say this, however, is not to endorse any of the arguments of the primordial position.

Second, it is clear that an individual's sense of ethnic membership may – depending upon context – be internalised during early primary socialisation, along with many of the markers of ethnicity such as language, religion, non-verbal behaviour, etc. (Bentley, 1987). During this period the primary, deep-rooted social identities of selfhood, gender and human-ness are acquired (Jenkins, 1996b); ethnicity may be acquired also as an integral part of the individually embodied point of view of selfhood. Thus, ethnicity may, *under local circumstances*, be characterisable as a primary, even if not a primordial, aspect of identity.

Third, it is, however, also clear that internal or self-identification – whether by individuals or groups – is not the only mechanism of ethnic identity formation. People are not always in a position to 'choose' who they are or what their identity means in terms of its social consequences. Power differentials are important here. External categorisation is an important contributor to ethnicity, not least in the processes of primary socialisation but also in a range of other settings (Jenkins, 1994; 1997: 52–73).

The visibility of ethnicity in primary socialisation is likely to be a product of the local specificities of place and time. Growing up in Denmark in 1994, for example, is not the same as growing up in Northern Ireland in 1994. Ethnicity, or at least an awareness of it, is likely to figure in different ways, with different social costs and benefits attached, in each place. Other processes of ethnic categorisation also vary with context with respect to their effectiveness and intrusiveness. Thus, although ethnicity can be understood as a primary social identity, its salience, strength and manipulability are situationally contingent (to say which is to come very close to Geertz's position above). No matter how apparently strong or inflexible it may be, it is always socially constructed, in the first instance and in every other.

If the primordial position is largely unconvincing, that may be because, as an analytical model, it is largely a straw man. The debate about 'instrumentalism' and 'primordialism' often exaggerates the differences between, for example, Geertz and Barth and does neither justice. I am tempted to agree with Eller and Coughlan (1993) that the notion of the 'primordial' should be banished from the social science lexicon. However, the debate remains important. Crude primordialism – although it makes an occasional appearance in academic guise (for example Grosby, 1995) – is essentially a commonsense view, and one possessed of enormous power in the social world. An anthropological perspective, rooted in the constructionist assumptions of the discipline, has much to offer as a critique of the naturalisation of chauvinism and ethnic conflict.

## Culture and biology

In many respects this debate is homologous to the one which I have just discussed. It is at least as important, and for largely similar reasons: common sense continues to assert the reality and significance of 'race' and racism remains a blight.

Building upon the example set by Boas (1940), social and cultural anthropology have long offered an important challenge to dubiously scientific notions of 'race' (Benedict, 1983 [1942]; Lévi-Strauss, 1952). Unfortunately, however, the problem of 'race', of the relationship between biology and culture, seems to have receded from the anthropological agenda as the social constructionist model of ethnicity has, to borrow a notion from Kuhn, become a normal science paradigm within the discipline. Wallman, for example, has dismissed the debate about the distinction between 'race' and ethnicity as a 'quibble' (1978: 205), and elsewhere (1986: 229) she argues that phenotype or physical appearance is just one potential ethnic boundary marker among many. A similar position is taken by Eriksen in his recent textbook: 'Ideas of "race" may or may not form part of ethnic ideologies, and their presence or absence does not seem to be a decisive factor in interethnic relations' (1993: 5).

The adoption of such a view seems, in part, to be a refusal to risk the validation of biological models of ethnic difference. Interestingly, however, the naturalisation of ethnicity within a socio-biological framework can lead to a similar position. In van den Berghe's terms, for example, ethnicity is an extension of kinship, a manifestation of an adaptive nepotism between kin which has essentially genetic foundations. By this token, 'race' becomes nothing more than a 'special marker of ethnicity', a visible folk test of likely common ancestry (van den Berghe, 1981: 240).

There are, of course, anthropologists who neither gloss over the relationship between 'race' and ethnicity nor submerge the one in the other. Banton, in particular, has consistently explored and theorised the two concepts and the relationship between them. 'Race', he argues, is a categorical identification based on physical or phenotypical characteristics, denoting 'them', while ethnicity is about cultural group identification and 'us' (1983: 1–15). Ethnicity is thus voluntarily embraced, while a 'racial' identification is imposed. Banton has also written at length about the history of theories of 'race' (1987). In a recent article Wade (1993) has criticised Banton for taking phenotypical variation somewhat for granted, neglecting the social processes of categorisation which denote and signify the differences which make a difference. In this view physical differences are always highly socially constructed.

A closely related issue is the anthropological perspective upon racism. Two characteristic threads of the anthropology of ethnicity are its celebration of ethnicity as a 'good thing', as a cultural and social resource rather than a stigma, and an emphasis upon minority rather then majority ethnicities. These biases derive in part from the anthropological romance with exotic Otherness, in part from the interpretive cross-cultural advocacy role assumed by many anthropologists, and in part from the continuing legacy of structural functionalism which leads to a theoretical underplaying of conflict. There are exceptions (of which Eidheim (1969) is conspicuous in its excellence) and there is clear evidence that world events – in the

Balkans, Amazonia, Indonesia, the list could be a very long one – in tandem with the developing anthropological concern with nationalism, are finally effecting shifts within the discipline that are likely to prove durable.[4] None the less, racism remains an aspect of the social construction of ethnic differentiation which is relatively little explored by anthropologists (and, when it is, it is not always done well: see La Fontaine (1986) and Jenkins (1987)).

The arguments about the spurious nature of 'race' are too well known to require reiteration here and to do so would extend the scope of the discussion beyond its brief. Nor can I adequately engage with the complexities of how one might theorise the relationship between 'race' and ethnicity (Jenkins, 1996a; 1997: 74–87). My intention is simply to suggest that the 'problem of race' is currently underplayed within anthropology and that adopting a social constructionist model of ethnicity neither requires nor entitles us to indulge in such a neglect. Anthropology has, after all, for many years specialised in the study of classificatory systems. To reiterate Wade's point, 'race' is a set of classificatory social constructs of considerable historical and contemporary significance (an exemplary study of the social construction of 'racial' categorisation – albeit one not undertaken by an anthropologist – is Dikötter's monograph (1992) on modern China). Racism, as an ideology of ethnic identification and a folk cosmology, is also socially constructed, an everyday version of the primordial model. As such it too is an appropriate object for the anthropological attention – in research as well as in teaching – which, at the moment, it receives all too infrequently.

## The communal, the local, the national and the global

One of the most important insights which can be claimed by the anthropological perspective upon ethnicity is that, in as much as it is situational, ethnic identity is also likely to be segmentary and hierarchical. Although two groups may be differentiated from each other as A and B, in a different context they may combine as C in contrast to D (with which they may combine in yet other circumstances). One of the best articulations of this model of situational and hierarchical classification is in Moerman's classic paper dealing with Thailand (1965).

It is a model which is straightforward to communicate to students, and to which they can often relate on the basis of their own experience. But it does precipitate an interesting problem. When does an identity in the segmentary hierarchy of comparison and contrast become local or communal rather than ethnic? Consider the following, very incomplete sequence. The opposition East Swansea:West Swansea is subsumed under Swansea:Cardiff, which is subsumed under South Wales:North Wales, which is subsumed under Wales:England, which is subsumed under Britain:Europe. Precisely where in this sequence could one say that identity based on community or locality becomes identity based on ethnicity? And why? After all, each of these identificatory contrasts reflects 'the social organisation of culture difference' (Barth) and involves 'socially ratified personal identities' (Geertz).

In the anthropological literature these questions are thrown into sharp relief by the work of Anthony Cohen on cultural identity and the symbolic construction of community and communal boundaries (Cohen, 1982; 1985; 1986). There is a clear and obvious similarity between the ideas of Cohen and his collaborators and the Barthian, social constructionist view of ethnicity; indeed, many of the contributors to the edited volumes (1982 and 1986) make the connection explicit, as does Cohen himself. Further, the subtitles of both of the edited collections invoke the idea of 'British cultures', a minor reification which suggests that each of the local research sites documented by the ethnographers concerned can be conceptualised, anthropologically at least, as a distinct domain of bounded cultural difference. Not quite ethnic groups or tribes, perhaps, but almost:

> 'Community' thus seems to imply simultaneously both similarity and difference. The word thus expresses a *relational* idea: the opposition of one community to others or to other social entities...the use of the word is only occasioned by the desire or need to express such a distinction. It seems appropriate, therefore, to focus our examination of the nature of community on the element which embodies this sense of discrimination, namely, the *boundary*.
>
> (Cohen, 1985: 12; original emphasis)

Substitute for 'community' the words 'ethnicity' or 'ethnic group', as appropriate, and one would have a perfectly sensible set of propositions (which would not look out of place in *Ethnic Groups and Boundaries*). Cohen's further emphasis upon the role of symbolism in the social construction of community boundaries is in fact, suitably modified, a powerful contribution to our understanding of ethnicity.

But this still leaves the question of whether, and how, we should distinguish the ethnic from the communal or the local. Nor is the question confined to locality or community. Heading in the other direction, towards the more macro and the more abstract, when does ethnicity become nationalism, and what is the relationship between them? This problem is also implicit in the Welsh illustration, above. From a different angle Eriksen (1993: 116–18) draws upon his Mauritian ethnography to discuss the possibility of a 'non-ethnic nationalism'. This turns the argument somewhat on its head: when does nationalism cease to be ethnic? Two things are in need of conceptual clarification here. The first has to do with levels of abstraction and analysis, the second with the developing character of nationalism in the modern world.

Debates about the nature of the modern world raise one final matter of importance here. Regardless of which particular view one wishes to adopt with respect to 'post-modernity', 'high modernity', or whatever, one consistent theme, about which there is some consensus within these debates, is that something called 'globalisation' is happening or has happened. New technology has facilitated a major shift in the nature, amount and communicative immediacy of information, while international travel has become an accepted part of the way of life of ever-larger sections of the world's population. The result – globalisation – is seen as a qualitative break with the past (Robertson, 1992)...or not (Frank and Gillis, 1993). However we see it, a range of commentators (Hannerz, 1990, 1992; Friedman, 1990, 1994; Hall, 1991; Waters, 1995: 133–9) are agreed that globalisation has consequences for ethnicity as a social phenomenon. There is, however, no suggestion that globalisation necessarily broadens the mind. Globalisation and heightened localisation, far from being contradictory, are inter-linked: the world is becoming smaller and larger at the same time. Localism and ethnicity are conceptualised as inextricably sides of the same coin, and each may (re)assert itself either as a defensive reaction to, or a result of, the increasingly global context of social life.

Whether or not to accept the 'global' as an appropriate or useful unit of analysis, particularly with respect to culture, is one question which is raised by this debate. Another concerns the way in which the local and the global are juxtaposed; there are a number of 'layers' in between which require some attention as well. It also takes for granted more than it should the close implication of the ethnic in the local. The jury is still out with respect to the shape which all of this will assume in the historical medium term, but, in the anthropological here and now, we are still only beginning to develop a response with respect to either theory or method (Eriksen, 1993: 150–2, 156–62; Marcus, 1992; Miller, 1995).

My own inclination is to retain ethnicity as a way of talking about one of the most general and basic principles of human sociability (Carrithers, 1992): collective identification, a sense of 'us' and 'them', socially constructed with some reference to culture. By this token the communal, the local, the national, and the 'racial' can be understood as historically and contextually specific social constructions on the basic ethnic theme: allotropes of ethnic identity. One could then also talk about ideologies of identification such as communalism, localism, nationalism, racism and ethnicism (Jenkins, 1997: 74–87). Whether or not we can look forward to talking about globalism remains to be seen (although, in the shape of socialism, it may already be something upon which we can only look back).

But mine is only one possible view. Regardless of how the question is to be answered, it remains on the table as something which must be broached in our research and theorising as well as in our teaching. Concerning the theoretical constitution of the topic and the pragmatic definition of the field for research purposes, the issue could not be more important.

## The importance of teaching

As a discipline we teach many more students than we train anthropologists. It is undergraduate students who, more than anything else, allow the communication of our ideas to the widest possible audience. And in some respects, teaching about ethnicity from an anthropological perspective does not present too many difficulties. The topic is a rising stock on the disciplinary exchange and there is an ever-growing anthropological literature, typically the kind of ethnographic material that students most enjoy, available as a teaching resource.[5] However, the fact that lots of anthropologists are talking to each other about ethnicity, combined with the disciplinary enthusiasm for detailed ethnography rather than theory, may lead to some things being taken for granted. Two major problems suggest themselves. The first is the problem of how to define anthropology, the second, and the more important, the problem of how to define ethnicity. Each is discussed above and offers eloquent testimony, as indeed does the subject matter itself, to the persistent importance of boundaries in the social world and in culture.

A further problem is the perpetual need to struggle, both in one's work and in the work of one's students, against the tendency to reify – and in the process, perhaps, naturalise – culture and ethnicity. Although we talk about them in these terms endlessly (and I have doubtless done so in this chapter), neither culture nor ethnicity are 'things' that people 'have'. They are, rather, complicated repertoires which people experience, use, learn and 'do' in their daily lives, upon which they draw for a sense of themselves and an understanding of their fellows.

One of the possible consequences of this reification is the construction of ethnicity as typically an attribute of the Other; it becomes something which characterises other people. So, how can one encourage one's students to understand that each and all of them participate in an ethnicity, just like 'them', just like the Other, just like the minorities? Some students, of course, as members of 'ethnic minorities', are perhaps only too aware of their own ethnicity. Students from culturally marked peripheries (such as, in the British Isles, Wales, Ireland or Scotland) can also appreciate this without too many difficulties. However, for other students – white, middle-class, metropolitan – it can be very difficult to appreciate. Yet its appreciation is arguably the first step towards understanding.

And the understanding is important. Perhaps more important at the present time than most things that we teach about. Although it is welcome, we should not *need* Eric Wolf's argument (1994) that 'race', 'culture' and 'people' are 'perilous ideas'. Newscasts if not history should teach us this. Nor – particularly bearing in mind my own argument that collective identification in terms of 'us' and 'them' should be understood as a general and basic foundation of the human social world – ought we allow ourselves to forget the uses to which our discussions and debates may be bent:

Classifying the most diverse historical forms of social identity as 'ethnic' creates the scientifically questionable but politically useful impression that all ethnicities are basically the same and that ethnic identity is a natural trait of persons and social groups....This is not an argument which bears up to historical scrutiny. Rather, it is a nominalist operation intended to provide scholarly legitimation for ethno-nationalist ideologies.

(Lentz, 1995: 305)

So we return, in closing, to the argument about the primordiality or otherwise of ethnicity.

Considerations such as these make anthropological teaching about ethnicity both urgent and troublesome. Because of its comparative global reach and its local-level research focus, its emphasis upon culture as well as social construction, anthropology offers a promise to the world beyond the academy: to relativise notions about ethnicity and to resist the naturalisation of ethnic identity and nationalist ideology. Among the most important contexts in which this can be done are our lectures, seminars and tutorials. There is, however, some way still to go, and some considerable conceptual clarification is necessary, before we can begin to live up to that promise.

## Notes

1  In a short chapter I cannot deal with the differences between cultural anthropology (typically North American) and social anthropology (typically European and, most specifically, British). This oversight is not critical: ethnicity is one of the areas in which the distinction has been of least moment, and for a number of reasons it is likely that the distinction is becoming less important, and that a new international domain of socio-cultural anthropology may be emerging.
2  Shortage of space prevents a consideration of the epistemological dimensions of disciplinary change, particularly with respect to the critique of ethnography (Bourdieu, 1990; Clifford and Marcus, 1986).
3  Although sociology, as the larger and less specialised discipline, tends not to be as sectarian in this respect as anthropology, both disciplines have suffered major intellectual losses as they have gradually drifted apart.
4  This can, for example, be seen in a range of recent contributions to the pages of the Royal Anthropological Institute's magazine *Anthropology Today*. The, mainly anthropological, contributions to *Identities*, a new journal edited in the USA since 1994, also illustrate the developing engagement of the discipline with change and conflict.
5  Not to mention, of course, ethnographic films.

# 7  'Race' in psychology
## Teaching the subject

*Karen Henwood and Ann Phoenix*

The 1990s is a timely historical moment, with racism resurgent in Europe, for psychologists to join other social scientists to consider teaching the subject of 'race'.[1] Many students attracted into psychology will pursue careers that involve the management and development of corporate 'individuals'. Reflecting somewhat different values, concern has begun to be voiced by some teachers of psychology (Jobanputra, 1995), and professional clinical and educational psychologists (Bender and Richardson, 1990), that psychology lacks alignment with multi-ethnic concerns, audiences and clients (Howitt and Owusu-Bempah, 1994). Psychology, as we shall see, is characterised by a chequered history in relation to the subject of 'race', at times supplying 'evidence' useful to those wishing to promote racist propaganda (Billig, 1979).

This chapter is largely concerned with the way 'race' is discussed in psychology, since without this an important part of the context for teaching the subject would be missing. One assumption to be challenged immediately, is that 'race' refers only to black people, since white people are racialised too (Ware, 1992; Frankenberg, 1993). Notwithstanding this, the lack of a subject of 'race' in the sense of treating 'race' as a sub-section of the discipline is a manifestation of the invisibility of black people and other minorities.[2] There are some notable exceptions: the featuring of 'race' and IQ in courses on 'individual differences' (where information has been popularised through the media); the topic of 'race' and mental health (which is relevant to courses on clinical – still sometimes called abnormal – psychology); cross-cultural psychology (which adopts a comparative, but typically apolitical, approach to cultural difference) and the social psychology of prejudice and discrimination. These are in themselves problematic since they underline a construction of black and other minority people as irrelevant to other psychological concerns, creating a 'normalised absence/pathologised presence' approach to 'racial' minorities (Phoenix, 1987).

The chapter also concerns the subject of 'race', as it refers to philosophical questions regarding the ways in which the psyche is conceptualised. As is well known, psychology is historically an Enlightenment discipline committed to the (illusory) ideal of detached, neutral, rational, scientific observation, that strives for single, accurate representations of an objectively present empirical world. Accordingly, psychology's subject is traditionally that of liberal humanism – the self-contained individual at the centre of consciousness and behaviour, whose attributes are then classified, counted and measured (and thereby objectified) by professional psychologists and researchers. However, by generally concentrating on the individual and viewing individuals and society as opposing entities, Enlightenment psychology treats racial difference as if it were natural, rather than socially produced. Black and other minority people are typically constructed, within this account, as deviations from a white (often) male majority ethnic group as the norm, which in itself results in the aforementioned problem of pathologisation (Wong, 1994). These characteristics mean that it is often difficult for minorities to use the intellectual idioms and languages of psychology 'to constitute themselves as self-conscious subjects, or find a self-representation that is not sexualised or racialised' (Stepan and Gilman, 1993: 177).

Nevertheless, the discipline of psychology is not unitary. Epistemological and metatheoretical developments, originating in other areas of social science (see, for example, Rabinow, 1984; Weedon, 1987), have facilitated a revised portrayal of psychology's subject as meaningfully produced within discourses that have ideological effects (Henriques *et al.*, 1984; Potter and Wetherell, 1987; Wetherell and Potter, 1992). The turn to discourse does not, in itself, integrate a concern for relations of dominance, oppression and racism into psychological work (Burman and Parker, 1990). Yet, subjection to racism has been a concern of the work mentioned, which has featured the way in which shifting, fragmented and multiple identities are constructed at points of intersection between categories such as gender, class and 'race' (Bhavnani and Phoenix, 1994; Burman, 1994a).

In this chapter we therefore seek to consider psychology's 'double role' as a set of institutional practices and discourses that are complicit with racism, while also seeking to explore and undermine racism as a serious social problem (Wetherell and Potter, 1992). The fact that there are fractures and fissures within psychological discourse means that teachers and students can succeed in opposing racism. Yet, because of the constraints placed on understanding by much existing psychological knowledge, it remains all too easy to become implicated in its reproduction. We consider two main topic areas, the first ('race' and IQ) in order to highlight psychology's relationship with old-style, crude (often biological) racism. The second (the social psychology of prejudice and discrimination) enables us to identify the problem of new, more subtle (often cultural) forms of racism in psychology, and productive strands of work illuminating this issue.[3] In the final section, we reflect upon some wider aspects of social and institutional context, and the discursively positioned subjectivities of teachers and students, as these necessarily complicate the teaching of psychology and 'race'.

## 'Race' and IQ

Since the French psychologists Alfred Binet and Theophile Simon devised what came to be seen as the first systematic intelligence test in 1905, intelligence quotient (IQ) tests have become part of a panoply of techniques for administration and control of populations (Henriques *et al.*, 1984; Rose, 1989). Initially intended to assess, in order to help, children who were lagging behind their peers, their subsequent use has been far from progressive (Evans and Waites, 1981; Lewontin *et al.*, 1984).

### *The essentials of the hereditarian argument*

The intersection of 'race' and IQ is long-standing. During the First World War, mass testing in the USA army provided data that black recruits scored less on IQ tests than their white counterparts. Genetic explanations of this were widely accepted and taken for granted in a historical context where some academics were also enthusiastic eugenicists (Milner, 1983). The area of 'race' and IQ was thus underpinned by essentialist arguments about black people's genetic intellectual inferiority to white people's. Black people were homogenised, reduced to low IQ scores and assumed necessarily to be different from white people. This form of essentialism pre-dated the development of IQ tests since it had for centuries been accepted as fact that white 'races' were naturally superior to black 'races' (Miles, 1989). Such long-standing beliefs helped to provide the conditions of possibility within which black people's inferior performance on IQ tests was accepted as natural (Gould, 1981).

The 'race' and IQ controversy arose when Jensen (1969) elaborated psychological hereditarian arguments suggesting, basically, that it was a waste of time and money to try to increase black children's IQ scores since they were genetically restricted. Within British and American academia, a lot of time and energy was spent on careful refutations of Jensen's arguments by white and black academics (see, for example, Guthrie, 1976; Rose and Rose, 1978). Outside the academy, much political activity was expended in opposition to the implications of hereditarian arguments. There were, for example, successful attempts by some black psychologists and parents in the USA to have standardised IQ tests legally banned for educational diagnosis of ethnic minority children (McLoughlin and Koh, 1982; Hilliard, 1992) on the grounds that they are racially and culturally biased. Psychologists, such as Richard Lynn and Hans Eysenck, together with the physicist William Shockley, provided support for Jensen's position (Lewontin *et al.*, 1984).

With concerted opposition to the hereditarian position espoused by Jensen and the loss of credibility generated by Kamin's (1974) demonstration that Cyril Burt[4] had manufactured the separated twin study data on which it was largely based, the hereditarian argument apparently declined.

However, hereditarians continued in productive work. Some, for example, sought to clear Burt's name (Milner, 1991) and the British Psychological Society (BPS) did eventually reinstate Burt. The 'race' and heredity debate resurfaced in Britain with the publication in the Bulletin of the BPS of a paper which argued that black people and white people had different reproductive strategies associated with different IQs, genitalia and family forms (Rushton, 1990). Current social concerns were thus incorporated into old hereditarian arguments (perhaps influenced by socio-biological ideas). Rushton's paper generated a furore. For the first time, the British psychology establishment was publicly criticised from within. Some psychologists threatened to withdraw from the BPS if it continued to lend support to scientific racism and if the honorary editors did not resign (see the *Psychologist*, the house journal of the BPS, 1990, vol. 3, nos 5 and 7). Despite the heat generated, the editors (who admitted that the offending article had not been refereed; Breakwell and Davey, 1990) did not resign and there was no official apology, despite the BPS's constitutional commitment to being apolitical. Hereditarian claims raised fresh controversies a few years later (see Richardson, 1994) and will, no doubt, continue periodically to do so.

BPS support for the politics of racism has also been challenged in other ways; for example, in the campaign to sever academic links between the BPS and South Africa in the apartheid period (Reicher, 1988a, 1988b; Henwood, 1994). The demonstration, in teaching, of disagreements between psychologists can potentially facilitate students' ability to refute hereditarian arguments.

## Implications for the teaching of psychology

The 'race' and IQ debate has implications for the teaching of 'race' in psychology in five ways. First, it presents a powerful message that black people are inferior to white people in ways deemed crucially important in 'meritocratic' societies. Despite refutations of arguments that black people's lower IQ scores, in comparison with white people's, result from their genetic inferiority, the quantity of work in this area of psychology and the continual necessity for refutations contribute to negative constructions of black people.

Second, it essentialises black and white lecturers and students within psychological narratives. For, although it is difficult to read off all the possible positionings that people occupy simply from knowing their colour and ethnicity (Phoenix, 1994), in the hereditarian 'race' and IQ story, skin colour is constructed as a major signifier of genes for high or low intelligence. 'Nature has colour-coded groups of individuals so that statistically reliable predictions of their adaptability to intellectually rewarding and effective lives can easily be made and profitably be used by the pragmatic man in the street' (Shockley, 1972: 307). Attempts to teach in a 'balanced' way leave open the question of whether or not lecturers (and students) hold hereditarian views. Students may well assume that lecturers and the majority of students accept racialised constructions of black people as inherently inferior to white people. Hunter, Simons and Stephens (1984: 10) quote a school teacher of English to make a similar point.

> I have always thought that my white liberalism was emblazoned all over me, but I will never forget the response of a black girl, whom I had taught for two years, to an outburst of mine condemning racists. She simply said 'I never knew you were one of us miss', because she had missed all the subtle responses and statements I had ever made concerning prejudice.

Third, the area of 'race' and IQ highlights one important way in which the discipline, despite claims to neutrality and objectivity by many of its practitioners, is political in its constructions and effects (Henriques *et al.*, 1984; Bohan, 1992; Burman, 1994b). Claims that black people are innately intellectually limited have been used to argue for differential treatment of black people and white people in social policy areas such as education and immigration. Although hereditarians generally claim to be apolitical, their work is not politically neutral. For example, Jensen's (1969) extended treatment of black–white differences in IQ in his 117-page paper was explicitly directed to halting the USA Head Start preschool intervention programme (which President Nixon did stop). Eysenck (1971) has also argued that black–white differences in IQ need to be taken into account in 'sensible' policies on immigration. Thus, potentially, the heritability and IQ position has directly negative effects on the ways in which black people are positioned within society and policies aimed at black people. In addition, extreme right-wing groups have seized upon Jensen's and Eysenck's work as proof of black inferiority (Billig, 1979). It is not possible therefore, as Eysenck (1971) has claimed, to keep 'scientific facts' about 'race' distinct from racist attitudes. Instead, the social and political context within which such research is reported underlines the interlinkages between scientific and popular discourses on 'race' and racism. Much ink has been expended on examining whether or not the proponents of hereditarian views are intentionally racist. This, arguably, is not entirely relevant to a consideration of the 'race' and IQ debate and hence the context in which 'race' is taught in psychology, since hereditarian work as discursive production has material effects regardless of the intentions of the authors.

The political nature of IQ testing is exemplified by the fact that intelligence test scores have been used to argue for social policies which have negative consequences for a particular minority ethnic group, regardless of whether that group scores well or badly. Thus, the higher Porteus test scores of Chinese and Japanese people in comparison with white people were used to argue against their being allowed to immigrate into Hawaii in the 1920s (Richards, 1997). Fourth, the recursive nature of the arguments in this debate has resulted in this being an area of stagnation within psychology (although it can help to advance metatheoretical understandings of the discipline).

> How little seems to have changed, and how little advance has been made since the days of Galton and Binet, in spite of a century of accumulating biological knowledge, the advent of quantitative genetics, and the potency of modern molecular biology. Why is this? Why can't we do better?
>
> Leaving aside the wilfull (sic) and pernicious misinterpretations of data, there appear to be two principal sources of confusion. The first is a widespread failure to understand what biology cannot yet tell us. The second is an equally widespread failure to understand what it can.
>
> (Odling-Smee, 1990: 653–4)

The only possible moves are either further to elaborate black–white differences in IQ, or continually to counter these arguments with detailed examinations of the shortcomings of the 'evidence' on which the hereditarian edifice is built while highlighting the contribution of environmental factors to test scores (Lewontin *et al.*, 1984). The debates are informed not only by psychology, but by irreconcilable ideological commitments (although these are consistently denied by hereditarians). Questions of whether or not IQ differences are hereditarily transmitted are, arguably, so archaic that the debate is akin to flogging an already dead horse (Brush, 1990). Yet, failure to counter hereditarian arguments would be seen by many to confirm their truth.

Finally, the popularisation of these ideas beyond psychology has an impact, not only in stereotyping psychology outside the discipline as stuck-in-the-mud, but in perpetuating racism.

> A number of years ago I was involved in a series of workshops which brought together psychologists, sociologists and black activists in considering how best to advance our understanding of racial inequality. It rapidly became clear that, for the sociologists present, psychology was at best a technique for ignoring power inequalities and structural determinants of discrimination, at worst an overt legitimation of racism. For the black activists, even liberal psychologies of 'race' were exercises in victim blaming. In most of the sessions, we psychologists were left trying to justify our right to speak on the issue and little time was left to see if we had any positive contribution to make.
>
> (Reicher, 1993: 121)

This is likely to have an impact on the students attracted into the discipline and hence on those who have any opportunity later to influence the discipline from within. While there are increasing numbers of black and minority students reading psychology in Britain and the USA, it is perhaps not surprising that more are attracted into the social sciences than into psychology.

## The social psychology of prejudice and discrimination

Our second topical focus, the social psychology of prejudice and discrimination, emerged as a research area in the USA in the 1920s and 1930s at a time of growing awareness of 'race' and racism in society, and in the 1940s as social scientists reflected upon the destruction wrought by Nazism during the Second World War (Samelson, 1978). Accordingly, its historical conditions of production involved tacit dissociation from the now tarnished notion of inherited racial difference, culminating in a societal shift of values that made apparent the unacceptability of discrimination on grounds of 'race'. The development of population genetics since this time has further discredited the view that racial classifications have any clear empirical basis in biological, genetic or other physical characteristics: contemporary science now points to the greater genetic variation within than between 'racial' groups and the dependence of evolution upon such variation for its operation (Harding, 1993). In one important respect, therefore, the social psychology of prejudice and discrimination is fundamentally less problematic than research premised on the possibility of establishing an innate, biological association between IQ and 'race'.

Nevertheless, as with psychology as a whole (Yee *et al.*, 1994), few social psychologists have shown a sustained interest in developing an alternative theorisation of 'race' that goes beyond society's global rejection of its derogatory, hierarchical and biological connotations. As a result, actively problematising existing theories where they reify culturally constructed 'racial' difference (Reicher, 1986) and/or tacitly justify cultural (or 'new'; Barker, 1981) forms of racism (Husband, 1986) provides one way of teaching the subject differently, by seeking to overcome the limitations of the material to be taught. The potential also exists to challenge the (still widely held) view within psychology, that its theories can represent universal, timeless truths that stand apart from society and history (Joseph *et al.*, 1990).

### Early developments: the focus upon irrational individual prejudice

The problematics of social psychological research on prejudice and discrimination may be traced to Gordon Allport's (1954) *The Nature of Prejudice*, and to other texts utilising the concept of attitude (Thomas and Znaniecki, 1919). The principles of liberal, Enlightenment psychology define prejudice as a problem that occurs when people deviate from their optimal functioning as rational, human agents, consciously controlling thought and behaviour. Within this account, rationality becomes the ideal of democratic society and individuals the site where it can break down (Henriques *et al.*, 1984). The majority of social psychologists today still follow Allport in attributing biased, faulty, irrational (that is, prejudicial) beliefs and attitudes to the distorting effects of cognitively necessary acts of prejudgement, to unwanted intrusions by emotional, unconscious, libidinal concerns into cognitive process, or to both.

Allport located the cognitive, emotional and attitudinal components of prejudicial dispositions at the 'personality level' within his multi-layered model (also containing 'historical', 'socio-cultural', 'situational', 'phenomenological' and 'stimulus object' levels), and there is a current preference for converting this into an integrated account (Duckitt, 1992). However, such eclecticism merely entrenches theories which divide the individual from society with reductive effects (Henriques *et al.*, 1984; Parker, 1989, 1992). One widely popularised approach within psychology (Dollard *et al.*, 1939; Hovland and Sears, 1940) and beyond (see, for example, Storr, 1979), for example, explains 'racial' hatred as the outcome of frustrated individual needs and desires, leading to displaced or generalised aggression. Since frustration need not lead to aggression and aggression may not result from frustration (it may simply be instrumental in securing desired goals), an early reformulation proposed that a build-up of anger will be released only on the appearance of learned environmental cues (Berkowitz, 1971; 1972). Yet, this again merely reduces society to observable, physical properties of the environment (for example, physiognomic features, weapons), neglecting the fact that ideological forces, bound up with power relations, necessarily structure human relations (Billig, 1976; Tajfel, 1978a). In order to become – in Berkowitz's behaviourist terms – cues for aggression, particular physical features must have been selected by discourses that presuppose racism since, in themselves, they are devoid of social significance (van den Berghe, 1967: 11).

Social psychology's second main mid-twentieth-century account of irrational individual prejudice – authoritarian personality theory (Adorno *et al.*, 1950) – marks a welcome break with individualistic reductionism by insisting that historical social formations and political ideologies are essential to explaining prejudicial attitudes and behaviour. It also strives to understand individual–society functioning by exploring how social forms can reach into the depths of individual psychology, by interweaving ideological with personal themes (Wetherell and Potter, 1992). Within this account, specifically capitalist economies and anti-democratic ideologies are associated with harsh, punitive parenting, leading to the development of a particular constellation of personality characteristics (including excessive deference to authority, disdain for weakness, repressed sexuality and cognitive rigidity), which then predispose authoritarians to find totalitarian ideologies appealing.

Social criticism has not been the main reason behind this theory's attraction for social psychologists. Researchers have simply adopted the F(predisposition to fascism)-scale as a convenient measure of personal authoritarianism, or subjected the empirical work to methodological scrutiny. Nevertheless, the explanatory weakness of the approach has been identified by observations of inconsistencies between society-wide levels of prejudice and numbers of individuals measuring high on personal authoritarianism (Pettigrew, 1958); in the behaviour of individuals in different contexts (Minard, 1952); and revelations of the anti-authority opinions of fascist youth (Billig, 1978a; 1978b). Proposing an ideologically specific account has been valuable in illuminating the psycho-social dynamics of one form of prejudice; ultimately, however, it obscures other forms of prejudice from view.

### Social cognition and social identity theory

Two more recently developed perspectives – 'social cognition' (also called 'cognitive social psychology') and 'social identity theory' (SIT) claim to be advances on earlier research. Modern social cognition starts from Allport's earlier view of prejudice as irrational belief, locating this within today's cognitive *Zeitgeist* which models internal mental functions as computer systems, sometimes considering its interface with affect and emotion (Nisbett and Ross, 1980; Hamilton, 1981; Miller, 1982; Fiske and Taylor, 1984; Mackie and Hamilton, 1993). A variety of 'basic', cognitive structures (that is, categories, prototypes, stereotypes) have been designated as the relevant information stores, and a range of information-processing errors (also called cognitive heuristics or biases) proposed as explanations of prejudice's irrational basis.

The fundamental problem with this work is its assumption that categories of people, like categories of objects, are more or less useful to the extent that they accurately predict behaviour, since by this reasoning the racist insults which can accompany the deployment of such categories are effectively naturalised, obscured or denied. Accordingly, its acceptance has been dubbed 'metalevel racism' (Condor, 1988). Similarly the proposal that undesirable stereotyped attributes result when associations (including metaphorical and temporal) are made between vivid physical (for example, black/white faces, thick/thin lips) and corresponding psychological and social characteristics (for example, laziness/endeavour) (McArthur, 1982) must be questioned. A flawed and rigid commitment to naive empiricism in this case reinforces a highly racialised view of external reality, including the view that the undesirable characteristics attributed to certain groups merely reflect certain objective facts about them. This amounts to a form of racism called 'reification of "race" categories' (Condor, 1988).

Attributing prejudice and discrimination to information-processing biases may appear to promote racial harmony, by denying that racism originates in real differences between races. However, it parallels the multi-culturalist ideal that people are all the same under the skin, and that differences are merely skin-deep. As critiques of multiculturalism have shown, this argument merely denies socially constructed 'racial' categories and divisions, and hence avoids rather than adequately theorises racial difference. Furthermore, space is re-created for a victim-blaming interpretation of racism, by casting prejudice as the 'natural effect of information-processing mechanisms' (Henriques, 1984: 74).

Social identity theory is, again, rooted in the tradition of cognitive social psychology, having pioneered empirical studies of the processes and effects of cognitively categorising stimuli into discrete groups (Tajfel, 1969; 1981). Yet, it differs in viewing such findings as the psychological analogue of social categorisation and differentiation, where groups compete to position themselves favourably in relation to others in societies stratified along dimensions of power and privilege (Tajfel, 1978b, 1981; Turner and Giles, 1981; Tajfel and Turner, 1979; Hogg and Abrams, 1988; 1990). The central concept of social identity refers to interiorised feelings of group belonging, which facilitate and guide collective action (Reicher, 1982). Potentially, therefore, SIT provides a necessary psychological dimension to socially constructed 'racial' difference (Turner and Oakes, 1986), and supports the view that 'race categories and their specification require an incorporation into the social ontology of collectivity and belongingness in order to be understood' (Anthias and Yuval-Davis, 1992: 1). The role assigned to social categorisation in instituting ingroup/outgroup boundaries and identifications also accommodates the analysis that intersecting categories (for example, 'race', gender, age, nationality) jointly mediate the effects of discrimination (Deschamps and Doise, 1978; hooks, 1982; Essed, 1994).

While SIT distances itself from viewpoints that marginalise prejudice and discrimination as problems of individual psychology, it is not wholly successful in avoiding the reification of racial difference. It has contributed little to interrogating the historical and cultural construction of social categories such as 'race' and gender (Potter and Litton, 1985; Potter and Wetherell, 1987), and it routinely uses 'race' as an experimental variable and standardised measures of racial stereotypes, thereby contributing to the further racialisation of reality (Reicher, 1986). The approach simply may have moved too quickly to study content-free mechanisms of ingroup/outgroup division within a discipline that understands little about the social meanings of 'race', their diffuseness, the complex and contradictory emotions that can become attached to them (Hall, 1992), and their cultural and historical specificity (Husband, 1986). It is important to understand how beliefs about social groups can 'merge into a generic neo-racist discourse' (Wodak and Matouschek, 1993: 225). However, comprehending specific racisms (for example, British, with its legacy of colonialism, and European, which links economic competition and immigration) is also necessary to appreciate the power of racist imagery (Balibar, 1991).

Social identity theorists have preferred to study the attitudes and behaviours of powerful groups in order to avoid problematising minorities and absolving responsibility for white racism. Yet this must not displace an equal concern for the experiences of those subjected to racism (Harrison, 1974). This latter standpoint fosters an acute awareness of more subtle forms of racist abuse (Essed, 1988; 1991), and also suggests how these appear within psychology itself. It is difficult to distinguish between SIT's insistence that biologically necessary acts of cognitive categorisation and ingroup favouritism are inextricably linked, and the new racist idea that it is simply natural to belong to one's 'own' group and to defend its cultural traditions. Positions have begun to emerge in social psychology to undermine the thesis that prejudice is inevitable. It is reasonable to suppose, for example, that the process of categorisation has no greater biological necessity than its opposite, particularisation, thereby making space for tolerance (Billig, 1985). Yet, the concept of tolerance has its own limitations, since it presupposes a hierarchy rather than an equality of difference (Husband, 1986). If tolerance is the best that can be achieved from a position of bigotry, then social psychologists can seek more than this (Howitt and Owusu-Bempah, 1994).

### The turn to discourse

The development of a new tradition of work, described here as the turn to discourse, has facilitated theoretical understanding of the shortcomings of earlier work and added a changed face to 'empirical' social psychological research. Some early commentators on the 'crisis of confidence' in social psychology (Elms, 1975) perceived the initial flaw in the view that social, moral and political problems can be solved by following the axioms of science, when they argued for a greater openness regarding the values and assumptions that necessarily underpin scientific work (Armistead, 1972; Israel and Tajfel, 1972). The turn to discourse has reinforced this position with its insight that all knowledge regimes – true and false; lay, scientific and psychological – embody normative beliefs that presuppose an applied ethics (Henriques *et al.*, 1984; Parker, 1989, 1992; Parker and Shotter, 1990).

There has been a proliferation of discourse work, some of which fuses together cognitive psychology, linguistics and various social science themes to analyse the reality defining power of elites, as manifested in many genres of institutional (media, legal, educational) and everyday discourse (van Dijk, 1984; 1987; 1988; 1993). The same interdisciplinary approach has informed studies of the way dominated groups jointly produce and resist discursively produced power relations (Essed, 1991; van Dijk, 1993). Discourse analysts have also criticised contemporary social psychology's cognitive-perceptual metatheory (where a lone perceiver generates a cognitive model reflecting empirical reality – Potter and Wetherell, 1987; Edwards and Potter, 1992), and social theories that are insensitive to the thoroughgoing interpellation into economic relations of ideologies such as those of 'race' (Wetherell and Potter, 1992). An integral point here is that psychological and ideological representation is never merely reflective, since objects of knowledge are always culturally constituted within complexes that intertwine meaning and power (Parker, 1992; Burman and Parker, 1993). A further analytic strand emphasises the rhetorical, argumentative or dilemmatic ideologies that pervade – and indeed in this approach make possible – common sense, thought and talk (Billig, 1988; Verkuyten et al., 1994a, 1994b). Here the ideological nature of thought and the thoughtful nature of ideology are juxtaposed, identifying the limitations of both sociological and social psychological approaches to the historical subject.

Using discourse theory, it is therefore possible to explain that racial difference is neither fixed in stone nor merely illusory, because it is the outcome of practices of (de)racialisation which position groups and subjects in more or less advantageous and discriminatory ways. The contribution of discourse analytic research then is to demystify the various discursive features, strategies or manoeuvres which construct racial difference and express racism. For example, interpretative repertoires (limited sets of descriptive and referential terms, using particular stylistic and grammatical constructions, and often organised around specific metaphors and figures of speech – Potter and Wetherell, 1987; Wetherell and Potter, 1988) may be studied as they are used flexibly to construct 'race'. By going beyond simple categorical images, research has demonstrated how deeply sedimented aspects of common sense can be activated to amplify self–other distinctions in ways which promote crude, colonial racism or, conversely, how they are subjected to anti-racist interrogation (van Teeffelen, 1994).

With the emergence of a societal norm against racism, deracialising practices have come to have the greater ideological potential. Accordingly, a more typical preoccupation of discourse analytic work is with the way in which categories, differences and categorical preferences may be related to taken-for-granted cultural principles widely assumed to stand in opposition to totalitarianism and racism (for example, rationality, freedom, equity, justice and individual rights). For instance, studies have found that negative beliefs about minorities are expressed, but in a way which disclaims any basis in irrational personal dislike by appealing to external, factual reasons made more compelling and vivid by concrete details of personal experience (Billig et al., 1988; Wetherell and Potter, 1992; van Dijk, 1993; Verkuyten et al., 1994a, 1995).

A number of explanatory frameworks have been proposed to encompass findings such as these. Van Dijk (1992) argues that many follow a familiar pattern of disclaiming or denying racism to avoid face-threatening attributions of racism, while simultaneously justifying inequality. Billig *et al.* (1988) (see also Billig, 1988 and Verkuyten *et al.*, 1994a, 1994b) interpret them as manifestations of genuine ideological dilemmas experienced by historical subjects as they struggle to reconcile conflicting values and beliefs such as opposition to racism and support for equal rights. Wetherell and Potter (1992) suggest that psychological activities such as warranting, blaming, arguing and legitimating function within complexes of power and domination, and that analysis should therefore attend to the interactional and broader ideological effects of such discourse acts.

Elements of each explanation appear in the other accounts, hence they are not mutually exclusive. In addition, they jointly emphasise the reasoned, argued and moral tone to contemporary racism. We may question whether this is an entirely new form of racism, since there is evidence that red-necked racists saw the value of circumventing attributions of racism (Billig, 1988, quoting Myrdal, 1944). Nevertheless, discourse analytic work has clarified why assumptions of clear distinctions between prejudice and tolerance cannot be sustained. The concepts are inextricably interlinked and ambivalent, each presupposing and shading into the other in racist discourse which simultaneously denies, justifies and legitimates inequality between those designated, for whatever reason, as 'us' versus those who are 'other' or 'different'. Statements or actions may not arise from old style bigotry, but this is of little import if the alternative – tolerance – amounts to nothing more than reasonable grounds for discrimination. As Billig *et al.* (1988) note, this is prejudice in all but name.

This analysis has profound implications for anti-racist teaching and practice, since it suggests that it is impossible to separate prejudiced sheep from tolerant goats, or to identify one single, definitive version of racist ideology. Instead, the exercise becomes one of considering how various (conservative, liberal, or social reformist) political ideologies can be plundered to reproduce or challenge racism (Wetherell and Potter, 1992). There is a danger that discourse analysis can be depoliticised (Burman and Parker, 1993), for example by 'denuding subjects of identities altogether' (Rattansi, 1994: 71). An outstanding project therefore is to consider the mobilisation of multiple, fragmented and contradictory subjectivities in the service of anti-racism.

## Reflections on teaching 'race' in psychology

The above discussion has demonstrated psychology's contradictory and ambiguous position with regard to 'race' and racism.

> Psychology has often assisted the theory and practice of racism. From its infancy, sometimes through innocence or ignorance, but most frequently through the intrusion of its beliefs about the nature of

racial groups, Psychology has embodied racism quite as much as it has opposed it.

(Milner, 1991: 1)

While psychology is often treated as if it is unitary and has clear-cut effects, it is important not to reify it, since its practitioners are differentiated in their approach to the discipline. However, the background to the teaching of 'race' in psychology is one in which the psychological material available to be taught does not generally start from a position of opposition to racism (see discussion above). The current 'norm against prejudice' (Billig, 1991; Essed, 1991) is so strong that it would be surprising if psychologists considered themselves racist. Yet, since there has been no general questioning within the discipline of the ways in which psychology helps to maintain and reproduce racist ideologies even when lecturers consider that they are teaching from a 'neutral', 'objective' perspective, it cannot be assumed that 'race' and psychology courses contribute to opposition to racism. The option of not directly addressing issues of 'race' on psychology degrees is not surprising given psychology's traditional lack of concern with social processes.

'University teachers do not speak often about what they actually do' (McNeil, 1992: 19). While this is likely to change as more assessments are made of teaching quality in universities and peer review of teaching becomes increasingly common, little is currently known about what goes on behind classroom doors. With regard to the teaching of 'race' and psychology, we know the material available, but not what is taught. In the absence of published reflections, we have taken this opportunity to reflect on issues raised from our own pedagogic engagement with 'race' and psychology.

## Situated knowledges: teaching and the wider context

Some challenges to racism within psychology have come from within the discipline. For example, in Britain, a few, relatively new, psychological organisations aim to resist (among other things) the reproduction of racism within psychology (for example, the Association of Black Psychologists; Psychology, Politics, Resistance; the special interest group of the BPS Division of Clinical Psychology on Race and Culture; Alliance of Women in Psychology). In addition, some journals have attempted to put issues of racism on the psychological agenda through the production of special issues and invitations to debate (for example, *Feminism and Psychology*); some individuals have directly addressed such issues (Joseph *et al.*, 1990; Reicher, 1993; Howitt and Owusu-Bempah, 1994) while others have consistently routinely addressed issues of 'race' in their work (see, for example, Billig, 1978a, 1978b; Essed, 1988; Bhavnani, 1991; Griffin, 1993). Partly because it has more psychologists who are black and from other minority ethnic groups, the USA has a longer history of addressing such issues within psychology (see, for example, Guthrie, 1976). The American Psychological Association and its societies, such as the Society for the Study of Social Issues, have addressed issues of racial equality over the last twenty years.

The institutional context is important to the teaching of 'race' and psychology. The more black students there are in educational institutions and, hence, on psychology courses, the more pressure they are likely to exert for issues of 'race' to be addressed. Teaching staff in such institutions are less likely than those where almost all the students are white, to be able to reproduce ideas which serve to maintain and/or reproduce racist ideologies in the name of 'objective neutrality'. It is difficult to imagine, for example, that lecturers in some of the new universities with well over half of their students coming from black and other minority ethnic groups and where, in some cases, black nationalist groups flourish, could teach about 'race' and IQ as if assertions about the intellectual inferiority of black people to white people were neutral fact. This is particularly the case since an increasing number of black students complain of racial discrimination (Commission for Racial Equality (CRE), 1997). The impact of increasing numbers of black students on psychology courses should not be over-played, since the presence of women students on psychology courses and a trickle of women lecturers did not disrupt the 'normalised absence/pathologised presence' treatment of women. Significant numbers of students working in concert can, however, make a difference.

Psychology, while mostly insulated from many of the developments within the social sciences, has been modified by those within it whose work is informed by insights from post-modernism and other specialisms such as sociology and psychoanalysis (Henriques *et al.*, 1984; Parker, 1989). Such insights have made the study of racism part of the cutting edge of new, popular areas of psychology. Those studying discourse analysis (Wetherell and Potter, 1992) or the dilemmas inherent in ideology (Billig, 1991) are often also introduced to 'race' and psychology (see discussion above). Student reactions to teaching are also constrained or facilitated by the other disciplinary options available. In departments where cultural studies or social science options are routinely taken by psychology students, the teaching of 'race' and psychology is likely to differ from those where no such options are available.

The optional nature of courses on 'race' and psychology is not necessarily problematic, but, since 'race' is not an integral part of psychology courses, it can lead to the marginalisation of the subject. This can be particularly the case if it is predominantly taught only in the few psychological departments which have black members of teaching staff, there being few black psychologists in clinical psychology as well as academia (Bender and Richardson, 1990).

## The intersection of student/teacher positionings

Since issues of 'race' and racism are complex and contradictory within psychology, it is not surprising that their teaching is often a complicated process, affected by the multiple positioning of the participants; for example, with regard to the colour and ethnicity of teachers and students (Phoenix, 1994).

As lecturers, one of us black and the other white, we are positioned differently within classrooms. In addition, we studied in different places with different teachers, then specialised in different areas. However, we share commonalities of (different) histories of committed opposition to racism (including within psychology, see Phoenix, 1987; Henwood, 1994) and of struggle with psychological material on 'race'. All these factors (colour, history in the discipline and opposition to racism) have an impact on the ways in which we and our students (who equally bring diversity into the classroom) teach, learn and are received. This impact is not, however, transparently evident, but we can attempt to tease apart some of the ways in which psychological material, the institutions in which psychology is taught, ourselves as teachers and our students all intersect.

Some psychology students (whatever their colour or ethnicity) are not sure what to expect from lectures, courses or modules on 'race'. There are numerous reasons for students wanting (or, negatively, not wanting) to study 'race' within psychology: to be informed; to study with a particular lecturer (sometimes to be taught by a black lecturer); to attempt to gain the upper hand on a psychology course (for minority students); to study black nationalist ideas or 'black psychology' (which starts from black perspectives rather than focusing on black people); to learn easily about the psychology of those constructed as Other; to raise consciousness; and to take an easy option because racism is an everyday issue (and, therefore, to avoid theoretical complexities). Students also differ in their readiness to consider social processes relevant to psychology and, hence, in their definitions of what constitutes proper psychological subject matter. Some black students privately express fear that they will be victimised or subjected to unwanted scrutiny if they address issues of 'race'. Others are resentful that white teachers make essentialist assumptions that they will, automatically, take options on 'race'. Students bring not only different expectations but also many, competing ideologies to courses aiming to avoid the (re)production of racism. As a result, the study of 'race' and psychology is popular with many students, fails to please others, and produces unpredictable and contradictory processes in teaching.

## Notes

1 We follow the convention of placing quotation marks around the term 'race'. This is to indicate that 'race' is a social construction, that racial difference is socially produced, and to break with discourses that naturalise 'race' and

(even) racism. Where exceptions exist, our explanatory framework should be suggested by other aspects of text and context.

2 Innovatory courses have begun to appear. However, the British Psychological Society does not specify that issues of 'race' and racism should be taught, other than those mentioned, at any level. There are moves to change the status quo in the development of certain 'A' level curricula (Jobanputra, personal communication).

3 A choice of topic areas was demanded by space limitations. Also, similar analytic work would have been done in sections on 'race' and mental health (as has been done in 'race' and IQ) and cross-cultural psychology (as in the social psychology of prejudice and discrimination).

4 Sir Cyril Burt's place in the annals of psychology is a singular one. He rose to prominence early in the twentieth century by adopting the Binet intelligence test for use in England, and was subsequently appointed the first school psychologist. The data he collected from studies of school children with different social backgrounds, and of twins, was for many years held as evidence for the heritability of IQ. He died in 1971 and it was after this that claims that he had falsified the twin studies data came to light. (For further details see R. C. Lewontin, S. Rose and L. J. Kamin *Not in Our Genes: Biology, Ideology and Human Nature*, 1984, NewYork: Pantheon Books.)

# 8   Political science encounters 'race' and 'ethnicity'

*Rupert Taylor*

Up until the mid-1960s issues relating to 'race' and 'ethnicity' were hardly studied by political scientists; until this time, unlike sociology or history, the number of books addressing this topic hardly filled a library shelf. Prior to the Second World War there were just a few studies of 'race' by political scientists, in particular Harold Gosnell's (1935) *Negro Politicians: The Rise of Negro Politics in Chicago* and Ralph Bunche's (1936) *A World View of Race*. Bunche was, in fact, the first black person to obtain a Ph.D. in political science at Harvard, in 1934. But even in the decade or so after the war there was little serious consideration given to the subject. It was certainly the case that the first major voting behaviour studies – *Voting* (Berelson *et al.*, 1954), *The Voter Decides* (Campbell *et al.*, 1954) and *The American Voter* (Campbell *et al.*, 1960) – barely touched on the role of black Americans.

To understand why there was this neglect, and to render meaningful the subsequent extent to which, and in which way, 'race' and 'ethnicity' have been studied in political science one must turn to consider how the discipline's standards and theoretical orientation were set in the postwar era in the United States of America (where today some 75–80 per cent of the world's political scientists work). Here, the most consistent and significant trend, for more than several generations, has been towards developing a scientific outlook which seeks to model the study of politics in the image of the natural sciences – a trend which following the publication of David Easton's *The Political System* in 1953, led to what has been termed 'the behavioural revolution'.

Basically the behavioural approach, spearheaded by the nation's premier departments (Harvard, Yale, Chicago) and the American Political Science Association (APSA), has sought to apply precise and rigorous scientific methods – primarily through empirical survey research which readily enables quantification of individual decisions or expressions of opinion – to the study of observable political behaviour in the formal liberal democratic political system, especially with regard to voting and the actions of political leaders, legislators and judges. More broadly, focus has been directed to explaining patterns of political socialisation and political participation. In terms of this scientific outlook, value questions are avoided in the interests of objectivity and the imperative is to 'discover basic invariants, structures or laws that can serve as a foundation for theoretical explanations – explanations which will take deductive form' (Bernstein, 1979: 227). Despite the stress placed on separating facts from values, the rise of political science cannot, however, be divorced from its homeland and the issue of science for what? In truth, as has been increasingly acknowledged, the 'science of politics' is not value free; it has been in tune with a liberal democratic intellectual ethos and a clear normative commitment to serve the policy requirements of American society in the context of the Cold War. Thus, while the study of American government and politics has focused on the existing machinery of the democratic system, the major subfield of comparative politics has been concerned to focus on the process of nation-building and modernisation in 'developing' countries, through investigating the causal links between economic growth and democratic stability and promoting what has been understood to be democracy's inevitable spread overseas; as in such classic works as Gabriel Almond and James Coleman's (1960) *The Politics of Developing Areas*, David Apter's (1965) *The Politics of Modernization*, and Gabriel Almond and G. Bingham Powell's (1966) *Comparative Politics: A Developmental Approach*.

The crucial point to recognise in all this is that the scientific approach to politics became ascendant in America during a historical period – the 1950s and early 1960s – in which 'race' and 'ethnicity' did not (with the exception of events in Africa) appear to be at issue. In fact, this was a time, it was believed, in which 'in the English-speaking world...so many of the interesting political problems have been solved' (Dahl, 1958: 89). The upshot of this, with major significance for the discipline's future trajectory, was that 'race' and 'ethnicity' were treated as factors that could be left outside the discipline's main framework assumptions. Thus, it is not surprising that political science texts on the foundations of the discipline fail to include any discussion of 'race' and 'ethnicity'.

This general understanding was reinforced by the assimilationist view then dominant in sociology which treated 'race' and 'ethnicity' as transitional phenomena; an approach reflected in much political science literature that chose to discuss 'race' and 'ethnicity', the most notable example being Robert Dahl's (1961) *Who Governs?* Also, of course, because the scientific approach placed concern on the formal political system, the fact that African Americans were more or less excluded entirely from this arena – in 1960 there were barely one hundred elected black officials nationwide – added to the 'invisibility' of the subject. In addition, racism within the profession itself has been a factor. Even as late as the mid-1980s, while persons classified as black represented 12 per cent of the American population, at best only 3 per cent of APSA members were black, and black political scientists constituted around one per cent of faculty in predominantly white universities (Preston and Woodard, 1984).

This has meant that the way in which 'race' and 'ethnicity' have been studied by the discipline is one of encounter in response to observed current affairs, within the context of the major trends in American political science since the 1950s, the rise of the scientific study of political behaviour and comparative work on political development and modernisation. For it is the case that from the mid-1960s onwards, some political scientists have come to give 'race' and 'ethnicity' significant attention, primarily by relating the phenomena to the discipline's pre-existing analytical frameworks and central concerns.

## An encounter of one kind

Attention to 'race', in particular, came in the latter half of the 1960s, in the wake of the American political system being forced open by the Civil Rights movement, ghetto uprisings and the Black Power movement, and the transformation in black politics from social movement politics to electoral politics.

The Voting Rights Act of 1965 was a watershed, it gave rise to a new force in electoral politics: the black voter. Black voting power more than doubled between 1960 and 1968, from 1.5 to 3.1 million. Moreover, Jesse Jackson's presidential candidacy in 1984 and 1988 netted three-and-a-half and seven million votes respectively. In 1990, there were forty African Americans in the US Congress; African-American mayors in three of the nation's five largest cities; and over 8,000 African Americans in elected government positions.

Given these developments the political science mainstream, taking the idea of the scientific method as central to its work, came to view 'race' as a thing-in-the-world which could be picked up, listed and coded to analyse political behaviour. In terms of scientific dictates, data tying political decisions, preferences and attitudes to 'race' have been aggregated, placed in varying relation to each other, and correlated with a broad range of contextual conditions. Through such techniques political scientists have been able to ask a series of questions as to the relative impact 'race' has, when correlated with social and economic factors, on the political process; particularly with regard to electoral political phenomena (registration, campaigning, voting and participation) at city, federal or national level.

An important book which helped to pre-set the frame of analysis for the growing literature on black political behaviour was V. O. Key's (1949) *Southern Politics in State and Nation* – a work which clearly advocated the use of advanced statistical techniques to try and help understand politics in the American South. What is seen as the natural successor to Key's study, Donald Matthews and James Prothro's (1966) *Negroes and the New Southern Politics*, was one of the first books on black political behaviour.

Between them, these books laid the groundwork for a number of articles on black voting behaviour in the *Journal of Politics*, and to a lesser extent in the *American Political Science Review* and the *American Journal of Political Science*.

In the mid-1960s concern also came to be directed to what was seen as the persistence of ethnic voting in American elections; important articles by Raymond Wolfinger (1965) and Michael Parenti (1967) stressed the role of 'ethnicity' as an important independent variable in voting behaviour. Studies such as Mark Levy and Michael Kramer's (1972) *The Ethnic Factor: How America's Minorities Decide Elections* sought to link the 'ethnic vote' to party support. In fact, in more recent years, much discussion has been given over to racial/ethnic voting statistics and the importance of racial/ethnic arithmetic in political calculations and analysis. Here, since much empirical research has revealed that voting behaviour does not uniformly correspond to people's shared experiences as subjects of racial/ethnic groups, 'race' and 'ethnicity' have been correlated to other socio-economic indicators. A focus on questions relating to the conditions that account for and sustain various forms of racial/ethnic coalition politics has been a dominant theme in many of the city-wide studies of America's largest cities, notably Dianne Pinderhughes's (1987) *Race and Ethnicity in Chicago Politics*, Clarence Stone's (1989) *Regime Politics: Governing Atlanta 1946–1988* and Raphael Sonenshein's (1993) *Politics in Black and White: Race and Power in Los Angeles*.

Likewise, the literature on political socialisation and political participation, finding through empirical analysis that black political behaviour is not monolithic, has sought to link 'race', as an independent variable, to socio-economic status (SES) and other variables. For example, Paul Abramson's (1977) *The Political Socialization of Black Americans* endeavoured to correlate black socialisation to questions of socio-economic status; and Sidney Verba and Norman Nie's (1972) *Participation in America* attempted to correlate levels of black participation to questions of SES and degrees of group consciousness.

In addition to the above, there have also been a number of important studies on political leadership behaviour and judicial behaviour, such as Everett Ladd's (1966) *Negro Political Leadership in the South* and Charles Hamilton's (1973) *The Bench and the Ballot: Southern Federal Judges and Black Voters*.

There is, however, a fundamental problem with all these works, and that is that the scientific method has not actually proved that politics can be explained through 'race' and 'ethnicity'. It has not been shown how 'race' and 'ethnicity' determine political behaviour; for there are no 'laws', not even of the middle-range, which link political behaviour to 'race' or 'ethnicity'. The offering of correlations – which has in any event, in most cases, been weak – is the closest approximation to causal explanation that can be given, yet to demonstrate correlation is not to prove causation and the question of whether 'race' and 'ethnicity' constitute most useful tools of modern political analysis has remained unanswered. Even Key's *Southern Politics in State and Nation*, when all is said and done about its landmark status, is a work which despite its many correlations, its sixty-eight tables and seventy-five figures concerning political behaviour, concludes with the inverted logic that 'until greater emancipation of the white from the Negro is achieved, the southern political and economic system will labor under formidable handicaps' (1949: 665).

## An encounter of another kind

In the field of comparative politics, the rise of work on 'ethnicity', which has come to serve in place of 'race' as a designate of group membership, evolved out of the political development and modernisation paradigm, which came to dominance in the 1950s and held that all roads of political development, one way or another, lead to national integration. The 1950s and early 1960s were a time in which 'The doctrine of 'nation-building' reigned supreme' (Young, 1983: 655), and none of the leading texts on political development contained a chapter or major subheading on 'ethnicity'. However, this view became increasingly hard to sustain, given events in Africa (the then Belgian Congo and Nigeria) and in Western states themselves (Quebec, Northern Ireland and the Basque Country). These events signalled that 'modernisation' processes had not appeared to dissolve the saliency of 'ethnicity', and led to increasing concern being directed to the role of ethnic cleavages in mitigating the onward march of liberal democratic nation-building.

Thus, in a widely cited *World Politics* article, Walker Connor (1972) argued that 'nation-building is also nation-destroying', and Cynthia Enloe's (1973) *Ethnic Conflict and Political Development* posited that 'ethnicity' and political development are not necessarily inversely related, that the saliency of 'ethnicity' has actually increased through the diffusion of modernity. From the 1970s onwards there has been a wave of books dealing with the 'revival' of 'peripheral nationalisms' of minority ethnic groups within 'advanced' nation-states, in Western Europe and Canada, what were termed 'First World Nationalisms', the best-known works being Milton Esman's (1977) *Ethnic Conflict in the Western World* and Edward Tiryakian and Ronald Rogowski's (1985) *New Nationalisms of the Developed West*. Here, it was concluded, in the words of Milton Esman, that the ethnic dimension of politics would be 'part of the agenda of industrial and postindustrial societies for the indefinite future' (1977: 387).

Many of the leading political scientists working in this area have been guided by a framework for analysis which sees ethno-nationalism and ethnic politics as having re-emerged, like a genie out of a bottle, into history as destabilising forces. Indeed, by the late 1980s events in the Soviet Union, Eastern Europe and Yugoslavia seemed, when it came to 'race' and 'ethnicity', to signal with a vengeance the 'rebirth of history'; and this has been a constant theme in current affairs books like Misha Glenny's (1990) *The Rebirth of History: Eastern Europe in the Age of Democracy*. Thus, 'ethnicity' has come to serve as a way of 'explaining' the breakup of the former Soviet Union and conflicts within Eastern Europe. And as attention has also focused on the impact of politicised ethnicity in such areas as Southeast Asia and Southern Africa there have in recent years been an ever-increasing number of books and articles focusing on 'ethnicity and politics'. Today, it appears that 'ethnic divisions have replaced the Cold War as the world's most serious source of violent conflict' (Lijphart, 1994: 451), and one can present an ABC of ethnic conflicts around the world: Azerbaijan, Bosnia, Croatia....These developments have been seen to pose a new dilemma for political science's concern with advancing liberal democracy; namely, what is the proper role of government in controlling and resolving ethnic divisions? How can one work to engineer democracy in societies that appear to be deeply divided on ethnic lines? The issue of ethnic conflict regulation, particularly through constitutional engineering, has most notably been advanced by Arend Lijphart and Donald Horowitz; as in such works as Lijphart's (1977) *Democracy in Plural Societies: A Comparative Exploration* and Horowitz's (1985) *Ethnic Groups in Conflict*. More recently, John McGarry and Brendan O'Leary (1993), in their edited book *The Politics of Ethnic Conflict Regulation*, have developed a taxonomy of eight modes of ethnic conflict regulation and urge the search for 'laws of motion' which govern them.

Various mechanisms of conflict resolution, such as federalism, electoral reform, succession/partition, and affirmative action policies have been advocated, but at the forefront stands consociationalism. Principally developed by Arend Lijphart (1968; 1977) in the context of pluralist theory, the argument of consociationalism is that democracy can be built by protecting ethnic group interests through elite accommodation and co-operation, and following the principles of segmental autonomy, proportionality and mutual veto rights. Consociationalism has been advanced, and contested, in the pages of *World Politics*, *Comparative Politics* and the *British Journal of Political Science*. Reflecting Britain's past colonial concerns, consociationalism has had wide appeal to political scientists in the United Kingdom and South Africa. In fact, consociationalism has been highly influential on debates around constitutional reform in Northern Ireland (the 1973 Sunningdale conference and subsequent attempts at devolved power-sharing) and South Africa (the 1983 and 1994 Constitutions), as well as having guided constitutional engineering in other countries, most notably Cyprus, Lebanon and Malaysia.

Generally then, the subject of 'ethnicity' and politics has come to prominence, featuring in comparative politics journals and the activities of the International Political Science Association. The question that has to be asked, however, is whether the existing literature on 'ethnicity' actually rests on solid foundations? Central to the work on both ethno-nationalism and consociationalism is that it treats 'ethnicity' as an independent variable, accepting notions of ethnic causation for understanding politics. But what interpretation is advanced to explain the origin and persistence of 'ethnicity'? Where does 'ethnicity' come from? How does it constitute the source of division and conflict? How does 'ethnicity' provide an analytic tool to make sense of politics? At this level, the meaning of 'ethnicity' has been understood in terms of 'primordialist' and 'instrumentalist' perspectives. The 'primordial' view holds that: 'Before an individual becomes a member of society or nation, modernising or otherwise, he or she already has a sense of common origins, of cultural or physical sameness, or of simple affinity – of "our kind" ' (Greenberg, 1980: 14). The 'instrumental' view holds that only when 'ethnicity' is 'called-up' for political purposes, given certain contextual factors, does it become a significant force. In fact, these two approaches do not represent opposing views, as the overriding consensus is to understand 'ethnicity' in terms of both deep 'primordial' group loyalties and its being used as an instrument for economic and political advantage. Thus, as Joseph Rothschild has maintained, 'the relationship between the emotional component and the interest component of politicised ethnicity is dialectical. Neither is a mere epiphenomenon of the other...and neither functions alone' (1981: 163). But if this is so, if the two components are to be woven together, it still needs to be shown how 'ethnicity' has a significance independent of other variables. What are its causal dynamics? And how is it that it can take on an intractable nature? Answers have not been forthcoming.

Attempts, such as James Kellas's (1991) *The Politics of Nationalism and Ethnicity*, to develop an 'integrated theory' by positing a 'link between certain traits in human nature and ethnicity and ethnocentrism' (p. 6), ultimately come to rest on unproven and highly contestable assumptions about instinctive behaviour. Other moves to substantiate the 'primordial' dimension of 'ethnicity' through recourse to social psychological forces, as in the work of Horowitz (1985), fail to show a specific link to 'ethnicity' as opposed to other factors.

When it comes down to it, the presumed thinghood of 'ethnicity' has not been sufficiently substantiated. Consequently, many political scientists are reduced to the resting-point most recently taken by Ted Gurr (1994), who in an article on ethnic conflict simply states that he does not propose to resolve the theoretical debate (p. 348). On what grounds, however, can one then go on, as happens, to use 'ethnicity' as a tool of analysis? Nathan Glazer and Daniel Moynihan (1975) in their edited book *Ethnicity: Theory and Experience* remarked that those seeking to theorise on 'ethnicity' 'are all beginners' (p. 25). More than twenty years on, there is little evidence of illuminatory advance.

## New vision

Despite all the above developments, literature to date on 'race' and 'ethnicity' within political science does not constitute a great body of work. Generally, it remains true that few of the world's most-cited political scientists have given much consideration to 'race' and 'ethnicity' in their work, and even in the case of those who have – such as Key, Dahl and Verba – they are better known for their contribution in other fields (electoral/party behaviour, pluralist theory, political culture). Furthermore, if one takes the five top-quality mainstream journals – namely, the *American Political Science Review*, the *American Journal of Political Science*, *World Politics*, *Comparative Politics*, the *British Journal of Political Science* – and analyses (through a computer keyword search of the *Social Science Citation Index*) the number of articles over the ten-year period 1987–96, there are only twenty-two articles out of 1,700 that explicitly address the topic of 'race' and 'ethnicity', that is 1.9 per cent.

However, the most vital issue is not the extent to which there has been continuing neglect, but how 'race' and 'ethnicity' have been dealt with when they have been approached. For the important point to be made is that while 'race' and 'ethnicity' have come to be incorporated into the discipline through their perceived impact on pre-existing concerns pertaining to the functioning and consolidation of liberal democracy, it has not actually been made clear how 'race' and 'ethnicity' help to 'explain' politics. 'Race' and 'ethnicity' have been employed to try and help to 'explain' patterns of political behaviour, the breakup of states, and the preconditions for democracy, but in the final analysis there has been, and remains, a failure to establish a coherent position that offers valid answers as to the thinghood of 'race' and 'ethnicity'.

If political science is ever to advance thinking on 'race' and 'ethnicity', it is clear that new vision is required. And here, as a first step, it has to be recognised that the reasons for failure lie within the discipline itself; in particular, through the misdirection caused by political science's presumption, under the sway of the scientific method, to attribute causes as being intrinsic to what has been called 'race' and 'ethnicity'. It has been held that 'race' and 'ethnicity' are entities having an independent existence of their own, with real effects in understanding politics. Why, though, when the existence of 'race' and 'ethnicity' themselves has not been scientifically established, should it be accepted that politics can be explained through 'race' and 'ethnicity'? For mainstream work, the dilemma that this question poses has been foreclosed by simply refusing to interrogate what knowledge of 'race' and 'ethnicity' is presupposed in the politics as science project.

What has transpired is that political science's specific commitment to the scientific method has dictated that 'race' and 'ethnicity' be taken as 'things' in themselves that we encounter, rather than prompting the need to see 'race' and 'ethnicity' as being problematic in themselves. To advance understanding, however, it is necessary to develop a wider and more deliberately philosophical political science which redirects the established relationship between politics and science, and recognises that the issue of 'race' and 'ethnicity' has to be moved from one of 'encounter' to one of investigating how the political system itself, broadly defined, has worked to create the belief that there are such things as 'race' and 'ethnicity'. To break free of the belief that 'race' and 'ethnicity' are forces that we 'encounter' in history, there is a need to reject totally notions of racial/ethnic determinism and shift focus to the material conditions and social relations which work to generate and reproduce 'race' and 'ethnicity', to show how they have been socially constructed, especially through state-making imperatives, as conceptual systems for constituting reality and establishing relations of power and forms of inequality.

In fact, such concerns have begun to be advanced by a few political scientists who have taken an interdisciplinary focus and accept a wider definition of what is 'political'. There is a body of work including, for example, Robert Miles and Annie Phizacklea's (1984) *White Man's Country* and Manning Marable's (1985) *Black American Politics*, which shows how state policies, particularly with regard to class interests and immigration issues, have been organised around, and continue to operate through, racial and ethnic constructions in order to justify exploitation. And lately a handful of comparative political scientists have moved to show how 'race' has been constructed and reconstructed in the process of nation-building; most noteworthy in this regard are Kathryn Manzo's (1995) *Creating Boundaries* and Anthony Marx's (1998) *Making Race and Nation*. These studies remain, however, on the margins of the discipline and much is left to be done to unmask the false starting-point presently taken in approaching 'race' and 'ethnicity'.

## Acknowledgements

The author is grateful for the guidance and comments of Martin Bulmer, Victoria Hattam, Ira Katznelson, Anthony Marx and Adamantia Pollis.

# 9 'The approval of Headquarters'

Race and ethnicity in English studies

*Maria Lauret*

> I remembered an old poem I had been made to memorize when I was ten years old and a pupil at Queen Victoria Girls' School. I had been made to memorize it, verse after verse, and then had recited the poem to an auditorium full of parents, teachers, and my fellow pupils....[L]ater they told me how nicely I had pronounced every word, how I had placed just the right amount of special emphasis where that was needed, *and how proud the poet, now long dead, would have been to hear the words ring out of my mouth.*
>
> (Kincaid, 1991: 17–18; my italics)

This extract from Jamaica Kincaid's 1991 novel *Lucy*, in which the protagonist remembers her experience of English literature at school in the Caribbean as one of colonisation of her mind and tongue, illustrates the title for this chapter on the problematic relation between English as a discipline on one hand, and issues of race and ethnicity on the other. Lucy's experience of having to recite Wordsworth's 'Daffodils' is here represented as an exercise in colonial mimicry of the Queen's English ('how nicely I had pronounced every word'), the success of which is measured in an invocation of Wordsworth's imagined, and emphatically posthumous, approval. In the particular dead poet's society of Queen Victoria Girls' School, English literature in its most canonical form still rules. The Lucys of that society have no recourse to 'a literature of their own'[1], since literature equals the English classics, yet Kincaid makes us aware in no uncertain terms of the oppressive powers of a colonial education. Such an education results in a split consciousness, as the rest of Lucy's reminiscence makes clear:

> I made pleasant little noises that showed both modesty and appreciation, but inside I was making a vow to erase from my mind, line by line, every word of that poem. The night after I had recited the poem, I dreamt, continuously it seemed, that I was being chased down a narrow cobbled street by bunches and bunches of those same daffodils that I had vowed to forget, and when finally I fell down from exhaus-

tion they all piled on top of me, until I was buried deep underneath them and was never seen again.

(Kincaid, 1991: 18)

Death by daffodils is obviously a metaphor for the death of not just a young girl's identity, but more importantly of Caribbean culture, choked and crushed by the ostensibly so benevolent and enlightened 'gift' of an education in the Major Writers and Received Standard Pronunciation. Lucy's predicament, caught between the rewards and the costs of assimilation, parallels that of any colonial subject in the history of the British empire, and of the post-colonial writer too. George Lamming saw his position as a migrant from the Caribbean to England, in an early essay entitled 'The occasion for speaking', as one of exile. In 'the country which has colonised his own history...each exile has not only got to prove his worth to the other, he has to win the approval of Headquarters, meaning in the case of the West Indian writer, England', he wrote (Lamming, 1995: 12–13). The post-colonial writer, post-colonialism, is thus still subject to the rule of the dominating power, because that power involves cultural as well as political institutions, and the former may be harder to dislodge.

## 'English' and English studies

I take Lamming's words as my title because it seems to me that despite the considerable incursions which the study of race and ethnicity has made in the teaching of English in the past two decades or so, approval from Headquarters still matters. By Headquarters I here mean not 'England' so much as a (Platonic?) idea of English in some pure and unadulterated sense, an idea which can materialise as a body of texts (Major Writers), as a practice (of writing and speaking a standardised form of a highly variegated language), or indeed as the demand for 'standards'. This idea is immensely powerful, perhaps precisely because it lives as a fantasy, an object of desire or nostalgia.[2] As such it continues to exert pressure – like the daffodils in *Lucy* – on those who would want to change syllabi, personnel and pedagogical conventions in order to take account of the importance of race and ethnicity in contemporary society and scholarship. At the same time those demands for change emerged from the field of English itself, insofar as that field has expanded in recent years to include research and teaching at the intersection with various other disciplines, notably cultural, post-colonial, women's, film and media studies. We are then concerned with at least two different versions of English: one, which I call 'English' and is narrowly defined as consisting of the classics and RSP. This 'English' is either idealised as a 'Paradise Lost' or, conversely, unmasked as the ideological construct that Lucy identifies in 'Daffodils'. The other, much more broad and diverse English is what I have termed English studies in my title. 'English' and English studies co-exist, not just in different sectors of education or in different institutions, but often in the same institution and even in the same department. Another way of putting this is to say that the familiar image (and discourse) of margin and centre is relevant to English as a discipline, with English *literature* at the centre and women's, post-colonial 'black' and ethnic *writing* at the periphery. As this spatial imagery suggests, however, the demarcations are unclear and changing. Depending on where you stand, the centre can be seen to be contracting *and* expanding – Salman Rushdie, Alice Walker and James Joyce (as Irish) are taught as Major Authors, but English students may get their BA without ever having studied Chaucer, if not quite Shakespeare. The marginalised are no longer content to stay in their ghettoes, if they ever were. Forays are made, inroads constructed, and the flow of traffic is being directed this way and that – not just from margin to centre, but vice versa as well. To put this in more concrete terms: the rise of racial and ethnic studies within English has led *both* to the introduction of new writers (usually already culturally approved, because 'prize-winning') *and* to new readings of canonical texts. After Fanon, one cannot read *Othello* or *The Tempest* with the same eyes, just as Jean Rhys's *Wide Sargasso Sea* forever changes one's view of *Jane Eyre*. And since Toni Morrison won the Nobel Prize, no academic – black, feminist or black feminist – could be accused of serving special interests by including Morrison on her twentieth-century survey course.

## What changed English?

I started with post-colonial examples because most obviously and expectedly this is where challenges to 'English', as a form of cultural imperialism, have come from first and foremost. A concern with race and ethnicity is, however, not the exclusive preserve of post-colonial studies; there are other factors which have contributed to the questioning of the canon of English literature as well.

If we take as our starting point a quotation from the critic F. R. Leavis, who dominated the discipline for several decades, then the measure of change in the teaching of English will be readily apparent. In *The Great Tradition* Leavis wrote by way of an opening statement:

> it is well to start by distinguishing the few really great – the major novelists who count in the same way as the major poets, in the sense that they *not only change the possibilities of the art for* practitioners and readers, but that they are significant in *terms of the human awareness* they promote; *awareness of the possibilities of life*.
>
> (Leavis, 1973: 2)

I have italicised this quotation in exactly the way I dutifully underlined it as an undergraduate student in Amsterdam in the 1970s. This was what

English, for a long time, was about: awareness of the possibilities of Life and of Art, without any questioning of whose life, or whose art, or the kinds of possibilities available in either. And that tradition persisted well into the 1980s, as Arun P. Mukherjee testifies when he describes English in a Canadian university. Noting that the students completely ignored the colonial theme of a story by Margaret Laurence, 'The Perfume Sea', reading it purely in terms of interpersonal relationships, Mukherjee observes:

> Their analysis, I realised, was in the time-honored tradition of…criticism which presents literary works as 'universal'. The test of a great work of literature, according to this tradition, is that despite its particularity, it speaks to all times and all people.
>
> (Mukherjee, 1995: 2)

My reading of Leavis in Amsterdam and Mukherjee's of universality in the Canadian classroom are both good reminders of what English was like 'before theory' (more about that in a moment), but also of the fact that 'English' outside Anglophone countries or in post-colonial contexts tended to be an ossified version of what was going on in Britain and America about twenty years before.[3] The two reminders are not, of course, unconnected. English literature lost its purported universality at the point when all kinds of other now-called master narratives (history, empirical science, liberal humanism, modernism) lost their authority as well.

'Theory' is what marks off Leavisite or New Critical English from the diversified English studies I mentioned earlier. Beginning in the 1970s with the influence of Althusserian, and later Gramscian Marxism, the study of literature was politicised in the course of a decade so as to become virtually unrecognisable to itself. Ideology critique and the analysis of class relations in texts as well as in literary institutions (such as authors, the publishing industry, and of course the curriculum itself) opened the way for a radical questioning of English literature's relevance in the world post 1968. Marxist, or rather: neo-Marxist literary theory then brought in its wake the notorious host of other -isms imported, as English departments experienced it, from 'the continent': structuralism, post-structuralism and deconstruction, discourse theory, psychoanalytic theory, new historicism, cultural materialism, and – neither last nor least – post-modernism. All of these in their various ways contributed to the demise of the aforementioned master narratives and previous critical orthodoxies; 'theory' was, after all, not just about literary texts but about questioning the fundamental precepts of Western culture.

The 'theory wars' which raged in English departments in Britain and elsewhere during the 1980s have by now been won. Perhaps it is because of 'theory's now hegemonic status in research – if not quite yet in teaching – that it has come to occupy a peculiar position in relation to race and ethnicity (and perhaps to gender, too). On one hand, it seems to enable the kinds of questioning and self-questioning that the study of race and ethnicity requires of any discipline. On the other, the notoriously exclusionary and highly professionalised language that many theorists employ, as well as their philosophical (implicitly rather than overtly political) concerns alienate those who want to see a more direct relation between the academy and society, and between historical or philosophical enquiry and the racist legacies of empire.[4]

In part such intellectual ambivalence arises, I think, from the practice of identity politics in the academy during the 1980s and early 1990s and its attendant fetishisation of 'experience' as a source of knowledge and power (deriving from the women's movement's slogan 'the personal is political'). In English studies, 'experience' can be used as a weapon in the battle for syllabus change ('we should teach texts that more closely reflect our students' experience') and for making new appointments in new fields (feminism, post-colonialism), preferably with personnel to match (white women and men and women of colour).[5] It can also be used, and commonly is, as a weapon against 'theory', which is counter-intuitive, demanding and in its post-modern guises resolutely relativist. Depending where and in whose hands it is wielded, the weapon of identity politics can be sharp or blunt; it can function as 'strategic essentialism' in admissions and appointments policies, or it can manifest itself as anti-intellectualism in the classroom.

It may seem somewhat paradoxical then that precisely those new areas of study within English which were initially most engaged with identity politics – i.e. post-colonialism, cultural studies, feminism and lesbian and gay studies – are the most effective in changing the face of the English curriculum and its attendant pedagogy. This is because identity politics arose from activism and insists on activist teaching and scholarship. But those areas of study which had their roots in identity politics have also been forced to question their own blind spots in the way they conceived of identity, which was often in unexamined, single-category essentialist terms. As the African-American feminist Toni Cade put it as early as 1970: '[H]ow relevant are the truths, the experiences, the findings of white women to black women? *Are women after all simply women?* (Cade, 1970: 9; my italics). The same question has been and is still being asked of men, of class, of national, racial and ethnic identities, and the various answers are generating new modes of theorising identity which can no longer appeal to a homogeneous or self-evident notion of 'experience'.

In terms of race and ethnicity, feminism and cultural studies are good examples of disciplinary discourses which lent themselves to the analysis of race and ethnicity, but only belatedly recognised it. Since doing so they have flowered precisely because of the rethinking that race and ethnicity has forced upon them, and their influence in English studies is growing.

Post-colonialism is a case in point where 'theory' has radically revised the study of race and ethnicity, and where pressure on 'English' is most acute.

I briefly want to sketch the contributions of each of these three areas, in order to give a better measure of their achievements and failures with regard to race and ethnicity in English studies in Britain; in the US, as we shall see, the situation is quite different.

## UK: feminism, cultural studies, post-colonial studies

At the very tail-end of the women's movement, feminism in the 1980s rapidly gained an academic following in its demands for syllabus reform and the correction of gender bias in criticism and pedagogy, including the call for the practice of gender-neutral language. Because of the traditionally large proportion of female students of English, and a larger-than-average number of female faculty compared with other disciplines, feminism was a major force in the transformation of English, even if progress at the time seemed slow, frustrating and often painful to achieve. But that transformation – so visible now – for a long time did not extend to the intersection of gender with race and ethnicity. The editors of the first black women's studies reader made this clear in the title of their 1982 collection: *All the Women Are White, All the Men Are Black, But Some of Us Are Brave.* It was this anthology of black women's writing and criticism which questioned white feminists on their credentials regarding global sisterhood, and demonstrated that the then emerging euphoria over the growth of 'women's writing' and 'feminist' criticism was a little premature.[6]

Fifteen years later the situation looks much different. Most self-respecting English departments in the late 1990s have courses on their books in women's writing, which include such authors as Toni Morrison, Maya Angelou, Zora Neale Hurston, Alice Walker and Audre Lorde. Some even run courses in black women's writing, exclusively; both the literature and black feminist criticism are expanding and becoming more available for study, as publishers' catalogues show. It is no coincidence, however, that all of the authors just mentioned are African-American, since that is where the market seems to be. The theoretically correct imperative to give due attention to race and gender (class has slipped in the ratings rather, of late) in English studies may also have something to do with it, however. That imperative tends to be narrowly interpreted, and the dangers of tokenism are real and present.[7] African-American women writers are immensely popular with students, which counters the tokenism somewhat because student demand is for more, not less of race and ethnicity on the curriculum and in the library. If, furthermore, we are nurturing the next generation of academic teachers and researchers in the work that we do on our MA programmes and in Ph.D. supervision, then further growth is likely, if also likely to be slow. But the drawback of a narrow interpretation of race and gender is that black men's writing tends to lose out, whereas other ethnicities (Asian-British, Caribbean or, in American literature, Chicano or Native American) are only just beginning to get attention in this country (with Irish studies as a possible exception).

Cultural studies has had a different kind of impact on English as regards race and ethnicity. It began to make its presence felt in the 1980s, particularly in its interdisciplinary concern with mass and popular culture. If the canon of Major Writers had been under fire for some time for its exclusivity in terms of class and gender, now it mattered less who was or wasn't in it than that the very idea of a canon was questioned. Work produced by the Centre for Contemporary Cultural Studies thus attracted a good number of disaffected English majors, who wanted to shift their attention from literature to film and media studies, youth culture, and popular literature and music. This move away from high culture towards more popular and contemporary forms, combined with an explosive political climate around race and ethnicity under Thatcherism, invited, if it did not force, critical thinking about popular discourses involving a newly revitalised and highly reactionary construction of (white) Britishness.[8] As with feminism, so with cultural studies: race and ethnicity were put on the agenda by black intellectuals, and as with feminism also the belated response to that agenda has been taken up more energetically in the United States than in Britain. Ironically, such energy has to a significant extent been generated by the work of several Birmingham-affiliated cultural critics – Hazel Carby, Kobena Mercer, Paul Gilroy and Stuart Hall among them, all of whom have taught or are now working in the US. This brain drain, which was so regrettable in many ways, nevertheless has had a positive effect in that it produced the 'diasporic intellectual' (the phrase is Stuart Hall's and I am using it rather more sloppily than he does) whose ideas travel well and fast and enable a hitherto unprecedented level of cross-fertilisation between Britain and America. This cross-fertilisation yields benefits especially in the study of race and ethnicity (Chen, 1996: 484–503). I am thinking here particularly of Hall's essay 'New ethnicities' and of the work of Paul Gilroy (*The Black Atlantic*) and Homi Bhabha (*The Location of Culture*; *Nation and Narration*), which are inspiring new research in English at the moment around revisions of (post-)modernity and (post-)modernism, hybridity, and the relation between nationalism and race and ethnicity in literature and popular culture.

Post-colonial studies, finally, is probably the major representative of racial and ethnic studies within English. Important figures such as Stuart Hall, or indeed Bhabha, or Gayatri Chakravorty Spivak (*In Other Worlds)* or Chandra Talpade Mohanty ('Under Western eyes') straddle various disciplinary discourses and are frequently cited and taught in English studies. Robert Young's transformation from post-structuralist theorist into a major voice in post-colonial studies is evident in his *White*

*Mythologies* and *Colonial Desire*, both of which force a critical re-examination not just of Western discourse but also of that of post-colonial theory itself.

A whole different periodisation of English from the one which has been in place for some time (e.g. medieval, Renaissance, eighteenth century, Romanticism, Victorian period, modernism, post-modernism) will be necessary, however, if post-colonialism is to become central to the English curriculum. Ken Parker suggested this in his contribution to the pivotal collection *The Black Presence in English Literature*, edited by the poet and scholar David Dabydeen. Parker wrote:

> If one recognises the extent to which literatures in English have to do with England's past (conquest in the seventeenth century; slavery in the eighteenth century; imperialism in the nineteenth century; decolonisation in the twentieth century) one cannot help but interpret [the absence of race in the theory wars] as a salutary indication of the extent to which 'the black presence' is treated – ignored, as if it did not exist.
>
> (Parker, 1985: 187)

This was in 1985. Whilst it can no longer be said that 'the black presence' is ignored, Parker's radical revision of the periodisation of English literature has not taken place either. Again an analogy with gender studies might be illuminating. Women writers can fairly easily be added to the study of any period of English literature, and even if feminist readings of the canon do undermine its presumed universal status, neither form of gender-intervention challenges the conventional mode of periodisation in the way that a focus on race and ethnicity must.

Publishers' catalogues are instructive in this regard. A quick survey shows that an 'English' core curriculum is still very much in evidence and that the conventional periodisation, which hives off 'race' to North American literature and ethnicity to the twentieth century, persists. True, there are new readings of Conrad, say, who seems to be enjoying a revival because of his colonial subject matter, and Fanon is now prominent on various theory lists. Every major academic publishing house also seems to have one or more textbooks in post-colonial theory or post-colonial literatures, and some have anthologies of Caribbean writing, African literature, Scottish and Welsh short stories as well as a further proliferation of books in Irish studies – by now a well-developed field. None of this would have been the case ten, or even five years ago. But as far as primary texts in cheap editions (Worlds Classics or Penguin) go, lists are far more conservative. To some extent teaching in English is necessarily publishing-led – we do need our primary texts as well as our criticism and theory – but only the classics as-we-know-them are widely available. This is very different from the United States, where the Schomburg Library of Nineteenth

Century Black Women Writers, edited by Henry Louis Gates Jr, for example has made hitherto obscure or unobtainable texts available to teachers and students. The impression from publishing, but also from curriculum development concerning race and ethnicity within English is that in Britain, Headquarters rules OK (albeit a little more democratically than before), whilst in the US that rule is rapidly crumbling. This is largely a result of those post-1960s developments in American universities which have come into public debate as the Culture Wars of the 1990s.

## US: the culture wars

Whilst it is problematic, in my view, to regard America as itself a post-colonial society, its colonial history vis-à-vis Britain and France may have something to do with the so-called Culture Wars which have received such hysterical media attention. In the early 1990s developments in the humanities which had been going on for some time, such as the proliferation of 'theory', of black and women's studies courses and departments, and of ethnic studies (Asian-American, Chicano, Italian- and Irish-American and also Native American) came under fire from right-wing cultural commentators and liberal academics. Apart from changes in the teaching of literature (notably of English), the attack also concerned affirmative action in hiring and admissions policies, and – most notoriously – the phenomenon of political correctness. The Culture Wars were then, to some extent, contemporaneous with and akin to the 'theory wars' in British academia, but they were of a much wider scope and had a much deeper impact. Allan Bloom's 1987 bestseller, *The Closing of the American Mind: How Higher Education Has Failed Democracy and Impoverished the Souls of Today's Students* fired the first shots. Bloom argued that expansion or revision of the canon on the grounds of cultural relativism, equality and affirmative action 'failed democracy and impoverished the minds of students'. Bloom defended, in what he clearly already recognised as a rear-guard action, a WASP literature curriculum which supports the universal rights of America's founders (or Founders, in his typography). The study of race and ethnicity ('outsiders') in his view was a threat to American identity: 'Only if [men] think their own things are good can they rest content with them....The problem with getting along with outsiders is secondary to, and sometimes in conflict with, having an inside, a people, a way of life' (Bloom, 1987: 37).

Another Bloom, Harold, followed in 1994 with *The Western Canon: The Books and Schools of the Ages*. As its title indicates, it is a wholesale defence of what I earlier called the Platonic idea of English as pure and unadulterated by politics or ideology. But this Bloom, likewise, is aware of his book's obsolescence; the first chapter is entitled 'An elegy for the canon' and here he defines canonical texts as those which are 'authoritative in our culture' because of their time-honoured 'aesthetic value'

(Bloom, 1994: 1). In his scathing comments on cultural studies, multicul-turalism, Afrocentrism, Marxism and feminism, which he collectively names the School of Resentment, Harold Bloom seeks to reinstate the (white, male) individual reader and evaluative (rather than analytical) criti-cism as sovereign, as if 'theory' never happened and other kinds of readers never existed (ibid.: 20). Henry Louis Gates Jr, the biggest gun in African-American literary studies of the past decade, responded in Lucy-like manner to the Blooms and others of similar mind: 'The return of "the" canon, the high canon of Western masterpieces, represents the return of an order in which my people were the subjugated, the voiceless, the invisible, the unrepresented and the unrepresentable' (Gates, 1992b: 197). The Culture Wars provoked Toni Morrison to write, in a similar vein, her highly influential critique of American literary history *Playing in the Dark: Whiteness and the Literary Imagination* (1992) and Gates himself followed up with *Loose Canons: Notes on the Culture Wars* in the same year. Writers like Morrison and prolific critics like Gates (*Black Literature and Literary Theory*; *The Signifying Monkey*; *'Race', Writing and Difference*), Houston A. Baker (*Modernism and the Harlem Renaissance*; *Blues, Ideology and Afro-American Literature*) and bell hooks (*Ain't I a Woman*; *Yearning*; *Outlaw Culture*) have generated the growth of African-American studies in English departments in the US and in Britain, and the burgeoning interest in other literatures of race and ethnicity which follow their lead.[9]

## English literature or...a bomb?

Yet I think it is premature to conclude, as the writers of a seminal work in post-colonial literary studies, *The Empire Writes Back*, put it in 1989 that:

> Not only the canon of 'classical texts', the disruption of which by new, 'exotic' texts can be easily countered by a strategy of incorporation from the centre, but the very idea of English literature as a study which occludes its own specific national, cultural, and political grounding and offers itself as a new system for the development of 'universal' human values, is exploded by the existence of post-colonial literatures.
>
> (Ashcroft *et al.*, 1989: 196)

For such an 'explosion' of the idea of English literature to take place more is required than the mere 'existence of post-colonial literatures', of course. As the writers themselves indicate, and as George Lamming pointed out, the approval from Headquarters can be and is increasingly extended to post-colonial writers, but whether this comes in the form of incorporation into universality or as a concession to cultural diversity doesn't much matter. What matters is the *sense* of incorporation and concession that teaching the literature of race and ethnicity in English departments often has and in turn imparts to its students; the sense of 'special options' or alternatively of a Rushdie or a Morrison having made the grade of becoming Major Authors.

Since the advent of theory in literary studies universality is no longer an avowed criterion in the construction of the English syllabus. Such humanist notions, along with more formalist approaches to counter it which dominated earlier modes of literary criticism, are now considered *outré* in the academic teaching of English, even if they may persist for a few more years in A-level teaching and Access courses. Yet an anxiety, even on the part of the most politically correct of students and faculty, regarding the abandonment of a core tradition of English literature manifests itself every time course choices are required ('Should I not choose something more traditional?') or new appointments are made ('The research is impressive, but can s/he teach the bread-and-butter English courses [Shakespeare, the Victorian Novel, Romanticism] as well as Caribbean fiction and the special option in post-colonialism?'). These questions belie the junking of the universal and self-evidently Great in favour of diversity and difference; they imply that some texts are more universal than others and that some kinds of difference are simply too great. Yet they are serious questions, they concern the business of English in the (post-) modern world, and they deserve to be asked and answered. What underlies them is an uncertainty about disciplinary identity in the face of challenges from that very trinity which literary theory for some time now has held sacred: race, gender and class (add ethnicity, add sexual orientation, and stir). Students – increasingly pragmatic about their education – ask what version of English is likely to yield most cultural capital, whereas faculty – in whose gift it is to bestow such capital, or so we would still like to believe – are reluctant to divide the inheritance.

What it takes for English literature to explode is not for it to disappear as a body of valued texts with a long history and widespread influence, but for the questions posed above not to make sense anymore. My quick survey of publishers' catalogues showed some evidence of 'Englishness' and 'British studies' as emerging areas of study. The English language, likewise, in all its variety of uses both at home and abroad, should become more of an object of scrutiny than at present it is – English departments and English curricula usually do not include any study of language *per se*. Yet as Lucy's experience at the beginning of this chapter demonstrated, or as the debate over Ebonics (or black vernacular English) in the US has shown, language is central to the study of race and ethnicity. As long as the 'universality' of English as a language is taken for granted and remains unexamined and unproblematic, just so long will English as a discipline remain complicit with the legacy of empire. Only when English is no longer 'a study which occludes its own specific national, cultural, and political grounding' can it become a discipline, in a very important sense, 'in its own right' rather than one which perpetuates cultural imperialism in the very act – these days – of disavowing it.

## Notes

1 I am citing here the title of Elaine Showalter's path-breaking book of feminist literary history, *A Literature of Their Own* by way of analogy.

2 Ever since English took over from Classics as the queen of humanities, it has been the subject of debate. A living language and culture cannot, by definition, be the stable and safe haven of values that defenders of Platonic English would want it to be.

3 In my original draft I wrote 'in the leading universities of Britain and America', but of course for English, that is not true. If one considers Oxford and Cambridge as two of Britain's leading universities, then they have certainly not been at the forefront of innovation (theoretical or otherwise) – quite the contrary.

4 Within feminist literary studies that view was most eloquently expressed in Barbara Christian's article 'The race for theory', in which she noted an increasing division between black writers and white theorists, a division which she correctly identified as hierarchical and critiqued for being such.

5 I should qualify this. The well-known problems of equal opportunities policies (in fact equal opportunism, as often as not) do not need reiterating here. Many white women and non-white men and women entered English departments through such appointments in feminism and post-colonialism, and that is a good thing. The problem lies with the implicit assumption that 'you teach what you are' —which comes out of identity politics. Does it mean that you can't teach or research well in anything else?

6 In the British context this critique of white middle class feminism's complacency was reluctantly and belatedly acknowledged, and followed from a preceding critique of feminism's class status. In the United States the bitter irony of feminism's white bias, given the fact that women's studies courses were modelling themselves on the black studies departments which had been established in the 1960s as a result of African-American political activism, alienated many African-American women from the beginning.

7 Yet African-American women's writing on English syllabi at the moment (and this goes for A-level study, too) also comes as a result of the writers' increasing international prominence – as evidenced by sales figures and literary prizes and honours (for example Maya Angelou's reading at President Clinton's inauguration ceremony).

8 As late, or as recently as 1987, Paul Gilroy wrote about the 'invisibility of "race"' within the field of cultural studies; his seminal *There Ain't No Black in the Union Jack* was written in part to counter 'the forms of nationalism endorsed by a discipline which, in spite of itself, tends towards a morbid celebration of England and Englishness from which blacks are systematically excluded' (p. 12).

9 The University of Chicago in particular is a centre for African-American literature and theory, whilst U. C. Berkeley is renowned for its scholarship in Asian-American studies. A Web search of English curricula in US universities further testifies to the proliferation of courses on race and ethnicity and makes those syllabi widely available.

# 10 Constructions of 'race', place and discipline

## Geographies of 'racial' identity and racism

*Alastair Bonnett*

Geography's relationship to 'racial' studies evidences almost continuous theoretical and empirical reformulation. Over the past thirty years, the racialised object of geographical enquiry has been constantly reconstituted in the light of changing perceptions both about the nature of the discipline and 'racial' identity. This chapter aims to chart this shifting terrain within contemporary British human geography. Drawing on key student texts, it will explain how and why geographers' engagements with 'race' have developed and diverged.

The chapter is divided into three parts. Each of its sections reflects a different formulation of the 'proper' object and method of geographical 'racial' enquiry. In the first section I address the empiricist tradition. This paradigm has been characterised by a narrow view of the legitimate topics of geographical 'racial' enquiry and by a reliance on quantitative methodologies. Although still a flourishing pedagogical and research force, critiques of empiricist work have enabled the development of two principal alternative perspectives. The approach dominated by the geography of 'race relations' is addressed in the second section of the chapter. The social constructionist paradigm, which has represented the 'cutting edge' of the sub-field since the mid-1980s, is discussed in the third section. As we shall see, social constructionists have significantly expanded the range and theoretical depth of geography's contribution to the study of the racialisation process.

As the above outline perhaps implies, from being wedded to a very limited and specialist range of topics and approaches (for example, the enumeration of visible minority settlement patterns), the sub-field has widened in recent years to embrace interdisciplinarity and the spatial contingency of all racialised discourse. This process is also reflected in the narrative of geography's changing disciplinary ambitions and self-image that threads its way through this chapter. More specifically, two antithetical currents are discerned. The first is characterised by the maintenance and policing of clear academic borders and a coherent, stable, disciplinary identity. The second tendency is towards disciplinary permeability. As we shall see, this latter process institutes an unstable, and potentially crisis prone, conception of the boundaries of the sub-field.

## Empiricist geographies of 'race'

Empiricist geographies of 'racial' difference may be traced throughout the twentieth century. Thus, although the paradigm's hegemonic postwar moment was in the 1960s and early 1970s, it is important to appreciate both its continuation within the 1990s and, perhaps even more revealingly, its resonances with much earlier work.

For, if we define empiricist 'race' research as the objectivist abstraction of racialised meaning into quantifiable 'facts', then a long geographic tradition comes into view. A tradition that stretches from the 'racial geography' practised at the turn of the century to contemporary statistical manipulations of census data. Since the intellectual and historical significance of the latter can only be fully understood in the context of the former, I will begin this survey with a brief historical overview.

Today it is not widely recognised, inside or outside the discipline, that 'race' was once central to the geography curriculum (though see Livingstone, 1992; 1994). Indeed, what was termed 'racial geography' was not merely a well-established sub-discipline but at the core of the subject; its theoretical assumptions and global perspective permeating both its physical and human branches.

The political and intellectual axis of this dominance revolved around the imputed influence of the physical environment upon the social and intellectual characteristics of different 'races'. 'The ultimate problem for geography', H. R. Mill (1905: 15) noted in 1905, is 'the determination of the influence of the surface forms of the Earth on the mental processes of its inhabitants'. Sir Thomas Holdich, one-time vice-president of the Royal Geographical Society, elucidated Mill's point by explaining that, 'The indolent sun-loving people of Southern latitudes have everywhere proved more easy to dominate than those who have been nurtured in a colder atmosphere' (Holdich, 1916: 13).

These beliefs encouraged 'racial geographers' to amass sets of 'objective' 'racial' data. Thus, we find geographers of the period enumerating the nature and movements of different 'races' and plotting and quantifying their migratory and mental potentials (for example, Huntington, 1924; for discussion see Livingstone, 1992; Hudson, 1977).

The presumed utility, and widespread popularity, of 'racial geography' were eventually corroded by, amongst other factors, the decline of Britain's imperial ambitions. Between 1940 and 1960 British geographers turned away from the subject of 'racial' difference, apparently unable to reconceptualise, and thus revitalise, its relevance to their work. As this absence implies, this period represents a time of stagnation rather than the development of any explicit critique of the assumptions and methodology of 'racial geography'. This intellectual vacuum is significant because it provides testimony to both (a) how completely wrapped up the issue of 'race' was in the imperial project, and (b) geographers' continued adherence to empiricist, and racially reifying, suppositions. Thus when 'race' was rediscovered by British geographers in the 1960s, it was interpreted from within an unbroken empiricist tradition. 'Race' continued to be understood as connoting a set of objective facts amenable to quantification and correlation. Instead of being subjected to scrutiny, 'racial geography's' essentialist notions of 'race' were, albeit unconsciously, reproduced and reworked as part of the common sense of an intellectually highly conservative discipline.

The timing of British geographers' rediscovery of 'race' can itself be correlated to the period of large-scale 'non-white' immigration into the United Kingdom. 'Race' returned to geography when the 'Empire returned' to Britain. Prompted by the influx of explicitly racialised minorities, geographers once again set about plotting and mapping biologically defined, discrete, 'racial' entities (see, for example, Lee, 1973 and 1977; Jones, 1978; Dalton and Seaman, 1973). Influenced by the quantitative, urban models and indices developed by the American inheritors of the Chicago School, British geographers also began tracing the effects of an 'objective' environmental influence (understood as 'space') on 'non-whites'' movements and behaviour. Indeed, Peach summarised his popular 1975 student text, *Urban Social Segregation*, in the following terms: '[The book's] basic hypothesis is that the greater the degree of difference between the spatial distributions of groups within an urban area, the greater their social distance from each other' (Peach, 1975a: 1).

Yet although empiricist echoes may be heard reverberating between these remarks and 'racial geography', by the 1960s geographers' estimation of their own social and intellectual role had changed. Under the influence of a quantitative revolution within the discipline, geographers were attempting to carve out a highly specialised academic niche for themselves as 'spatial scientists' (for discussion see Billinge, Gregory and Martin, 1984). This tendency became woven with a more general drift within the social sciences towards a welfare managerialist, policy oriented, research agenda. These two trends encouraged geographers to identify a number of very specific and limited topics of legitimate and useful geographical enquiry. The two central social processes that were deemed to fulfil these conditions, and which came to preoccupy the empiricist tradition, were the mapping of 'non-white' immigrant settlement and the development of indices of 'racial' segregation. In the 1960s and 1970s these interests, which dominated both the student and research literature, became established as representing *the* geographical perspective on issues of 'racial' difference.

However, empiricist hegemony was not long lived. Although remaining a strong tradition within the discipline, from the mid-1970s critiques of its theoretical and empirical limitations became increasingly common. Peter Jackson, whose work has, in recent years, helped create a decisive shift away from empiricism, quotes an early remark of Peach as an exemplar of its disadvantages. 'A criticism made of this geographical work', Jackson notes:

is its tendency to regard the nature of ethnicity as unproblematic or to proceed from the disingenuous assumption that ethnicity can be regarded straightforwardly as 'the linkage of a particular cultural mode with a particular genetic stock'.

(Jackson, 1985: 100)

A similar critique is articulated by Berg (1993) in his response to a study in the empiricist tradition by Waddell (1992). In a paper titled 'A multino-mial logit model of race and urban structure' Waddell attempts to quantify 'the influence of race on urban spatial structure' (127), that is, the impact different 'races'' residential choices have upon urban residential structure. With the erosion of empiricist hegemony the premises of such models, Berg suggests, have become highly vulnerable. In Berg's terms 'they change complex social processes into things for quantitative analysis' and, thereby, 'contribut[e] to the ongoing process of racialisation' (1993: 194–5; for Waddell's response see Waddell, 1993).

Interestingly, as its limited methodology and empirical foci have made the empiricist tradition seem suspect for social geographers, others are being freshly attracted to its statistical clarity. For empiricist work has, in recent years, become a source of growing fascination for those geographers involved in the burgeoning sub-field of computer-generated social modelling and data collection. This relationship has meant that the empiri-cist tradition is, in many geography departments, as likely to be taught and researched by GIS (Geographical Information Systems) and other computer specialists as it is by social geographers.

The relationship between computer literacy and empiricist research has been further strengthened by the sizeable grants made available by various agencies (most importantly, the Economic and Social Research Council) to interpret the 1991 national census. The census, which contained, for the first time, a self-assessed ethnic identity question (along with the more traditional 'place of birth' question), has provided researchers with a mass of data to map and correlate (see, for example, Rees and Phillips, undated; Burton and Stewart, 1994; Peach and Rossiter, 1994).

Although much of this work is still in progress, it has already shown itself capable of producing some useful pedagogical material. For example, Daniel Dorling's (1995a) mapping of the second largest ethnic (self-assessed) and nationality (place of birth) groups in British electoral wards, provides a useful source for discussion of, for example, the concentration of self-assessed 'non-white' ethnicities in urban areas and the significance of Scottish settlement in rural England.

However, whatever the value of specific pieces of empiricist work, the grander ambitions of this paradigm to represent (a) the sole legitimate methodology of geographical 'race' study, and (b) an objective representa-tion of unproblematic 'racial' categories, are no longer credible. Indeed, these assumptions are now widely rejected even by those active in teaching and researching quantitative methods. Rather than offering 'the geograph-ical perspective', many contemporary empiricists are more likely to claim that they are merely making a limited, problematic, yet strategically useful, contribution to the wider debate on 'race' and place (Taylor, 1997; Dorling, 1995b).

As I have already noted, within the sub-field, the decline in empiricist hegemony began in the mid-1970s. At this time a number of geographers interested in 'race' and ethnicity made attempts to position their work as essentially interdisciplinary and engaged with wider theoretical debates within the social sciences. This reorientation developed into what I term the geography of 'race' relations.

## Geographies of 'race' relations

The 1970s and early 1980s saw a series of attempts to expand, both theo-retically and, to a lesser extent, empirically, the geographical perspective on 'race'. Most importantly, a new willingness to relate geography to social theory encouraged an interest in sociological theories of 'race' rela-tions.

The 'race' relations paradigm is characterised by its attempts to analyse the social, cultural and economic interactions of different 'races' or ethnic groups. The identity of these groups is viewed by the paradigms more sophisticated adherents as historically contingent (for example, Banton, 1987; 1991). Yet, as Miles has suggested (1993), even where this is the case, the 'race' relations problematic, by focusing on the relationship between communities and individuals as *determined* by their 'racial' identi-fication, often comes to instate 'race' as a real, concrete, social agent. With the application of reflexive discursive interventions, this tendency could be resisted. However, geographical studies in 'race' relations have not been notable for such interpretative nuances. Indeed, as the key student texts reviewed below suggest, geographers have tended to be drawn to theoreti-cally naive, highly empiricist, and 'racially' essentialist forms of 'race' relations research and teaching.

I will take two important edited collections as examples of the nature and impact of the 'race' relations paradigm: Jackson and Smith's *Social Interaction and Ethnic Segregation* (1981) and Peach, Robinson and Smith's *Ethnic Segregation in Cities* (1981). Revealingly, both books contain chapters that reflect the continued vitality of straightforwardly empiricist approaches (for example, Baboolal, 1981; Lieberson, 1981). They also contain a number of, largely critical, engagements with Marxism. However, the majority of their contributors offer statistically based studies of 'inter-racial' conflict and accommodation.

A more detailed picture of geographers spatialisation of the race rela-tions tradition may be taken from Phillips's chapter (in Jackson and Smith) on 'The social and spatial segregation of Asians in Leicester'. Phillips draws on data from the Register of Electors, and her own questionnaire, to trace different Asian groups' attitudes to, and involvement with, residential segregation. She observes:

> Polarisation of black and white living space may be attributed to one or more of several segregating processes, including spatial sorting due to differences in socio-economic status, social avoidance through voluntary segregation by the minority, and forced segregation through rejection and exclusion of the coloured immigrants by the white majority.
>
> (Jackson and Smith, 1981: 103)

At the end of her study Phillips concludes that, 'While all [the surveyed Asian groups] exhibit superficial signs of acculturation and limited structural assimilation through secondary inter-group contact, most remain culturally isolated' (118).

The work of geographers writing in this tradition is framed by a specific set of assumptions concerning the legitimate geographical approach to 'race' issues. Their focus is on the spatial consequences and causes of visible minority agency and constraint. Thus 'racial' and ethnic groups are seen to be making spatial decisions in the context of 'racial' discrimination, assimilation, voluntary separation and so on. It is equally evident, from these contributions, that 'racial' identity is being reified, whilst the process of racialisation, of the contingent social production and management of 'racial' meaning, is neglected.

It is also noticeable that 'race' relations geography has tended to focus on very conventional spatial topics (that is, topics that were established as legitimate and proper areas of geographical study during the period of empiricist hegemony). Thus, nearly all the essays in Jackson and Smith's and Peach, Robinson and Smith's texts focus on the residential spread and segregation of 'non-white' people. Indeed, Peach and Smith (1981) justify, and summarise, the contents of *Ethnic Segregation in Cities* by noting that 'a sound basis for empirical enquiry continues to centre on the graphic summary indices of the dissimilarist school' (10).

However, the interdisciplinary ambitions that fed into the development of the 'race' relations paradigm, have provided encouragement to other geographers to look beyond the issues of segregation and dispersal. Another influential student text provides us with an example of this more original trajectory: Clarke, Ley and Peach's (1984) *Geography and Ethnic Pluralism*. Ley, Peach and Clarke introduce this edited volume by noting that 'until recently there has been very little sensitivity within human geography to...sociology or social theory' (1). As the subsequent chapters indicate, this willingness to engage with sociology qua sociology, rather than focus on the limited tradition of 'spatial sociology', opens up a range of research horizons. In so doing, the book blurs the lines, not just between geography and sociology, but between the sub-disciplines of 'racial' studies, development studies and urban geography.

The central intellectual claim of Clarke, Ley and Peach's text is the spatial contingency of ethnic interaction. This notion is unpacked in a variety of settings in both the First and Third World. Thus, for example, Porteous (1984) provides an historical essay on the interaction between the indigenous population of Easter Island and their Chilean and Spanish colonisers. Ley (1984), on the other hand, takes as his object of study the inter-ethnic dynamics that framed the incorporation of ideologies of pluralism and multiculturalism within the local and federal Canadian state.

Although these analyses represent fairly conventional applications of the 'race' relations perspective, their refusal of the sub-field's narrow parameters lends them a certain boldness. Clarke, Ley and Peach's text advances the notion that national and regional identities and ideologies are ethnicised phenomena, amenable to both historical and spatial analysis. This proposition clearly signals that issues of ethnicity and 'race' are relevant to a number of geography's manifold sub-disciplines. It also undermines the assumption that issues of segregation and dispersal are, in some way, more essentially and legitimately 'geographical' than other spatially differentiated racialisations.

However, with this seemingly unlimited expansion of empirical focus comes a crisis of sub-disciplinary identity. The distinctive and specialised topics of study that geographers had become associated with are superseded by work that could be said to have emanated from many other branches of the social sciences. Although this process reflects a more general drift within geography, it provokes an interesting sub-text of identity crisis and self-legitimation within Clarke, Ley and Peach's book. This sub-text attempts to assert the essentially geographical nature of their work whilst defending its increasingly broad empirical range. Thus, for example, Ley, Peach and Clarke (1984: 1) open their collection by noting both that geographers need to become more conversant with social theory, and by stating that the intended subject of *Geography and Ethnic Pluralism* is 'the sociology of place'. Given the specific associations within geography, in the 1970s and early 1980s, of 'place' as a term for 'humanistic', 'experiential' analysis, and the focus of the book's chapters on national political formations, Ley, Peach and Clarke's phrase seems, at first sight, to be a rather ill-suited choice. However, in the context of the volume's contribution to the significant realignment of inter- and sub-disciplinary boundaries, their selection of words appears entirely politic. It reflects, in other words, less an attempt to encapsulate the book's contents, than a desire to affiliate it with a traditional, indisputably geographical, category ('place') whilst signalling the need to expand geography's empirical and theoretical ambitions. As we shall see such slightly awkward self-definitions can also be found within social constructionist geography.

## Social constructions of 'race' and place

In 1987 Vaughan Robinson (1987: 162) described 'the accelerated development of ethnic geography in the UK'. From 'being a descriptive backwater', he noted, the sub-field has developed 'to its current position as part of a revived social geography which is in the vanguard of the discipline's development and growth'.

This section addresses the 'vanguard' work in 'ethnic geography' to which Robinson alludes. More specifically, it looks at how a group of social geographers (the most prominent of whom is Peter Jackson) have reconstituted, and promoted, the sub-field under the influence of the theory of 'social constructionism'. Social constructionism is a broad and, as yet, rather ill-defined current. The term may be understood, loosely, as referring to the interrogation of the formation of socio-spatial meaning. Jackson and Penrose (1993b: 3) explain that 'social constructionist theory rejects the longstanding view that some categories are "natural"'. Constructionism, they continue, 'works by identifying the components and processes of category construction'. For geographers, such categories include notions of national, regional and other territorial and spatial identities, as well as the idea of 'race' itself.

Signalling a move away from the 'race' relations paradigm and towards the study of processes of racialisation, Jackson opines that, although 'the idea of race as a naturally occurring category is a remarkably persistent one', 'As geographers we can contribute to its general dissolution by tracing its specific constitution and variable effects in particular historical and geographical circumstances' (Jackson, 1992: 190). As this concern with the 'dissolution' of 'racial' reductionism implies, Jackson, and other social constructionists, tie their studies to an explicitly egalitarian political project. The 'knowledge' produced by constructionist study, Jackson and Penrose argue, can.

> be used to reconstruct categories in ways that allow their inherent power to be used in the pursuit of equality. Alternatively, we can use the theory to deconstruct categories such that their power to engender inequality is dissolved.
>
> (Jackson and Penrose, 1993b: 3)

Jackson and Penrose's perspective betrays the influence deconstructionism and neo-Marxism have had upon the social constructionist perspective within human geography. More specifically, their critical agenda brings into an uneasy alliance the deconstructionist tendency to privilege the discursive, category bound, nature of meaning and a neo-Marxist cultural politics. As this implies, although social constructionism has a long and complex theoretical lineage within sociology, its impact within geography has been largely mediated through two relatively recent and innovative theoretical traditions. This somewhat modish focus may, in part, be explained by reference to human geographers' wish to finally extricate themselves from the narrow and intellectually 'provincial' concerns that dominated the discipline in the past. However, despite this embrace of contemporary critical theory, social constructionist geographers have remained relatively reticent about the tensions, and discontinuities, that exist between their two favoured theoretical influences. More specifically, they have rarely confronted the fact that whilst deconstructionism draws from an anti-foundationalist concern to view all meaning as inherently fluid, unstable and contingent, the predominating tendency within neo-Marxism is to engage with an overtly politicised, and foundationalist, set of debates grounded within the 'socially concerned' and/or materialist analysis of power (for example, Miles, 1982; Centre for Contemporary Cultural Studies, 1982). In summary, geographers appear to want the best of both worlds: to embrace anti-foundationalism *and* foundationalism; to be post-modernists with a modernist ethical foundation. I will return to this tension later. However, before doing so, a more detailed portrait of constructionist writing within geography needs to be supplied.

The following three sub-sections may be summarised as follows. In the first I draw on the writings of Peter Jackson to explain the paradigm break that the social constructionist school has attempted to make with both the 'race' relations and empiricist traditions. I will also explain how constructionism has managed and legitimised its own transgression of disciplinary identity. The second sub-section looks at some examples of social constructionist study found within student texts. In the third and final section I return to the tension isolated above and critique constructionism's lack of reflexive rigour.

### Reconstituting the sub-field

Despite the continued strength of both the empiricist and race relations traditions within geography, the last ten years has seen the social constructionist paradigm achieve significant institutional advances. Indeed, in terms of published output and debate, it appears, within the United Kingdom at least, to be achieving dominant (but not hegemonic) status. The rapidity and ease of this process has been assisted by the immanent and explicit tendencies already at work within 'race' relations approaches. Thanks to the latter, an orientation to interdisciplinarity and social theory is widely considered a valuable characteristic of the sub-field.

Despite this legacy, constructionists have been at pains to distance themselves from what they tend to cast as the dated formulations of alternative models. Peter Jackson's (1987) introduction to his edited collection *Race and Racism: Essays in Social Geography* provides a vigorous example of this trend. 'This volume' he writes, 'is intended to mark a firm departure from the established tradition in studies into the geography of racial and ethnic minorities' (4). The 'established tradition' to which Jackson refers is characterised, he argues, by its failure to ask 'questions about the meaning or significance of segregation'. Instead, he continues, it has focused:

> on describing the spatial pattern of minority-group concentration, with gestures towards an explanation in terms of opposing forces of 'choice' and 'constraint'....Not surprisingly, this tradition of research drew often angry criticism from more radical scholars and from those involved in black political struggles who found this work guilty of 'narrow empiricism' at best and 'socio-cultural apologism for racial segregation' at worst.
>
> (4)

In another contribution Jackson (1989) differentiates the new geographies of racialisation and racism from the trajectory mapped out by Clarke, Ley and Peach:

> Recent attempts to recast this work in terms of broader theories of ethnic pluralism (Clarke *et al.*, 1984) have not resolved the issue satisfactorily, failing to recognise that questions of ethnicity and ethnic identity involve social relations in which differences of power are fundamentally at stake.
>
> (176)

Jackson's references to the issue of 'power' and 'black political struggle' indicate the radical inclinations of constructionist debate. More specifically, the language and themes of constructionist politics betray the influence of British black radical scholars, most notably those writers associated with the Institute of Race Relations and Race and Politics group of the Centre for Contemporary Cultural Studies. The latter groups assertion that racism, rather than 'race', should be the focus of academic study finds a variety of echoes in the constructionist agenda. Jackson (1989) approvingly draws on both Sivanandan and Stuart Hall before concluding that, 'Social geographers are now moving away from an exclusive interest in patterns of immigration, segregation and assimilation to focus on racism and its geographical ramifications' (179).

Such attempts to privilege the study of racism provide a new identity, a new coalescing principle, for the sub-field. This process evidences a paradoxical concern to, on the one hand, maintain and justify the existence of a distinctive and discrete 'geographical contribution' to 'racial' studies whilst, on the other, suggesting that the racialisation process is inherently geographical, and cannot be properly understood otherwise.

As with the disciplinary transgressions of Clarke, Ley and Peach cited earlier, many constructionists have attempted to manage this tension through ambiguous rhetorical forms. In this regard it is not flippant to note that constructionist geographers tend to insert the words 'geography' and 'space' at seemingly every available opportunity throughout their work. The sub-headings of one short, and not untypical, paper (Jackson, 1989) read 'geography, race and racism'; 'the territorial basis of racial oppression'; 'the geography of apartheid' and 'the geography of racist attacks'. The same article also introduces 'a geography of resistance'; the 'geography of black people's struggles', and 'the geography of race-related urban unrest'. So much 'geography'! Yet the intent of all these references is difficult to interpret. Is it to suggest that geographers have a specialist and separate perspective on such issues? Or that geography is inherent to their formation, categorisation and valid academic interpretation?

There is clearly a certain awkwardness to such repetition. As with Ley, Peach and Clarke's self-definition quoted earlier, it is awkwardness that reflects the difficult process of both reproducing and transgressing the boundaries of the sub-field. The constructionists appear to be both missionaries for, and subverters of, 'the geographical contribution'.

## Geographies of racialisation

The majority of geographical work within the social constructionist paradigm has been focused on the way places are assigned 'racial' meaning(s). Thus geographers have studied how different areas of cities, and different national and international categories, have literally and metaphorically been developed and 'invented' through their racialised interpretation. Examples of such study include Jackson's work on the Notting Hill carnival (1988) and 'race' and crime in Toronto (1993; 1994); Bonnett's (1997; forthcoming) geographies of white identity; Jacob's studies of Aboriginal 'sacred land' (1988; 1993); Jackson and Penrose's writings on national identity and Smith's work on Scottish regional identity (Smith, 1989a). A distinctive feature of recent debate has been the interest of historical and feminist geographers in the theme of 'race'. More specifically, an increasingly influential body of researchers have sought to integrate constructionist and post-colonial theory within the study of the gendered and racialised nature of the spatial ideologies and practices of British imperialism (Jacobs, 1996; Blunt, 1994; Blunt and Rose, 1994; Crowhurst, 1997).

In order to work through the implications of the constructionist approach in more detail I will outline two studies on the racialisation of particular places. The first is Kay Anderson's work on the Australian suburb of Redfern. My second example is Michael Keith's writings on the spatialised construction of 'race' and 'riots' in 1980s London.

Kay Anderson's previous work has been focused on constructions of Chinatown (see Anderson, 1987; 1988; 1991). More specifically, she has undertaken an historical study of the different and dynamic urban constituencies which have helped shape the 'racial' boundaries and meanings associated with Vancouver's Chinatown. The 'space of knowledge called Chinatown', she explains (Anderson, 1988: 146), 'grew out of, and came to structure, a politically divisive system of racial discourse that justified domination over people of Chinese origin'. In her more recent studies Anderson has continued her interest in the historical analysis of what she terms 'the interlocking semiotic *and* material processes' (1993a: 85) behind the racialisation of urban space. This work has been focused on the development of 'racial' meanings in the 'Aboriginal suburb' of Redfern in Sydney (Anderson, 1993a; 1993b). 'Aboriginal Redfern', Anderson comments, 'was constructed out of multiple and contradictory discourses and practices, the deconstruction of which clears the way for a non-essentialised theorisation of not only Aboriginal identity but also of the place of "Redfern"' (1993a: 87).

Anderson isolates two competing discourses that have racialised Redfern. The first emerges from 'Aboriginal rights' arguments that position the suburb as at the heart of 'the Aboriginal community'; a physical site that symbolically coalesces the multiplicity of indigenous voices into a 'pan-Aboriginal struggle against White Australia' (1993a: 86).

Anderson concentrates her attention on how this 'cultural and political invention' has come into conflict with racist, white, constructs of Redfern and Aboriginally during the early 1970s. With the help of archive and interview material she shows how '[p]oliticians and officials...drew on an established (pejorative) set of images of Aboriginality, not out of any simple "prejudice", but in order to win the support of local White residents' (1993a: 86–7). This process, Anderson continues, helped 'construct a negatively racialised Redfern that has not eroded with time'.

Thus Redfern became a central and disputed category in a socio-spatial conflict between white and black activists and sympathisers. As Anderson stresses, this process of spatialised racialisation needs to be understood as historically contingent. This point has also been made by Keith in his studies on the antagonistic 'racial' geographies of the police and 'black community' in London. However, Keith's work draws on a wider range of semiotic vocabulary and ideas than Anderson. Thus, for example, he makes the valuable suggestion that the study of the generation of spatial meanings should be accompanied by the analysis of their 'closure' or contingent completion.

The suggestion that 'places are moments of arbitrary closure' (Keith, 1991b: 187) is supported by Keith in his book *Race, Riots and Policing: Lore and Disorder in a Multi-racist Society* (1993; see also Keith, 1987; 1988a; 1988b; 1991a; Keith and Pile, 1993). This work focuses on the way that those areas of London 'associated with' the Afro-British community have been racialised in different ways by Afro-Britons and the police. Keith pays particular attention to the multiple symbolism of 'Front Lines' (that is, those streets, such as Railton Road in Brixton, that are seen to be at the front line in the conflict between the police and black people). These locations are analysed as being subject to metaphoric, metonymic and syntagmatic interpretation. I will elucidate Keith's argument by looking at each of these forms of meaning in turn.

Front lines, such as Railton Road, he explains 'can be seen as metaphorically linked. They are not precise replications of each other, but in terms of the sign system involved they are almost mutually interchangeable' (1993: 165). Keith then proceeds to explain the difference between the metonymic and syntagmatic meaning of front lines. He suggests that 'black people' understand police action in front line areas from an historical vantage point; police action connotes (metonymically) a history of racism and police brutality. The police, on the other hand, possess an historically shallow perspective; the front line connotes (syntagmatically) day-to-day operational burdens. Thus:

> [B]lack perceptions are constructed as a form of 'local knowledge' and are fundamentally metonymic in the reading of the social world; the police action is seen as part of a historical whole, invoking a 20 to 30 year history of black experience in a particular 'place'. For the police, operational goals have priority and 'place' as a sign is read syntagmatically; the action is part of an expected sequence, an anticipated repertoire of behaviour that occurs wholly in the present....It is this very structure of police practice in such areas which guarantees that the policing institution acts as a 'machine for the suppression of time' – history is lost.
>
> (1993: 166)

However, Keith implies, that the closure of these metaphoric, metonymic and syntagmatic associations is provisional, contingent and arbitrary. The meanings arrived at by different groups may reflect the unconscious, common-sense, formation of prejudice or self-conscious, strategic, forms of 'race-place' essentialism (for example, the ghetto as focus of black pride). Yet, in either case, they are geographically and historically mutable, liable to change, challenge and reformation.

## A critique of social constructionist geography

The constructionist approach is now the dominant paradigm for geographical 'racial' study. It is an approach with far more confidence in the relevance of the discipline to a broad range of 'racial' issues than evidenced by the empiricist and 'race' relations traditions. And, by the same token, it offers students a refreshingly, if somewhat dauntingly, interdisciplinary intellectual trajectory. However, there are a number of problems within social constructionism that need to be addressed. I will highlight two of the most important: the incoherence of anti-essentialism and the tension between constructionist politics and theory.

The intellectual strain between constructionist theory and politics encourages the paradigm's adherents to 'ring fence' or 'bracket off' categories deemed to be 'egalitarian' and 'progressive' from rigorous critique. Thus, for example, notions of 'equality', 'racism' and 'anti-racism' tend to appear in constructionist work, not as objects for scrutiny, or as explicitly strategic essences, but as taken-for-granted foundations, providing 'common-sense' moral and political coherence and direction.

Indeed, constructionists, when not assuming the meaning of such terms to be obvious, will often attempt to communicate their 'real' and single essence by *defining* them. 'Racism', notes Jackson (1987: 3) on the opening page of *Race and Racism* 'is a set of interrelated ideologies and practices that have grave material effects'. For Smith (1989b: 594), on the other hand, 'Racism...is essentially a doctrine of biological inequality.' Such definitions fix and universalise the central moral categories of constructionist thought. The implication is clear: the racialisation process is historically and geographically contingent and contested but the meanings of 'racism', 'equality' and 'anti-racism' are not.

Jackson and Penrose provide an interesting reflection on this process when they note that, 'While some constructions may be more defensible than others (according to our humanly constructed powers of persuasion and legitimisation), no constructions are more intrinsically "real" than others' (1993b: 3). The reference to 'humanly constructed powers of persuasion' appears to suggest that the political content of constructionist work need not be problematised because an intersubjective agreement (a consensus?) can be, or has been, reached concerning the meaning of the relevant categories ('equality', 'racism' etc.). The most valued categories of constructionist authors can thus, 'legitimately', be closed off from inspection. Yet, as constructionist study itself shows, meaning is neither fixed or uni-dimensional nor is it ever innocent of power relations. The unreflexive political categories of constructionist work are, then profoundly at odds with the theory's own deconstructive agenda.

I have attempted in my own work to provide an historical geography of British anti-racism (Bonnett, 1993a; 1993b; 1993c). Thus, for example, in *Radicalism, Anti-racism and Representation*, I seek to show how different definitions of racism and anti-racism have been arrived at by teachers in different parts of England. This analysis is designed to subject radical ideas to critique. However, its purpose has not been to depoliticise constructionism. It is rather an attempt to encourage political reflexivity amongst radicals, especially amongst radical public professions, a group whose definitions and categories can often be so powerful in setting the terms of emancipatory debate.

However, this work may itself be criticised, both for its very restrictive focus on public professionals qua public professionals (thus excluding consideration of gender and 'racial' differences) and, perhaps, more pertinently, for implying that anti-essentialism can, or should, simply be extended, continued further. For, as Fuss (1989) has argued, essentialism cannot be dispatched; it can only be deferred. In an important, yet sympathetic, critique of constructionist thinking, Fuss explains that:

> the strength of the constructionist position is its rigorous insistence on the production of social categories like 'the body' and its attention to systems of representation. But this strength is not built on the grounds of essentialism's demise, rather it works its power by strategically deferring the encounter with essence, displacing it, in this case, onto the concept of sociality.
>
> (6)

Thus Fuss is asking why 'the category of the social automatically escapes essentialism'. She contends that 'social constructionism can be unveiled as merely a form of sociological essentialism, a position predicated on the assumption that the subject is, in essence, a social construction' (6). Fuss's challenge is difficult to refute *not* because 'the social' *cannot*, in purely theoretical terms, be thought of in anti-essentialist manner, but because of the way it has, in practice, been used by constructionists. For constructionist geographers tend to treat 'the social' in precisely the cavalier fashion Fuss describes; escaping deconstruction or any other form of critical investigation, it is accepted as a common-sense category; a totalising and total 'explanation' (see also Schor and Weed, 1994; Smaje, 1997; Craib, 1997). It seems that the irony of social constructionism is that it is unprepared to investigate the construction of its own defining term, 'the social'.

## Conclusions: the end of the anxious geographer?

We have seen how 'racial' studies in British geography has been dominated by three competing paradigms: empiricism, the geography of 'race' relations and social constructionism. I have argued that the postwar empiricist tradition represents a reformulation of the objectivist, and 'racially' reifying, assumptions associated with imperial 'racial geography'. 'Race' relations geography also incorporates some of these assumptions. However, as we have seen, it has also encouraged the growth of interdisciplinarity and social theorisation within the sub-field. The last tradition I have explored, social constructionism, whilst defining itself against both the empiricist and 'race' relations schools, has developed this intellectual trajectory.

Each of these approaches is a vibrant and living force within British geography. Each feeds into current research and teaching in the discipline. None, it is true, has yet established 'racial' studies as an essential course within university geography curricula. 'Race' has, however, been successfully introduced as a core component of a wide variety of geography's sub-disciplines. Thus contemporary courses in urban geography, social geography, political geography and, to a lesser extent, development geography, will usually engage with at least some of the literature cited above. Indeed, with the rapid growth in sociologically orientated approaches throughout human geography, as well as the emergent interest of quantitative geographers in empiricist perspectives, interest in 'racial' issues is probably more widespread today than at any time since the hey-day of imperial 'racial geography'.

However, despite its increased profile, the sub-field's self-image remains somewhat uncertain. More specifically, many of those involved still appear to experience a sense of intellectual vertigo when faced with the potentially vast expansion of empirical and theoretical terrain augured by the interdisciplinary direction of spatial 'racial' studies.

It is now increasingly widely accepted, inside and outside the discipline, that geography should be as central to the study of racialisation and ethnicisation as history or sociology; that it is impossible to understand the categories of 'race' ('European', 'African' etc.), or the development of different 'racial' identities, without the assistance of spatial analysis. Yet, for many geographers, the restrictive, self-deprecating, tradition of offering 'geographical perspectives', of bolting spatial data onto what are perceived to be essentially aspatial phenomena, retains its stultifying grip. Thus, even within the social constructionist paradigm, geographers still communicate a certain disciplinary anxiousness: the word 'geography' is repeated a little too often; the truism that 'space matters' arrived at a little too breathlessly.

Ironically, such nervousness would be unnecessary if geographers were completely confident that space really does 'matter'. Keith's work, mentioned earlier, provides us with an impressive, yet all too rare, example of the removal of any lingering doubts on the issue. Keith sees the racialisation of place as central to the analysis of police–minority relations in London. Yet he never suggests he is taking 'a geographical perspective'; indeed he rarely mentions geography at all. The importance of geography emerges as he tries to explain the social issue he is concerned with, not the other way round. Thus geography, history and sociology are woven together as equally necessary components of a fully interdisciplinary account.

Clearly the approach Keith has taken requires that geographers become even more alert to developments within other disciplines. It also suggests that geographers' confidence in the idea that 'space matters' will find its most accurate reflection in their refusal of disciplinary fetishism. The importance of geography, I would conclude, may only be made fully visible when 'the geographical perspective' is finally abandoned.

# 11 Peopling the past

## Approaches to 'race' and ethnicity in archaeology

*Siân Jones*

Archaeologists study the material culture of past societies – things discarded, left behind, actively consumed or lost – and it seems obvious that the first stage in subjecting these objects to analysis is to *identify* them. It is impossible to study anything without identifying what it is, in effect, naming it, and throughout the history of archaeological research two modes of identification have predominated, one relating to function and the other to cultural background. Thus, it is commonplace to read that, for instance, large, bucket-shaped ceramic objects with grooved impressions found in Britain associated with Neolithic sites such as Durrington Walls and Skara Brae are cooking pots of the 'grooved ware culture'. However, this attribution of identity to inanimate objects is by no means self-evident. Objects do not contain an intrinsic, original identity that archaeologists can simply extract and use as a seemingly objective foundation for the construction of hypotheses about past societies. Instead, they are attributed identities in the present within a complex framework of concepts and analogies that all too often remain implicit.

In what follows I intend to dissect these concepts and analogies, with particular attention to the attribution of racial and ethnic labels to archaeological remains. Like many disciplines in the human sciences, archaeology has been dominated until recently by an empiricist agenda intent on 'mapping' the temporal and geographical distribution of cultures and their corresponding ethnic groups. Within this empiricist tradition there has been little discussion of the nature of ethnic groups, or the relationship between ethnicity and cultural difference. Ethnic groups were simply assumed to represent bounded, homogeneous entities which can be objectively defined on the basis of cultural, linguistic, and sometimes biological, characteristics. Their very existence was taken as a given, part of the natural order of things, which provided an obvious focus for the classification and interpretation of archaeological remains. However, far from being part of some self-evident natural order, the particular modes of classifying human diversity that prevailed within empiricist archaeology can be traced back to the nineteenth century, where they have their origins in the study of racial difference.

## Race, culture and language

By the mid-nineteenth century, the study of archaeological remains was bound up with other emerging disciplines in the task of defining the 'races' of humanity on an empirical basis and examining their relationships with one another. The boundaries between various disciplines were relatively fluid at this time, and many of the individuals involved in this endeavour had training in a range of fields dealing with language, culture and anatomy/physiology. Nevertheless, two main disciplinary traditions can be identified, both of which provided the conceptual framework for the development of archaeological method in general, and frameworks for the identification of past peoples in particular.

One of these traditions, often referred to as the ethnological tradition, was closely related to comparative and historical linguistics and focused on tracing the genealogies of modern nations back into the past (see Stocking, 1973; 1987: 50). Within this framework historical linguistics tended to take priority in reconstructing the historical relations between 'races' (e.g. Prichard, 1813 [1973]), but before long archaeological remains were also being used to identify specific 'races' or nations, and their historical trajectories (see Sklenár, 1983: 91; Trigger, 1989: 155). By the turn of the twentieth century an explicit methodology was beginning to emerge, which enabled archaeological remains to be classified into culture areas on the basis of similarities in style and form, and for these culture areas in turn to be correlated with past ethnic/racial entities. For instance, drawing on his philological training the German scholar, Gustaf Kossinna, defined and systematically applied the concept of an 'archaeological culture'. His approach was based on the axiom that 'in all periods, sharply delineated archaeological culture areas coincide with clearly recognisable peoples or tribes' (as cited in Childe, 1956: 28). Cultures were defined on the basis of specific styles of material culture associated with archaeological sites in a particular region, and it was assumed that cultural continuity, like linguistic continuity, indicated ethnic continuity. On the basis of this methodology, he claimed that it was possible to identify major prehistoric ethnic cum racial groups, such as the Germans, the Slavs and the Celts and trace their relationships through time (Trigger, 1989: 165).

The other main tradition which dominated research into human difference during the nineteenth century stemmed from comparative anatomy and physical anthropology, where physical characteristics took priority in the definition of 'race' (see Stocking 1968; 1988: 4–5). Within this tradition there was a strong tendency to view race as a fixed and permanent form of human differentiation, and a direct link was often asserted between racial characteristics and mental capabilities. Human remains from archaeological sites played an important role in the development of racial typologies by physical anthropologists. Consequently, archaeologists were often able to use associations between material culture and skeletal material as the basis for the attribution of racial categories to specific archaeological cultures, as in the case of the 'Beaker culture' of the late Neolithic and early Bronze Age in Britain, and the Nordic culture of the late Neolithic period in Northern Europe (for further discussion see Childe, 1933; 1935). Furthermore, the incorporation of the idea of race as a physically defined type within an universalising framework of cultural evolution meant that archaeological evidence was also used as a means of placing specific 'races' at particular evolutionary stages often without direct association with human remains. Applied to colonial America or Africa, such approaches provided the basis for a racialist discourse which sought to place indigenous cultures lower down on the evolutionary ladder and European 'civilisation' at the top. So, for instance, in Africa archaeological monuments, such as Great Zimbabwe, deemed too sophisticated for the supposedly inert and backward negroid races, were thought to have been built by migrating races from north of the Sahara, which were ultimately attributed a Near Eastern, caucasoid racial origin (see Trigger, 1989: 129–38).

Different individual archaeologists drew on different strands of thought to come up with their own particular blend of biological and cultural explanation. However, one thing which can be said to characterise almost all the work carried out in the late nineteenth and early twentieth century was a tendency to conflate 'race', language and culture in the definition of human groups. Furthermore, whilst 'race' arguably provided the dominant mode for understanding human difference at this time, many scholars used terms such as 'tribe', 'ethnic group', 'nation', and 'people' interchangeably with that of 'race'. This mode of reasoning and use of terminology is encapsulated, for instance, in W. Greenwell's (1905: 306–7) interpretation of two late Iron Age burials in Yorkshire and it is worth quoting at length:

> [T]he two cemeteries may be treated as one, for though there are some differences between the articles discovered in the graves at the two sites, there is so much in common in their principal and more important features, that they must be regarded as the burial places of people whose habits and manner of life were similar [...] The first question which arises is that of the race or tribe who were buried at Danes Graves and Arras, and to what division of the human family they belonged.

In respect to this question, Greenwell argues that the 'most essential, and perhaps the principal factor is the physical characteristics of the skeletons themselves', but, he acknowledges, the site of Arras lacks good skeletal evidence, with only two skulls surviving. Nevertheless, he states, in the absence of evidence to the contrary, where such things as grave-relics 'are found to be similar in two districts, the presumption is strong that they were in the main occupied by people who were united by *affinity of blood*' (ibid.: 307; my emphasis).

## Culture history and typology

By the 1930s a critique of the concept of 'race' was emerging in archaeology, just as it was in social and cultural anthropology (for anthropology see, for example, Huxley and Haddon, 1935). This consisted less of an attack on the concept of race *per se*, as an objection to the correlation of cultural and physical groupings, and a questioning of the appropriateness of the concept of race for archaeological analysis. For instance, in a paper entitled 'Races, peoples and cultures in prehistoric Europe' the prehistorian, Gordon Childe (1933; see also 1935), argued that any confusion between sociological and linguistic similarity and physiological similarity should be studiously avoided:

> culture need not correspond to a group allied by physical traits acquired by heredity. Culture is a social heritage; it corresponds to a community sharing common traditions, common institutions and a common way of life. Such a group may reasonably be called a people.
> (Childe, 1935: 198)

He then went on to argue that in studying the material culture of past societies archaeologists should be able to identify past peoples, or ethnic groups, but not races, and therefore that 'prehistoric archaeology has a good hope of establishing an ethnic history of Europe, while a racial one seems hopelessly remote' (ibid.: 199).

Although influenced by developments in the science of genetics, such arguments were also specifically designed to counter the political use of archaeology in support of racial inequality in the present. So for instance, Childe's critique was directed at attempts to correlate the Indo-European culture and language group with the Nordic race, and he added that: 'Confusions between race and language persist only in the minds of the most superficial journalists and bigoted politicians' (Childe, 1933: 200). This concern to distinguish race from ethnic and cultural forms of differentiation was heightened following the Second World War and outrage at the political appropriation of the past under the Third Reich. The work of archaeologists, such as Gustaf Kossinna, had been explicitly concerned with demonstrating the geographical spread of German settlement in antiquity on the basis of the identification of Germanic cultural traits, and the results of such work were used to justify German claims to Polish territory during the First and Second World Wars (*see* Arnold, 1990: 467; Wijworra, 1996: 176). Furthermore, archaeological remains were also used to attribute a decisive role to the Germans in prehistory and hence substantiate Nazi propaganda about the inherent superiority of the Germanic race over others, such as the Slavs and the Jews (for further discussion see McCann, 1990).

As Ian Hodder (1991: x) has pointed out in his review of archaeological theory in Europe, 'few archaeologists in Europe can work without the shadow of the misuse of the past for nationalistic purposes during the Third Reich'. In the immediate aftermath of the Second World War, overt ethnic interpretations of archaeological remains were rejected due to the traditional conflation of ethnic groups with races. German archaeologists, in particular, retreated into a descriptive, empiricist approach with little reference to peoples such as the 'Germani' or the 'Indo-Europeans' (Härke, 1995: 56; Veit, 1989: 42). However, a strong empiricist tradition focusing on the identification of archaeological culture areas had already come to dominate the practice of archaeology. For instance, by the 1920s the archaeological literature in Britain was littered with references to cultures, such as the 'Dorian culture' (Casson, 1921: 212; see also Bosanquet, 1921; Hall, 1921) and the 'Halstatt culture' (Fox, 1923: 85). Furthermore, explicit statements about the basis for such reconstructions of the past, although few in number, reveal that the underlying epistemology was not far removed from that of Kossinna and others concerned with the identification of past races. So, for example, the British archaeologist O. G. S. Crawford stated that 'culture may be defined as the sum of all the ideals and activities and material which characterise *a group of human beings*. It is to a community what character is to an individual' (Crawford, 1921: 79; my emphasis). Archaeologists, he stated, should aim to discover 'homogeneous cultures' through the analysis of a broad range of types and their distribution in space and time (ibid.: 132).

By the mid-twentieth century, the definition of culture areas had become the principal means by which prehistory was delineated in space and time, expressed in maps, tables and charts as a mosaic of discrete, homogeneous peoples and cultures (e.g. see Figures 11.1 and 11.2). The only real distinction with earlier approaches was that the concept of race, and any attempt to correlate cultural and racial groupings, was increasingly rare in the archaeological literature. As Veit (1989: 42) has pointed out, the 'archaeological culture' became 'a quasi-ideology free substitute' for the terms 'race' and 'ethnic unit', but one which still takes for granted the idea that peoples must be lurking behind such archaeological groupings. Thus, irrespective of whether or not explicit reference was made to past peoples, or races, the same basic paradigm which was appropriated for political purposes with such success within Nazi Germany also came to form the rudimentary framework for a world-wide empiricist archaeology dominated by classification and typology.

As with all empiricist traditions, what was lacking from attempts to question essentialist representations of past races and ethnic groups within

*Figure 11.1* 'Early Bronze Age Europe'
*Source*: after Hawkes (1940, map VI)

archaeology was any critique of the underlying categories and assumptions which framed culture-historical archaeology (for a notable exception see Tallgren, 1937). For the most part, it is assumed that the classificatory concepts employed are derived from the object of study. So, for instance, it has often been argued that the adoption of a culture-historical approach in archaeology is a product of the need to establish a system for classifying the spatial and temporal variation evident in the archaeological record (e.g. Trigger, 1978: 86; Paddayya, 1995: 139). The implication is that culture-history involves the description and classification of variation in material remains without reference to any preconceived concepts or theory. Clearly, it cannot be denied that human ways of life vary in space and time and that this variation is frequently manifested in some form or another in material culture. However, the particular classificatory framework developed in archaeology in order to deal with such variation was, and still is, based on certain assumptions about the nature of cultural diversity.

The dominance of the culture concept in twentieth-century archaeology

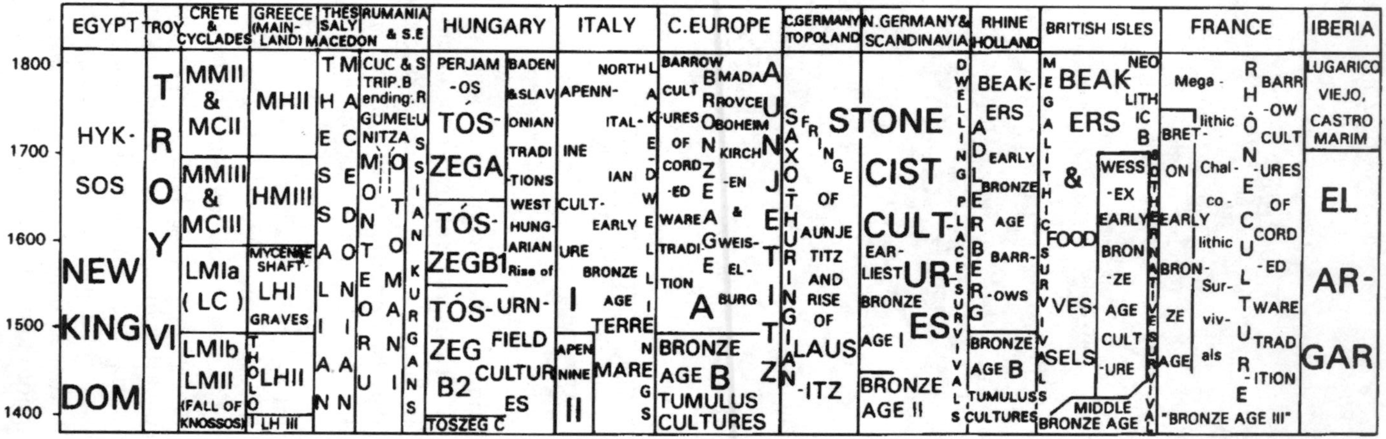

*Figure 11.2* 'The achievement of the European Bronze Age, 1800–1400 BC'
*Source*: after Hawkes (1940: table VI)

reflects an important shift away from the racial classifications of human diversity. Nevertheless, the normative concept of culture that replaced race carried over many assumptions that were central to nineteenth-century ideas, in particular an overriding concern with holism, homogeneity, order and boundedness. Normative theories of culture are based on the idea that within a given group cultural practices and beliefs tend to conform to prescriptive ideational norms or rules of behaviour. These norms are maintained by regular interaction within the group, and the transmission of shared cultural norms to subsequent generations occurs through the process of socialisation, which purportedly results in a continuous, homogeneous cultural tradition. Childe (1956: 8) was explicit about this process, arguing that:

> Generation after generation has followed society's prescription and produced and reproduced in thousands of instances the socially approved standard type. An archaeological type is just that.

A culture, comprised of a set of distinctive norms, was regarded as the product of a particular society, or ethnic group, and at the same time assumed to provide the distinguishing characteristics of that group. Within an archaeological framework such ideas led to the assumption of a fixed and one-to-one relationship between material types and particular ethnic groups. Furthermore, it enabled archaeologists to identify past peoples or ethnic groups through the identification of various supposedly objective (material) cultural types. Gradual changes in these types were attributed to internal drift in the prescribed cultural norms of a particular group, whereas sudden large-scale changes were explained in terms of external influences, such as diffusion resulting from culture contact, or the succession of one cultural group by another as a consequence of migration and conquest: 'Distributional changes [in diagnostic types] should reflect displacements of population, the expansions, migrations, colonisations or conquests with which literary history is familiar' (Childe, 1956: 135). It is these ideas which provided the underlying framework for the reconstruction of culture-history, but by the 1960s they were being challenged within archaeology as elsewhere in the human sciences.

## Recent approaches and debates

Up until the 1960s, archaeology had followed a similar path, in respect of its treatment of human differentiation, to other disciplines in the social sciences. In particular, a concerted shift from the concept of 'race' to that of culture can be observed in both anthropology and archaeology during the early–mid twentieth century, and many disciplines aside from archaeology were dominated by the empirical documentation of cultural diversity. At this point, however, the parallels cease. Whereas in anthropology a further shift from culture to ethnicity can be observed in the 1960s, the direction of archaeological research changed altogether. Ethnic groups became a marginal area of research due to the demise of culture history as a dominant paradigm, at least in Anglo-American archaeology. This shift was associated with what became known as the 'new archaeology' (or more broadly defined as 'processual archaeology'), and to some extent it was stimulated by disillusionment with the descriptive, empiricist nature of traditional archaeological research. Whilst traditional archaeology had been largely satisfied with tracing what happened in prehistory in terms of cultures and their movements, archaeologists in the 1950s and 1960s became increasingly concerned with *how* and even *why* cultural change occurred in the past (e.g. Willey and Phillips, 1958: 5–6).

The normative concept of culture which had dominated traditional archaeology was overturned within 'new archaeology'. It was argued that culture constitutes an integrated system, made up of different functioning sub-systems, and as a corollary archaeological remains must be regarded as the product of a variety of past processes, rather than simply a reflection of ideational norms (e.g. Binford, 1962, 1965; Clarke, 1978 [1968]). Culture was conceptualised as an adaptive mechanism, and a number of functionalist oriented ecological and neo-evolutionary approaches were developed with the aim of analysing various dimensions of past socio-cultural systems. In particular, research focused on the application of predictive law-like models in the interpretation of technological and economic systems, but other dimensions of society, such as ideology, political organisation and symbolism, also became distinct foci of analysis within the systemic approach (for an historical review see Trigger, 1989).

Thus, descriptive historical reconstructions of past cultures and peoples were pushed into the background of archaeological interpretation by the establishment of a new intellectual hegemony focusing on the functionalist and processual analysis of past socio-cultural systems. Within this new framework the identification of ethnic groups remained almost indelibly tied to traditional descriptive culture-history, and therefore confined to a sterile and marginal position in the interpretative agenda; a marginalisation which was reflected in a decline in explicit references to ethnic entities in the literature concerned with social analysis and explanation (Olsen and Kobylinski, 1991: 10). The main exception has been in the field of historical archaeology where the existence of references to specific ethnic groups in textual sources has resulted in the perpetuation of the 'ethnic labelling' of sites and objects.

Although the identification of archaeological cultures and their distribution in space and time ceased to be regarded as an adequate explanation of the archaeological record, or an end in itself, such concerns were not discarded altogether. Indeed, whilst recent archaeological studies have been committed to the explanation of settlement systems, trade networks, social ranking, political systems and ideology, the traditional culture unit has survived as the basic unit of description and classification, inevitably shadowed by the implicit connotation of a corresponding social or ethnic group, even where such a correlation has been criticised. For instance, Bradley (1984: 89, 94) makes frequent references to the 'Wessex Culture', Renfrew (1972: 187, 191) to the 'Phylokopi I Culture' and the 'Copper Age cultures of the Balkans', and Sherratt (1982: 17) refers to the 'Szakálhát' and 'Tisza' cultures.

For some (e.g. Binford, 1965) the retention of a normative culture concept was justified, because although functional aspects of material culture were no longer considered to be appropriate for the identification of cultures or ethnic groups, such information was still assumed to be held in non-functional stylistic traits. However, many people adopted a pragmatic position similar to Renfrew (1972; 1979; see also Hodson, 1980) arguing that the archaeological culture and the typological method were still necessary for the basic description and classification of the 'facts' prior to the process of explanation:

> While the simple narration of events is not an explanation, it is a necessary preliminary. We are not obliged to reject Croce's statement (quoted in Collingwood, 1946, 192): 'History has only one duty: to narrate the facts', but simply to find it insufficient. The first, preliminary goal of an archaeological study must be to define the culture in question in space and time. Only when the culture has been identified, defined and described is there any hope of 'taking it apart' to try to reach some understanding of how it came to have its own particular form.
>
> (Renfrew, 1972: 17)

This statement reveals the distinction between empirical description and classification ('where' and 'when' questions), and social explanation and interpretation ('how' and 'why' questions) which has been, and continues to be, intrinsic to a great deal of recent social/processual archaeology. Cultures and ethnic groups remain firmly located at the empirical descriptive level of archaeological research, whilst other aspects of society are seen as components making up a dynamic cultural system (e.g. Renfrew, 1972). Recently, such a distinction between empirical description and explanation has been the focus of critiques by those influenced by poststructuralist theory (e.g. Hodder, 1986; Shanks and Tilley, 1992 [1987]; Tilley, 1991). Nevertheless, these have not, for the most part, been associated with a reconsideration of the interpretation of group identity in archaeology, focusing instead largely on symbolic and ideological systems.

There are a number of exceptions to this general picture, all of which are rooted in the transposition of ethnic groups and ethnicity from the domain of description and classification to that of explanation and interpretation. Drawing on anthropological theories of ethnicity such as those developed by Barth (1969) and A. Cohen (1974), this shift involves a reconceptualisation of ethnicity as an aspect of social organisation often related to economic and political relationships, and in particular inter-group competition. Ethnic identity, it is argued, involves the active maintenance of cultural boundaries in the process of social interaction, rather than a passive reflection of cultural norms. Ethnicity thus becomes an aspect of social process, and yet another component of the social system, alongside subsistence, economics, politics, religion and so on, which requires processual analysis, in stark contrast to its previous status as a passive normative backdrop.

Within this framework, two main areas of research can be identified in archaeology. On the one hand, there have been a number of studies concerned with the relationship between material culture and ethnic symbolism (e.g. Haaland, 1977; Hodder, 1982; Larick, 1986; Praetzellis *et al.*, 1987; Shennan, 1989). For instance, on the basis of ethno-archaeological research, Hodder (1982) has argued that there is rarely a one-to-one correlation between cultural similarities and differences and ethnic groups. He demonstrated that the kinds of material culture involved in ethnic symbolism can vary between different groups, and that the expression of ethnic boundaries may involve a limited range of material culture, whilst other material forms and styles may be shared across group boundaries. On the other hand, there have been several studies focusing on the role of ethnicity in the structuring of economic and political relationships (e.g. Blackmore *et al.*, 1979; McGuire, 1982; Odner, 1985; Olsen, 1985; Tilley, 1991; Brumfiel, 1994). For instance, in a recent study of ethnicity in the Aztec state, Brumfiel (1994) argues that state representations of identity were fashioned to suit the needs of particular political factions. The Aztecs sought to override particularistic ethnic identities within regional elites, but at the same time promoted derogatory ethnic stereotypes which served to reinforce the superiority of the civil state culture.

Whilst focusing on ethnicity as an active social process, rather than a passive reflection of shared cultural norms, such approaches still perpetuate the idea of ethnic groups as discrete, coherent wholes. This emphasis on wholes is amply demonstrated by the prevalence of terms such as 'group' and 'boundary' which imply the existence of distinct entities (cf. R. Cohen, 1978: 386, with relation to anthropology). In the last decade, however, a few archaeologists have started to challenge the very existence of ethnic groups in the form of bounded, monolithic, territorially based entities (e.g. Shennan, 1989; Thomas, 1996; A. M. Jones, 1997; S. Jones, 1997). Instead, it is argued that the construction of ethnicity (and cultural identity in general) is a situational and dynamic process which can take diverse forms in different contexts of social interaction. The material world both informs such processes of identity construction and is used in the communication of similarity and difference which ethnicity inevitably entails. Thus, from an archaeological perspective, it cannot be assumed that there is any fixed relationship between particular material types and particular identities. And furthermore, that rather than neat, coherent cultural entities the resulting pattern is more likely to consist of a complex web of overlapping styles of material culture relating to the repeated realisation and transformation of ethnicity in different social contexts. Such an approach has important implications, both for the interpretation of ethnicity in archaeology, as well as the underlying classification of archaeological evidence, which still relies on normative conceptions of culture.

Considered together, the developments which have taken place in archaeology over the last three decades have overturned a number of the assumptions central to traditional culture-history: (a) the idea that a one-to-one relationship persists between cultures and ethnic groups; (b) the existence of discrete, homogeneous cultures; (c) and finally, the idea that group identities relate to distinct, territorially based social entities. However, studies focusing on ethnicity are sporadic and tend to be confined to specific, isolated case studies. Despite the important implications for archaeological enquiry generally, the impact of these recent studies on the discipline as a whole has not been extensive. Consequently, ethnicity, and the relationship between cultures and ethnic groups, remains a problematic area of archaeological analysis. On the one hand, the identification of ethnic groups is based upon implicit assumptions inherited from traditional archaeology, and located in the domain of the supposedly pre-theoretical description of the empirical evidence. On the other, ethnicity has been elevated, in a few instances, to the status of social process, subject to archaeological explanation. An artificial dichotomy between empirical description and social interpretation persists in a great deal of archaeological research, and the position attributed to ethnicity within this dichotomy is ambivalent.

## The present past

Of all the recent developments concerning identity in archaeology, perhaps the most significant in terms of its impact on the discipline as a whole is the recent concern with the role of archaeology in the construction and legitimation of modern identities. The 1980s and 1990s have witnessed an increasing body of conferences, symposia and publications dealing with the socio-politics of archaeology in general, and specifically with the ways in which archaeology intersects with the construction of identities in the present (for three recent examples see Atkinson *et al.*, 1996; Díaz-Andreu and Champion, 1996; Graves-Brown *et al.*, 1996). I have already suggested here that early attempts to equate archaeological remains with specific 'races' were tied up with the politics of empire and the legitimation of social inequality between different so-called 'races' in the present. Now, a much broader critique has emerged, dominated by a concern to expose the effects of nationalist interests on the discipline. This is epitomised by the definition of 'nationalist archaeology' as a specific type of archaeology by Trigger (1984: 385), a prominent historian of the discipline. Furthermore, numerous case studies have emerged documenting for instance, how Gallic resistance to the Roman Empire has played a key role in the construction of French national consciousness (Dietler, 1994: 584; Fleury-Ilett, 1996: 196, 204). Or, focusing on the way in which archaeology has been actively used to support a direct genealogical relationship between the modern state of Israel and the ancient Israelites, and hence to legitimate the former's territorial claims and right to existence (Glock, 1994; Whitelam, 1996).

It has also been shown that nationalism has had a more profound effect on the discipline through the very concepts of culture and identity that are employed (e.g. Díaz-Andreu, 1996; S. Jones, 1996). As Handler (1988: 8) points out:

> nationalist ideologies and social scientific inquiry [including that of archaeology] developed in the same historical context – that of the post-Renaissance European world – and...the two have reacted upon one another from their beginnings.

Nations, he argues, are considered to be 'individuated beings'; endowed with the reality of natural things, they are assumed to be bounded, continuous and precisely distinguishable from other analogous entities (ibid.: 6, 15). The idea of culture is intricately enmeshed with nationalist discourse; it is culture which distinguishes between nations and which constitutes the content of national identity. Moreover, 'culture symbolises individuated existence: the assertion of cultural particularity is another way of proclaiming the existence of a unique collectivity' (ibid.: 39).

There are striking similarities between the representation of culture in nationalist discourses and the conceptualisation of 'culture' used in academic theory and practice, where cultures are regarded as bounded, homogeneous entities, occupying exclusive spatio-temporal positions (see Clifford, 1988; Handler, 1988). The concept of an archaeological culture represents a particular variant of this formula. As discussed above, bounded material culture complexes are assumed to be the material manifestation of past peoples, who shared a set of prescriptive learned norms of behaviour. Archaeological cultures came to be regarded as organic, individuated entities, the prehistorian's substitute for the individual agents which make up the historian's repertoire: 'prehistory can recognise peoples and marshal them on the stage to take the place of the personal actors who form the historian's troupe' (Childe, 1940: 2; see also Piggott, 1965: 7). Moreover, as in the case of contemporary claims concerning the relationship between nations and cultures, the relationship between archaeological cultures and past peoples is based on teleological reasoning in that culture is both representative of, and constitutive of, the nation or people concerned:

the almost a priori belief in the existence of the culture follows inevitably from the belief that a particular human group...exists. The existence of the group is in turn predicated on the existence of a particular culture.

(Handler, 1988: 39)

Through the concept of an archaeological culture the past has been reconstructed in terms of the distribution of homogeneous cultures whose history unfolds in a coherent linear narrative measured in terms of objectified events, such as contacts, migrations and conquests, with intervals of homogeneous, empty time in between them.

The problem is that such an approach to the past enables history, place and people to be tied together in an exclusive and monolithic fashion reinforcing essentialist representations of ethnic and national identity in the present. Furthermore, the definition of ethnic or 'tribal' groups on the basis of the culture concept has traditionally invoked an inventory of cultural, linguistic and material traits. As Devalle (1992: 234) indicates, 'the resulting picture has been one of people with a 'museum culture', uprooted from the deep historical field, devoid of dynamism and meaning'. The consequences of such an approach are not restricted to academic studies and reports, but are also manifest in areas such as political policy, administrative practice, legislation, heritage management and education. For instance, in Zimbabwe a static, reconstructionist approach to the past has been adopted in some areas, such as at the site of Great Zimbabwe (for a detailed discussion see Ucko, 1994). At this site, one particular architectural phase in the highly complex past of the monument is being preserved and reconstructed. Such an approach leads to the reification of the monument as part of the heritage of the nation, and alienation and denial of contemporary, heterogeneous, beliefs and practices associated with the monument (ibid.: 271). Many other examples abound, ranging from Stonehenge (see Bender, 1993: 269–70) to Australian Aboriginal rock art (see Ucko, 1983: 33–6), where a static, reconstructionist approach has resulted in the reification of supposedly 'authentic', moments in the history of particular sites or material remains, and their extrapolation from ongoing social life.

In such contexts archaeology has often been used to provide a static set of reference points where previously there was negotiation and dynamism. Traditional culture-historical archaeology has contributed to such an objectification of culture, enabling a reconstruction of the past in terms of the distribution of homogeneous cultures whose history unfolds in a coherent linear narrative. Thus, attempts to identify past cultural entities in archaeology have been particularly suited to the construction of national traditions, which as Devalle (1992: 21) points out: 'are concerned with establishing a legitimating continuity with the past, not with understanding historical discontinuities and the evolution of social contradictions'. The challenge facing archaeology today is to pursue analytical approaches which can accommodate the multiple strands of practice involved in the reproduction and maintenance of ethnicity in the past and the present. Such approaches will inevitably involve a recognition of the subjective and constructed nature of ethnic identity; that ethnicity is never fixed or given, but rather continuously being made in changing social and historical contexts. It is only by accepting that the past is never dead, and that the material world is likely to be involved in the ongoing construction of diverse and fluid identities, that archaeologists will be able to facilitate dynamic and engaged relationships between archaeological monuments and living communities.

## Acknowledgements

I would like to thank Martin Bulmer and John Solomos for inviting me to contribute to this volume and Colin Richards for comments on a draft version.

# References

Abbott, P. and Wallace, C. (1990) *An Introduction to Sociology: Feminist Perspectives* London: Routledge.

Abercrombie, N. *et al.* (1994) *Contemporary British Society* Cambridge: Polity Press.

Abramson, P. (1977) *The Political Socialization of Black Americans* New York: Free Press.

Adam, H. and Moodley, K. (1993) *The Opening of the Apartheid Mind: Options for the New South Africa* Berkeley, CA: University of California Press.

Adorno, T. W., Frenkel-Brunswick, E., Levinson, D. J. and Sanford, R. N. (1950) *The Authoritarian Personality* New York: Harper and Row.

Alba, R. D. (ed.) (1985) *Ethnicity and Race in the U.S.A.: Toward the Twenty-First Century* London: Routledge and Kegan Paul.

Alcoff, L. (1988) 'Cultural feminism vs. poststructuralism: the identity crisis in feminist theory' *Signs* 13, 3: 405–36.

Alderman, G. (1992) *Modern British Jewry* Oxford: Clarendon Press.

—— (1983) *The Jewish Community in British Politics* Oxford: Clarendon Press.

All India Congress Committee (1930) 'Report' 18 July, Unpublished, Nehru Memorial Library Delhi.

Allen, T. W. (1994) *The Invention of the White Race* London: Verso.

Allport, G. (1954) *The Nature of Prejudice* Reading, MA: Addison-Wesley.

Almond, G. A. and Coleman, J. S. (eds) (1960) *The Politics of Developing Areas* Princeton, NJ: Princeton University Press.

Almond, G. A. and Powell, G. B. (1966) *Comparative Politics: A Developmental Approach* Boston, MA: Little, Brown.

Amos, V. and Parmar, P. (1984) 'Challenging imperial feminism' *Feminist Review* Special Issue, 'Many voices, one chant', 17, July.

Andersen, M. and Hill Collins, P. (eds) (1995) *Race, Class and Gender* Belmont, CA: Wadsworth Publishing Company.

Anderson, K. (1993a) 'Constructing geographies: "race", place and the making of Sydney's Aboriginal Redfern' in Jackson, P. and Penrose, J. (eds) *Constructions of Race, Place and Nation* London: UCL Press.

—— (1993b) 'Place narratives and the origins of the Aboriginal settlement in inner Sydney, 1972–1973' *Journal of Historical Geography* 19.

—— (1991) *Vancouver's Chinatown: Racial Discourse in Canada 1875–1980* Montreal: McGill-Queens University Press.

—— (1988) 'Cultural hegemony and the race-definition process in Chinatown, Vancouver: 1880–1980' *Environment and Planning D: Society and Space* 6: 127–49.

—— (1987) 'Chinatown as an idea: the power of place and institutional practice in the making of a racial category' *Annals, Association of American Geographers* 77: 580–98.

Anthias, F. (1992) 'Connecting "race" and ethnic phenomena' *Sociology* 26: 421–38.

Anthias, F. and Yuval-Davis, N. (1992) *Racialised Boundaries: Race, Gender, Colour and Class and the Anti-Racist Struggle* London: Routledge.

Appiah, K. A. (1992) *In My Father's House: Africa in the Philosophy of Culture* New York: Oxford University Press.

—— (1989) 'The conservation of "race"' *Black American Literature Forum* 23, 1: 37–60.

Appiah, K. A. and Gates Jr, H. L. (eds) (1995) *Identities* Chicago, IL: University of Chicago Press.

Apter, D. E. (1965) *The Politics of Modernization* Chicago, IL: University of Chicago Press.

Arendt, H. (1969) *On Violence* New York: Harcourt, Brace, Jovanovich.

Armistead, P. (1972) *Reconstructing Social Psychology* Harmondsworth: Penguin.

Arnold, B. (1990) 'The past as propaganda: totalitarian archaeology in Nazi Germany' *Antiquity* 64: 464–78.

Aronsfeld, C. C. (1962) 'German Jews in Victorian England' *Leo Baeck Yearbook* Vol. 7.

—— (1956) 'Jewish enemy aliens in England during the first world war', *Jewish Social Studies* Vol. 17.

Ashcroft, B., Griffiths, G. and Tiffin, H. (eds) (1995) *The Post-Colonial Studies Reader* London: Routledge.

—— (eds) (1989) *The Empire Writes Back: Theory and Practice in Post-Colonial Literatures* London: Routledge.

Association for the Study of Ethnicity and Nationalism (ASEN) (1994–5) *The ASEN Bulletin* 8, Winter.

Atkinson, J. A., Banks, I. and O'Sullivan, J. (eds) (1996) *Nationalism and Archaeology* Glasgow: Cruithne Press.

Baboolal, E. (1981) 'Black residential distribution in south London' in Jackson, P. and Smith, S. (eds) (1981) *Social Interaction and Ethnic Segregation* London: Academic Press.

Back, L. (1996) *New Ethnicities and Urban Culture, Racisms and Multiculture in Young Lives* London: UCL Press.

Baker, H. A. Jr (1987) *Modernism and the Harlem Renaissance* Chicago: University of Chicago Press.

—— (1984) *Blues, Ideology and Afro-American Literature: A Vernacular Theory* Chicago: University of Chicago Press.

Balibar, E. (1991) 'Racism and politics in Europe today' *New Left Review* 186: 5–19.

Ballard, R. (1992) 'New clothes for the Emperor? The conceptual nakedness of the race relations industry in Britain' *New Community* 18, 3: 481–92.

Banks, M. (1995) *Anthropological Constructions of Ethnicity: An Introductory Guide* London: Routledge.

Banton, M. (1991) 'The race relations problematic' *The British Journal of Sociology* 42, 1: 115–30.

—— (1987) *Racial Theories* Cambridge: Cambridge University Press.

—— (1983) *Racial and Ethnic Competition* Cambridge: Cambridge University Press.

—— (1967) *Race Relations* London: Tavistock.

—— (1955) *The Coloured Quarter: Negro Immigrants in a British City* London: Jonathan Cape.

Barkan, E. (1992) *The Retreat of Scientific Racism* Cambridge: Cambridge University Press.

Barker, M. (1981) *The New Racism* London: Junction Books.

Barth, F. (1994) 'Enduring and emerging issues in the analysis of ethnicity' in Vermeulen, H. and Govers, C. (eds) *The Anthropology of Ethnicity: Beyond 'Ethnic Groups and Boundaries'* Amsterdam: Het Spinhuis.

—— (1989) 'The analysis of culture in complex societies' *Ethnos* 54, 3–4: 120–42.

—— (1984) 'Problems in conceptualizing cultural pluralism, with illustrations from Somar, Oman' in Maybury-Lewis, D. (ed.) *The Prospects for Plural Societies (1982 Proceedings of the American Ethnological Society)* Washington DC: American Ethnological Society.

—— (ed.) (1969) *Ethnic Groups and Boundaries: The Social Organisation of Culture Difference* Oslo: Universitetsforlaget.

Bash, H. (1979) *Sociology, Race and Ethnicity: A Critique of American Ideological Intrusions Upon Sociological Theory* New York: Gordon and Breach.

Bauman, Z. (1992) 'Soil, blood and identity' *Sociological Review* 40, 4: 675–701.

Bender, B. (1993) 'Stonehenge – contested landscapes (medieval to present-day)' in Bender, B. (ed.) *Landscape, Politics and Perspectives* Oxford: Berg.

Bender, M. P. and Richardson, A. (1990) 'The ethnic composition of clinical psychology in Britain' *The Psychologist: Bulletin of the British Psychological Society* 3, 6: 250–2.

Benedict, R. (1983) *Race and Racism* London: Routledge and Kegan Paul [first published 1942].

Bentley, G. C. (1987) 'Ethnicity and practice' *Comparative Studies in Society and History* 29: 24–55.

Berelson, B. R. *et al.* (1954) *Voting: A Study of Opinion Formation in a Presidential Campaign* Chicago, IL: University of Chicago Press.

Berg, L. (1993) 'Racialization in academic discourse' *Urban Geography* 14, 2: 194–200.

Berger, C. (1970) *The Sense of Power: Studies in the Ideas of Canadian Imperialism 1867–1914* Toronto: University of Toronto Press.

—— (1969) *Imperialism and Nationalism, 1884–1914: A Conflict in Canadian Thought* Toronto: Copp Clark.

Berkhofer Jr, R. F. (1973) 'Native Americans and United States history' in Cartwright, W. H. and Watson, R. L. Jr (eds) *The Reinterpretation of American History and Culture* Washington DC: National Council for the Social Studies.

Berkowitz, L. (1972) 'Frustrations, comparison and other sources of emotion arousal as contributors to social unrest' *Journal of Social Issues* 28: 77–91.

—— (1971) 'The study of urban violence: some implications of laboratory studies of frustration and aggression' in Davies, J. C. (ed.) *When Men Revolt and Why* New York: The Free Press.

—— (1962) *Aggression: A Social Psychological Analysis* New York: McGraw Hill.

Berman, P. (ed.) (1992) *Debating P.C.: The Controversy over Political Correctness on College Campuses* New York: Bantam Doubleday Dell.

Bernstein, R. J. (1979) *The Restructuring of Social and Political Theory* London: Methuen.

Bhabha, H. (1994) *The Location of Culture* London: Routledge.

—— (ed.) (1990) *Nation and Narration* London: Routledge.

Bhat, A., Carr-Hill, R. and Ohri, S. (1988) *Britain's Black Population: A New Perspective* second edition, Radical Statistics Race Group, Aldershot: Gower.

Bhattacharyya, G. (1996) 'Black skin/white boards: learning to be the "race" lady in British Higher Education' *Parallax* 2: 161–71.

Bhavnani, K.-K. (1991) *Talking Politics* Cambridge: Cambridge University Press.

Bhavnani K.-K. and Phoenix, A. (1994) 'Shifting identities shifting racisms: an introduction' *Feminism and Psychology* 4, 1: 5–18.

Billig, M. (1991) *Ideology and Opinions* London: Sage.

—— (1988) 'The notion of "prejudice": some rhetorical and ideological aspects' *Text* 8, 1–2: 91–110.

—— (1985) 'Prejudice, categorisation and particularisation: from a perceptual to a rhetorical approach' *European Journal of Social Psychology* 15: 79–103.

—— (1979) *Psychology, Racism and Fascism* Birmingham: Searchlight Publications.

—— (1978a) 'The new social psychology and "fascism"' *European Journal of Social Psychology* 7, 4: 393–432.

—— (1978b) *Fascists: A Social Psychological Analysis of the National Front* London: Academic Press.

—— (1976) *Social Psychology and Intergroup Relations* London: Academic Press.

Billig, M., Condor, S., Edwards D., Gane, M., Middleton, D. and Radley, A. (1988) *Ideological Dilemmas: A Social Psychology of Everyday Thinking* London: Sage.

Billinge, M., Gregory, D. and Martin, R. (eds) (1984) *Recollections of a Revolution: Geography as Spatial Science* Basingstoke: Macmillan.

Binford, L. R. (1965) 'Archaeological systematics and the study of culture process' *American Antiquity* 31: 203–10.

—— (1962) 'Archaeology as anthropology' *American Antiquity* 28: 217–25.

Black Audio Film Collective (1986) *Handsworth Songs.*

Blackmore, C., Braithwaite, M. and Hodder, I. (1979) 'Social and cultural patterning in the late Iron Age in southern Britain' in Burnham, B. C. and Kingsbury, J. (eds) *Space, Hierarchy and Society. Interdisciplinary Studies in Social Area Analysis* Oxford: B.A.R.

Blalock, H. M. (1967) *Toward a Theory of Minority Group Relations* Chapel Hill, NC: University of North Carolina Press.

Blauner, R. (1972) *Racial Oppression in America* New York: Harper and Row.

Bloom, A. (1987) *The Closing of the American Mind: How Higher Education Has Failed Democracy and Impoverished the Souls of Today's Students* New York: Simon and Schuster.

Bloom, H. (1994) *The Western Canon: The Books and Schools of the Ages* New York: Harcourt Brace.

Blunt, A. (1994) *Travel, Gender and Imperialism: Mary Kingsley and West Africa* New York: The Guildford Press.

Blunt, A. and Rose, G. (eds) (1994) *Writing Women and Space: Colonial and Post-colonial Geographies* New York: The Guildford Press.

Boas, F. (1940) *Race, Language and Culture* New York: Free Press.

Bodeman, M. (1984) 'Elitism, fragility and commoditism: three themes in the Canadian social mythology' in Berkowitz, S. D. (ed.) *Models and Myths in Canadian Sociology* Toronto: Butterworth.

Bodnar, J. (1985) *The Transplanted: A History of Immigrants in Urban America* Bloomington, IN: Indiana University Press.

Bohan, J. (ed.) (1992) *Seldom Seen, Rarely Heard: Women's Place in Psychology* Boulder, CO: Westview Press.

Bolaria, B. S. and Li, P. S. (1989) *Racial Oppression in Canada* Toronto: Garamond Press.

Bonnett, A. (forthcoming) 'Who was white? The disappearance of non-European white identities and the formation of European whiteness' *Ethnic and Racial Studies*.

—— (1997) 'Geography, "race" and whiteness: invisible traditions and current challenges' *Area* 29, 3: 193–9.

—— (1993a) 'Contours of crisis: anti-racism and reflexivity' in Jackson, P. and Penrose, J. (eds) *Constructions of Race, Place and Nation* London: UCL Press.

—— (1993b) *Radicalism, Anti-racism and Representation* London: Routledge.

—— (1993c) 'The formation of public professional radical consciousness: the example of anti-racism' *Sociology* 27, 2: 281–97.

Bosanquet, R. C. (1921) 'Discussion of "The Dorian invasion reviewed in the light of new evidence"' *Antiquaries Journal* 1: 219.

Bourdieu, P. (1990) *The Logic of Practice* Cambridge: Polity Press.

Bradley, H. (1996) *Fractured Identities: Changing Patterns of Inequality* Oxford: Blackwell.

Bradley, R. (1984) *The Social Foundations of Prehistoric Britain: Themes and Variations in the Archaeology of Power* London: Longman.

Brah, A. (1996) *Cartographies of Diaspora* London: Routledge.

Breakwell, G. and Davey, G. (1990) 'Rushton and race differences' *The Psychologist: Bulletin of the British Psychological Society* 3, 7: 318.

Brown, C. (1984) *Black and White Britain: The Third PSI Survey* Aldershot: Gower.

Brumfiel, E. M. (1994) 'Ethnic groups and political development in ancient Mexico' in Brumfiel, E. M. and Fox, J. W. (eds) *Factional Competition and Political Development in the New World* Cambridge: Cambridge University Press.

Brush, F. R. (1990) 'Why does an already dead horse need to be flogged again?' Commentary on 'Are intelligence differences hereditarily transmitted?' (Pierre Roubertoux and Christiane Capron) *European Bulletin of Cognitive Psychology* 10, 6: 595–8.

Bunche, R. (1936) *A World View of Race* Washington DC: Associates in Negro Folk Education.

Burman, E. (1994a) 'Experiences, identities and alliances: Jewish feminism and feminist psychology' *Feminism and Psychology* 4, 1: 155–78.

—— (1994b) *Deconstructing Developmental Psychology* London: Routledge.

Burman, E. and Parker, I. (eds) (1993) *Discourse Analytic Research*, London: Routledge.

—— (1990) 'Differing with deconstruction: a feminist critique' in Parker, I. and Shotter, J. (eds) *Deconstructing Social Psychology* London: Routledge.

Burton, P. and Stewart, M. (1994) 'Concentration and segregation: the implications for urban policy' paper presented to OPCS Seminar, 5–6 September, University of Leeds.

Butler, J. (1993) 'Poststructuralism and postmarxism' *Diacritics* Winter 1993: 3–11.

Cade, Toni (1970) *The Black Woman: An Anthology* New York: Mentor 1970.

Cambridge, A. X. and Feuchtwang, S. (1990) 'Histories of racism' in Cambridge, A. X. and Feuchtwang, S. (eds) *Anti-racist Strategies* Aldershot: Avebury.

Campbell, A. *et al.* (1960) *The American Voter* New York: Wiley.

—— (1954) *The Voter Decides* Evanston, IL: Row, Peterson.

Carby, H. V. (1992) 'Multicultural wars' in Dent, G. (ed.) *Black Popular Culture* Seattle: Bay Press.

Carmichael, S. and Hamilton, C. V. (1968) *Black Power: The Politics of Liberation in America* London: Jonathan Cape.

Carrithers, M. (1992) *Why Humans Have Cultures: Explaining Anthropology and Social Diversity* Oxford: Oxford University Press.

Carter, B., Harris, C. and Joshi, S. (1987) 'The 1951–55 Conservative government and the racialisation of black immigration' *Immigrants and Minorities* 6: 335–47.

Cashmore, E. and McLaughlin, E. (1991) *Out of Order? Policing Black People* London and New York: Routledge.

Casson, S. (1921) 'The Dorian invasion reviewed in the light of some new evidence' *The Antiquaries Journal* 1: 198–221.

Castles, S. (1984) *Here for Good* London: Pluto Press.

Castles, S. and Kosack, G. (1973) *Immigrant Workers in the Class Structures of Western Europe* London: Oxford University Press.

Castles, S. and Miller, M. J. (1993) *The Age of Migration: International Population Movements in the Modern World* Basingstoke: Macmillan.

Centre for Contemporary Cultural Studies (1982) *The Empire Strikes Back: Race and Racism in 70s Britain* London: Hutchinson.

Cesarani, D. (1994) *The Jewish Chronicle and Anglo-Jewry, 1841–1941* Cambridge: Cambridge University Press.

—— (ed.) (1990) *The Making of Modern Anglo-Jewry* Oxford: Blackwell.

Chen, K.-H. (1996) 'The formation of the diasporic intellectual: an interview with Stuart Hall' in Morley, D. and Chen, K.-H. (eds) (1996) *Stuart Hall: Critical Dialogues in Cultural Studies* London: Routledge.

Childe, V. G. (1956) *Piecing Together the Past: The Interpretation of Archaeological Data* London: Routledge and Kegan Paul.

—— (1940) *Prehistoric Communities of the British Isles* London: W. and R. Chambers.

—— (1935) 'Changing methods and aims in prehistory. Presidential Address for 1935' *Proceedings of the Prehistoric Society* 1: 1–15.

—— (1933) 'Races, peoples and cultures in prehistoric Europe' *History* 18: 193–203.

Christian, B. (1987) 'The race for theory' *Cultural Critique* 6: 51–63.

Clarke, C., Ley, D. and Peach, C. (eds) (1984) *Geography and Ethnic Pluralism* London: George Allen and Unwin.

Clarke, D. (1978) [1968] *Analytical Archaeology* London: Methuen.

Clifford, J. (1988) *The Predicament of Culture* Cambridge, MA: Harvard University Press.

Clifford, J. and Marcus, G. E. (eds) (1986) *Writing Culture: The Poetics and Politics of Ethnography* Berkeley: University of California Press.

Cohen, A. (ed.) (1974) *Urban Ethnicity* London: Tavistock Publications.

Cohen, A. P. (1985) *The Symbolic Construction of Community* Chichester and London: Ellis Horwood and Tavistock.

—— (ed.) (1986) *Symbolising Boundaries: Identity and Diversity in British Cultures* Manchester: Manchester University Press.

—— (ed.) (1982) *Belonging: Identity and Social Organisation in British Rural Cultures* Manchester: Manchester University Press.

Cohen, P. and Bains, H. S. (eds) (1988) *Multi-Racist Britain* Basingstoke: Macmillan.

Cohen, R. (1987) *The New Helots* Aldershot: Avebury.

Cohen, Ronald (1978) 'Ethnicity: problem and focus in anthropology' *Annual Review of Anthropology* 7: 379–403.

Cole, G. D. H. (1947) *A Short History of the British Working Class Movement* London: George Allen and Unwin.

Colpi, T. (1991) *The Italian Factor: The Italian Community in Great Britain* Edinburgh: Mainstream Publishing.

Colvin, I. (1915) *The Germans in England, 1066–1598* London: National Review Office.

Commission for Racial Equality (1997) *Casebook of Racial Discrimination in Education* London: Commission for Racial Equality.

Condor, S. (1988) ' "Race stereotypes" and racist discourse' *Text* 8, 1–2: 69–89.

Connor, W. (1972) 'Nation-building or nation-destroying?' *World Politics* 24, 3: 319–55.

Conzen, K. N. (1976) *Immigrant Milwaukee, 1836–1860: Accommodation and Community in a Frontier City* Cambridge, MA: Harvard University Press.

Cornell, S. and Hartmann, D. (1998) *Ethnicity and Race: Making Identities in a Changing World* Thousand Oaks: Pine Forge Press.

Council for National Academic Awards (1988) *Review of Sociology: Courses and Teaching* London: CNAA.

Cox, O. C. (1948) *Caste, Class and Race* New York: Doubleday.

Craib, I. (1997) 'Social constructionism as a social psychosis' *Sociology* 31, 1: 1–15.

Crawford, O. G. S. (1921) *Man and his Past* London: Oxford University Press.

Crowhurst, A. (1997) 'Empire theatres and the empire: the popular geographical imagination in the age of empire' *Environment and Planning D: Society and Space* 15: 155–73.

Cuningham, W. (1897) *Alien Immigrants in Britain* London: Swan, Sonnenschein and Co.

Dabydeen, D. (ed.) (1985) *The Black Presence in English Literature* Manchester: Manchester University Press.

Dahl, R. A. (1961) *Who Governs? Democracy and Power in an American City* New Haven, CT: Yale University Press.

—— (1958) 'Political theory: truth and consequences' *World Politics* 11, 1: 89–102.

Dalton, M. and Seaman, J. (1973) 'The distribution of New Commonwealth immigrants in the London borough of Ealing 1961–66' *Transactions of the Institute of British Geographers* 58: 21–38.

Daniels, R. (1993) *Prisoners Without Trial: Japanese Americans in World War II* New York: Hill and Wang.

—— (1975) *The Decision to Relocate Japanese Americans* Philadelphia, PA: Lippincott.

—— (1962) *The Politics of Prejudice: The Anti-Japanese Movement in California and the Struggle for Japanese Exclusion* Berkeley and Los Angeles: University of California Press.

Daniels, R. and Kitano, H. H. L. (1990) *Coming to America: A History of Immigration and Ethnicity in American Life* New York: Harper Collins.

—— (1988) *Asian Americans: An Emerging Minority* Englewood Cliffs, NJ: Prentice Hall.

—— (1970) *American Racism* London: Prentice Hall International.

Danielson, D. and Engle, K. (1995) 'Introduction' in Danielson, D. and Engle, K. (eds) *After Identity: A Reader in Law and Culture* New York: Routledge.

Davis, A. (1982) *Women Race and Class* London: Women's Press.

Davis, G. (1991) *The Irish in Britain 1815–1914* Dublin: Gill and Macmillan.

Deloria, V. (1985) *American Indian Policy in the Twentieth Century* Norman, OK: University of Oklahoma Press.

—— (1984) *The Nations Within: The Past and Present of American Indian Sovereignty* New York: Pantheon.

Denvir, J. (1892) *The Irish in Britain* London: Kegan Paul, Trench, Trubner and Co.

Deschamps, J. C. and Doise, W. (1978) 'Crossed category memberships in intergroup relations' in Tajfel, H. (ed.) *Differentiation Between Social Groups* London: Academic Press.

Devalle, S. B. C. (1992) *Discourses of Ethnicity: Culture and Protest in Jharkhand* London: Sage.

Díaz-Andreu, M. (1996) 'Constructing identities through culture: the past in the forging of Europe' in Graves-Brown, P., Jones, S. and Gamble, C. (eds) *Cultural Identity and Archaeology: The Construction of European Communities* London: Routledge.

Díaz-Andreu, M. and Champion, T. C. (eds) (1996) *Nationalism and Archaeology in Europe* London: University College London Press.

Dickie, C. H. (1923) *Official Report of Debates in the House of Commons* Ottawa: King's Publisher, Vol. V, 4,661–2.

Dietler, M. (1994) ' "Our ancestors the Gauls": archaeology, ethnic nationalism, and the manipulation of Celtic identity in modern Europe' *American Anthropologist* 96: 584–605.

Dikötter, F. (1992) *The Discourse of Race in Modern China* London: Hurst.

Dinnerstein, L. (1994) *Antisemitism in America* New York: Oxford University Press.

Dinnerstein, L., Nicols, R. L. and Reimers, D. M. (1990) *Natives and Strangers: Blacks, Indians and Immigrants in America* second edition, New York: Oxford University Press.

Dollard, J., Doob, L. W., Miller N. E., Mower, O. H. and Sears, R. R. (1939) *Frustration and Aggression* New Haven, CT: Yale University Press.

Dominguez, V. (ed.) (1995) '(Multi)culturalisms and the baggage of "race" ' Special Issue of *Identities: Global Studies in Culture and Power* 1: 4.

Dorling, D. (1995a) *A New Social Atlas of Britain* Chichester: John Wiley.

—— (1995b) Unpublished letter to Alastair Bonnett, 10 January.

Downing, J. (1970) 'Teaching race relations' *Race* 12, 1: 100–2.

Drimmer, M. (1968) *Black History: A Reappraisal* Garden City, NY: Doubleday.

D'Souza, D. (1991) *Illiberal Education: The Politics of Race and Sex on Campus* New York: Free Press.

Du Bois, W. E. B. (1935) *Black Reconstruction in America* New York: Harcourt Brace and Co.

—— (1903) *The Souls of Black Folk* Chicago, IL: A. C. McClurg.

Duckitt, J. (1992) 'Psychology and prejudice: a historical analysis and integrative framework' *American Psychologist* 47, 10: 1,182–92.

Dummett, A. (1973) *A Portrait of English Racism* Harmondsworth: Penguin.

Dyer, R. (1997) *White* London and New York: Routledge.

Easton, D. (1953) *The Political System* New York: Knopf.

Edwards, D. and Potter, J. (1992) *Discursive Psychology* London: Sage.

Eidheim, H. (1969) 'When ethnic identity is a social stigma' in Barth, F. (ed.) *Ethnic Groups and Boundaries* Oslo: Universitetsforlaget.

Elkins, S. (1959) *Slavery: A Problem in American Institutional and Intellectual Life* Chicago, IL: University of Chicago Press.

Eller, J. D. and Coughlan, R. M. (1993) 'The poverty of primordialism: the demystification of ethnic attachments' *Ethnic and Racial Studies* 16: 185–202.

Elms, A. C. (1975) 'The crisis of confidence in social psychology' *American Psychologist* 30: 967–86.

Endelman, T. M. (1990) *Radical Assimilation in English-Jewish History, 1656–1945* Bloomington, IN: Indiana University Press.

—— (1979) *The Jews of Georgian England: Tradition and Change in a Liberal Society* Philadelphia, PA: Jewish Publication Society of America.

Enloe, C. H. (1973) *Ethnic Conflict and Political Development* Boston, MA: Little, Brown.

Epstein, A. L. (1978) *Ethos and Identity: Three Studies in Ethnicity* London: Tavistock.

Erickson, C. (1957) *American Industry and the European Immigrant* Cambridge, MA: Harvard University Press.

Eriksen, T. H. (1993) *Ethnicity and Nationalism: Anthropological Perspectives* London: Pluto.

Esman, M. (ed.) (1977) *Ethnic Conflict in the Western World* Ithaca, NY: Cornell University Press.

Essed, P. (1994) 'Contradictory positions, ambivalent perceptions: a case study of a black woman entrepreneur' *Feminism and Psychology* 4, 1: 99–118.

—— (1991) *Understanding Everyday Racism: An Interdisciplinary Theory* Newbury Park, CA and London: Sage.

—— (1988) 'Understanding verbal accounts of racism: politics and heuristics of reality constructions' *Text* 8, 1–2: 5–40.

Evans, B. and Waites, B. (1981) *IQ and Mental Science: An Unnatural Science and its Social History* Basingstoke: Macmillan.

Eysenck, H. (1971) *Race, Intelligence and Education* London: Temple Smith.

Ferguson, R., Gever, M., Minh-La, T. and West, C. (eds) (1990) *Out There: Marginalization and Contemporary Cultures* Cambridge, MA: MIT Press.

Fielding, S. (1988) 'The Irish Catholics of Manchester and Salford: aspects of their religious and political history, 1890–1939' Coventry: University of Warwick Ph.D. Thesis.

Finnegan, F. (1982) *Poverty and Prejudice: A Study of Irish Immigrants in York, 1840–1875* Cork: Cork University Press.

Fiske, S. and Taylor, S. (1984) *Social Cognition* New York: Random House.

Fleury-Ilett, B. (1996) 'The identity of France: archetypes in Iron Age studies' in Graves-Brown, P., Jones, S. and Gamble, C. (eds) *Cultural Identity and Archaeology: The Construction of European Communities* London: Routledge.

Flynn, J. R. (1990) 'Explanation, evaluation and a rejoinder to Rushton' *Psychologist* 3, 5: 199–200.

Forman, S. (ed.) (1994) *Diagnosing America: Anthropology and Public Engagement* Ann Arbor: University of Michigan Press.

Foucault, M. (1982) *The Archaeology of Knowledge* trans. A. M. Sheridan Smith, New York: Pantheon.

—— (1977) *Discipline and Punish* London: Allen Lane.

—— (1975) *The Birth of the Clinic* trans. A. M. Sheridan Smith New York: Vintage Books.

Fox, C. (1923) *The Archaeology of the Cambridge Region* Cambridge: Cambridge University Press.

Frank, A. G. and Gillis, B. K. (eds) (1993) *The World System: Five Hundred Years or Five Thousand?* London: Routledge.

Frankenberg, R. (1993) *White Women, Race Matters: The Social Construction of Whiteness* London: Routledge.

Franklin, J. H. (1948) *From Slavery to Freedom: A History of American Negroes* New York: Alfred Knopf.

Frazier, E. F. (1957) *Race and Culture Contacts in the Modern World* New York: Knopf.

Freeman, M. (1993) *Re-Writing the Self* London: Routledge.

Friedman, J. (1994) *Cultural Identity and Global Process* London: Sage.

—— (1990) 'Being in the world: globalisation and localisation' in Featherstone, M. (ed.) *Global Culture: Nationalism, Globalisation and Modernity* London: Sage.

Fuchs, L. H. (1990) *The American Kaleidescope: Race, Ethnicity and the Civic Culture* Hanover, NH: University of New England.

Fuss, D. (1989) *Essentially Speaking: Feminism, Nature and Difference* New York: Routledge.

Gainer, B. (1972) *The Alien Invasion: The Origins of the Aliens Act of 1905* London: Heinemann.

Gallagher, C. A. (1995) 'White reconstruction in the university' *Socialist Review* 24, 1 and 2: 165–87.

Garcia, M. T. (1991) *Mexican Americans: Leadership, Ideology and Identity, 1930–1960* New Haven, CT: Yale University Press.

—— (1981) *Desert Immigrants: The Mexicans of El Paso*, New Haven, CT: Yale University Press.

Gardner, J. B. (1993) 'Jobs lag as new PhDs continue to increase' *Perspectives* 31, 1: 2–4.

Garrard, J. A. (1971) *The English and Immigration, 1880–1910* London: Oxford University Press.

Garrow, D. J. (1986) *Bearing the Cross: Martin Luther King Jr and the Southern Leadership Conference* New York: William Morrow.

Gartner, L. P. (1960) *The Jewish Immigrant in England, 1870–1914* London: George Allen and Unwin.

Gates, H. L. Jr (1992a) *Loose Canons: Notes on the Culture Wars* Oxford: Oxford University Press.

—— (1992b) 'Whose canon is it, anyway?' in Berman, P. (ed.) *Debating P.C.: The Controversy over Political Correctness on College Campuses* New York: Bantam Doubleday Dell.

—— (1989) *The Signifying Monkey: A Theory of African-American Literary Criticism* Oxford: Oxford University Press 1989.

—— (ed.) (1986) *'Race', Writing and Difference* Chicago, IL: University of Chicago Press.

(ed.) (1984) *Black Literature and Literary Theory* London: Methuen.

Geertz, C. (1973) *The Interpretation of Cultures: Selected Essays*, New York: Basic Books.

Gellner, E. (1994) *Conditions of Liberty: Civil Society and its Rivals* London: Hamish Hamilton.

Gillespie, M. (1995) *Television, Ethnicity and Cultural Change* London and New York: Routledge.

Gilman, S. L. (1986) 'Black bodies, white bodies: toward an iconography of female sexuality in late nineteenth-century art, medicine, and literature' in H. L. Gates, Jr (ed.) *'Race', Writing and Difference* Chicago and London: University of Chicago Press.

Gilroy, P. (1993a) *The Black Atlantic: Modernity and Double Consciousness* London: Verso.

—— (1993b) *Small Acts: Thoughts on the Politics of Black Cultures* London: Serpent's Tail.

—— (1987) *There Ain't No Black in the Union Jack: The Cultural Politics of Race and Nation* London: Unwin Hyman.

Glass, R. (1960) *Newcomers: The West Indians in London* London: George Allen and Unwin.

Glazer, N. and Moynihan, D. P. (eds) (1975) *Ethnicity: Theory and Experience* Cambridge, MA: Harvard University Press.

Glenny, M. (1990) *The Rebirth of History: Eastern Europe in the Age of Democracy* Harmondsworth, UK: Penguin.

*Globe and Mail* 17 June 1992, Toronto.

Glock, A. (1994) 'Archaeology as cultural survival: the future of the Palestinian past' *Journal of Palestine Studies* 23: 70–84.

Goldberg, D. T. (1993) *Racist Culture: Philosophy and the Politics of Meaning* Oxford: Basil Blackwell.

Goldberg, D. T. (ed.) (1994) *Multiculturalism: A Reader* Oxford: Basil Blackwell.

—— (ed.) (1990) *Anatomy of Racism* Minneapolis: University of Minnesota Press.

Gooding-Williams, R. (1993) *Reading Rodney King, Reading Urban Uprising* New York and London: Routledge.

Gordon, L. (1995) *Bad Faith and Antiblack Racism* Atlantic Highlands, New Jersey: Humanities Press.

Gosnell, H. F. (1935) *Negro Politicians: The Rise of Negro Politics in Chicago* Chicago, IL: University of Chicago Press.

Gould, S. J. (1981) *The Mismeasure of Man* Harmondsworth: Penguin.

Graves-Brown, P., Jones, S., and Gamble, C. (eds) (1996) *Cultural Identity and Archaeology: The Construction of European Communities* London: Routledge.

Greenberg, S. B. (1980) *Race and State in Capitalist Development: Comparative Perspectives* New Haven, CT: Yale University Press.

Greenwell, W. (1905) 'Early Iron Age burials in Yorkshire' *Archaeologia* 60: 251–324.

Griffin, C. (1993) *Representations of Youth: The Study of Youth and Adolescence in Britain and America* London: Routledge.

Grimshaw, A. and Hart, K. (1995) 'The rise and fall of scientific ethnography' in Ahmed, A. and Shore, C. (eds) *The Future of Anthropology: Its Relevance to the Contemporary World* London: Athlone.

Grosby, S. (1995) 'Territoriality: the transcendental, primordial feature of modern societies' *Nations and Nationalism* 1: 43–62.

Gurr, T. R. (1994) 'Peoples against states: ethnopolitical conflict and the changing world system' *International Studies Quarterly* 38, 3: 347–77.

Guthrie, H. (1924) *Official Report of Debates in the House of Commons* Ottawa: King's Publisher, Vol. IV, 4,010–11.

Guthrie, R. (1976) *Even the Rat was White: A Historical View of Psychology* New York: Harper and Row.

Gutmann, A. (1992) 'Introduction' in Taylor, C. *et al. Multiculturalism and 'The Politics of Recognition'* Princeton, NJ: Princeton University Press.

Haaland, R. (1977) 'Archaeological classification and ethnic groups: a case study from Sudanese Nubia' *Norwegian Archaeological Review* 10: 1–31.

Hall, H. R. (1921) 'Discussion of "The Dorian invasion reviewed in the light of new evidence"' *Antiquaries Journal* 1: 219–20.

Hall, S. (1992) 'New ethnicities' in Donald, J. and Rattansi, A. (eds) *'Race', Culture and Difference* London: Sage.

—— (1991) 'The local and the global: globalisation and ethnicity' in King, A. D. (ed.) *Culture, Globalisation and the World-System* Basingstoke: Macmillan.

Hall, S., Critcher, C., Jefferson, T., Clarke, J. and Roberts, B. (1978) *Policing the Crisis: 'Mugging', the State and Law and Order* Basingstoke: Macmillan.

Hall, S. and du Gay, P. (eds) (1996) *Questions of Cultural Identity* London: Sage.

Hamilton, C. V. (1973) *The Bench and the Ballot: Southern Federal Judges and Black Voters* New York: Oxford University Press.

Hamilton, D. (1981) (ed.) *Cognitive Processes in Stereotyping and Intergroup Behaviour* Hillsdale, NJ: Erlbaum.

Hammond, J. L. and L. B. (1919) *The Skilled Labourer, 1760–1832* London: Longman.

Handler, R. (1988) *Nationalism and the Politics of Culture in Quebec* Madison: University of Wisconsin Press.

Handley, J. E. (1947) *The Irish in Modern Scotland* Cork: Cork University Press.

—— (1943) *The Irish in Scotland 1798–1845* Cork: Cork University Press.

Handlin, O. (1973) *The Uprooted: The Epic Story of the Great Migrations that Made the American People* second edition, Boston, MA: Little Brown [first edition, 1951].

—— (1959) *Immigration as a Factor in American History* Englewood Cliffs, NJ: Prentice Hall.

—— (1941) *Boston's Immigrants: A Study in Acculturation* Cambridge, MA: Harvard University Press.

Hannerz, U. (1992) *Cultural Complexity: Studies in the Social Organisation of Meaning* New York: Columbia University Press.

—— (1990) 'Cosmopolitans and locals in world culture' in Featherstone, M. (ed.) *Global Culture: Nationalism, Globalisation and Modernity* London: Sage.

Hansen, M. L. (1940a) *The Atlantic Migration, 1607–1860* Cambridge, MA: Harvard University Press.

—— (1940b) *The Immigrant in American History* Cambridge, MA: Harvard University Press.

(1927) 'The history of American immigration as a field for research' *American Historical Review* 32, 3: 500–18.

Harding, S. (1993) (ed.) *The 'Racial' Economy of Science: Toward a Democratic Future* Bloomington and Indianapolis, IN: Indiana University Press.

Härke, H. (1995) 'The Hun is a methodical chap' Reflections on the German tradition of pre- and proto-history' in Ucko, P. J. (ed.) *Theory in Archaeology: A World Perspective* London: Routledge.

Harris, T. (1984) *On Lynching* Bloomington: IN: Indiana University Press.

Harrison, G. (1974) 'A bias in the social psychology of prejudice' in Armistead, P. *Reconstructing Social Psychology* Harmondsworth: Penguin.

Haseler, S. (1996) *The English Tribe* Basingstoke: Macmillan.

Hawkes, C. F. C. (1940) *The Prehistoric Foundations of Europe To the Mycenean Age* London: Methuen.

Hennings, C. R. (1923) *Deutsche in England* Stuttgart: Institut für Auslandsbeziehungen.

Henriques, J. (1984) 'Social psychology and the politics of racism' in Henriques, J. et al. *Changing the Subject: Psychology, Social Regulation and Subjectivity* London: Methuen.

Henriques, J., Hollway, W., Urwin, C., Venn, C. and Walkerdine, V. (1984) *Changing the Subject: Psychology, Social Regulation and Subjectivity* London: Methuen.

Henwood, K. (1994) 'Resisting racism and sexism in academic psychology: a personal/political view' *Feminism and Psychology* 4, 1: 41–62.

Herrnstein, R. and Murray, C. (1994) *The Bell Curve: Intelligence and Class Structure in American Life* New York: Free Press.

Hewitt, R. (1986) *White Talk, Black Talk: Inter-racial Friendship and Communication amongst Adolescents* London: Cambridge University Press.

Higham, J. (1955) *Strangers in the Land: Patterns of American Nativism, 1860–1925* New Brunswick, NJ: Rutgers University Press.

Hilliard, A. (1992) 'IQ and the courts: Larry P. v. Wilson Riles and PASE v. Hannon' in Hurlew, A. K. H., Banks, W. C., McAdoo, H. P. and Azibo, D. A. (eds) *African American Psychology: Theory, Research and Practice* California: Sage.

Hocken, H. C. (1926) *Official Report of Debates in the House of Commons* Ottawa: King's Publisher, Vol. II, 1,054–9.

—— (1924) *Official Report of Debates in the House of Commons* Ottawa: King's Publisher, Vol. IV, 4,006–7.

Hodder, I. (1991) 'Preface' in Hodder, I. (ed.) *Archaeological Theory in Europe* London: Routledge.

—— (1986) *Reading the Past: Current Approaches to Interpretation in Archaeology* Cambridge: Cambridge University Press.

—— (1982) *Symbols in Action* Cambridge: Cambridge University Press.

Hodson, F. R. (1980) 'Cultures as types? Some elements of classificatory theory' *Bulletin of the Institute of Archaeology* 17: 1–10.

Hoerder, D. (1985) 'Labor migration in the Atlantic economies', in Hoerder, D. (ed.) *Labor Migration in the Atlantic Economies* London: Greenwood.

Hogg, M. and Abrams, D. (1988) *Social Identifications* London: Routledge.

—— (eds) (1990) *Social Identity Theory: Constructive and Critical Advances* New York and London: Harvester Wheatsheaf.

Holdich, T. (1916) *Political Frontiers and Boundary Making* Basingstoke: Macmillan.

Holmes, C. (1988) *John Bull's Island: Immigration and British Society, 1871–1971* Basingstoke: Macmillan.

—— (1979) *Anti-Semitism in British Society, 1876–1939* London: Edward Arnold.

hooks, b. (1994a) *Teaching to Transgress: Education as the Practice of Freedom* New York and London: Routledge.

—— (1994b) *Outlaw Culture: Resisting Representations* London: Routledge.

—— (1992) *Black Looks: Race and Representation* Toronto: Between the Lines.

—— (1990) *Yearning: Race, Gender and Cultural Politics* Boston: South End Press.

—— (1982) *Ain't I a Woman? Black Women and Feminism* Boston, MA: South End Press.

hooks, b. and West, C. (1991) *Breaking Bread: Insurgent Black Intellectual Life* Boston, MA: South End Press.

Horowitz, D. L. (1985) *Ethnic Groups in Conflict* Berkeley, CA: University of California Press.

Horton, P. B. and Hunt, C. L. (1980) *Sociology* fifth edition, New York: McGraw Hill.

Hovland, C. and Sears, R. (1940) 'Minor studies of aggression: VI. Correlation of lynching with economic indices' *Journal of Psychology* 9: 301–10.

Howe, S. (1992) 'Empire strikes back' *New Statesman and Society* 26 September: 36–7.

Howitt, D. and Owusu-Bempah, J. (1994) *The Racism of Psychology: Time for Change* Hemel Hempstead: Harvester Wheatsheaf.

Hudson, B. (1977) 'The new geography and the new imperialism: 1870–1918' *Antipode* 9: 12–19.

Hughes, C. (1991) *Lime, Lemon and Sarsaparilla: The Italian Community of South Wales, 1881–1945* Bridgend: Seren Books.

Hughes, E. C. (1948) 'The study of ethnic relations' *Dalhousie Review* 28, reprinted in Coser, L. A. (ed.) *Everett C. Hughes: On Work, Race and the Sociological Imagination* Chicago: University of Chicago Press, 1994.

Hughes, E. C. *et al.* (eds) (1952) *Where Peoples Meet* Glencoe, IL: Free Press.

Hull, G., Scott, P. B. and Smith, B. (eds) (1982) *All the Women Are White, All the Men Are Black, But Some of Us Are Brave: Black Women's Studies* Old Westbury, NY: The Feminist Press.

Humphrey, L. W. (1923) *Official Report of Debates in the House of Commons* Ottawa: King's Publisher, Vol. V, 4,648–9.

Hunter, B., Simons, M. and Stephens, J. (1984) 'Teaching against racism: literature and knowledge' *The English Magazine* 13: 5–11.

Huntington, E. (1924) *The Character of Races, as Influenced by Physical Environment, Natural Selection and Historical Development* New Haven: Yale University Press.

Husband, C. (1984) 'Working notes on social identification theory – potential limitations and possibilities' ESRC funded workshops on Social Identity Theory and Race Relations, University of Bristol, 1983–4.

—— (1986) 'The concepts of attitude and prejudice in the mystification of racism' paper presented at the British Psychological Society Social Section Conference University of Sussex (September).

—— (ed.) (1982) *'Race' in Britain* London: Hutchinson.

Huxley, J. S. and Haddon, A. C. (1935) *We Europeans: A Survey of 'Racial' Problems* London: Jonathan Cape.

Hyamson, A. M. (1908) *A History of the Jews in England* London: Chatto and Windus

India Office (1931) *Royal Commission on Labour in India, Report* London: HMSO.

—— (1930–1) *Proceedings of the Round Table Conference* London: HMSO.

Israel, J. and Tajfel, H. (eds) (1972) *The Context of Social Psychology: A Critical Assessment* London: Academic Press.

Jackson, A. (ed.) (1987) *Anthropology at Home* London: Tavistock.

Jackson, J. A. (1963) *The Irish in Britain* London: Routledge and Kegan Paul.

Jackson, P. (1994) 'Constructions of criminality: police–community relations in Toronto' *Antipode* 26.

—— (1993) 'Policing difference: "race" and crime in metropolitan Toronto' in Jackson, P. and Penrose, J. (eds) *Constructions of Race, Place and Nation* London: UCL Press.

—— (1992) 'The racialization of labour in post-war Bradford' *Journal of Historical Geography* 18, 2: 190–209.

—— (1989) 'Geography, race and racism' in Peet, R. and Thrift, N. (eds) *New Models in Geography* Vol. 2, London: Unwin Hyman.

—— (1988) 'Street life: the politics of carnival' *Environment and Planning D: Society and Space* 6: 201–27.

—— (1985) 'Social geography: race and racism' *Progress in Human Geography* 9, 1: 99–108.

—— (ed.) (1987) *Race and Racism: Essays in Social Geography* London: Allen and Unwin.

Jackson, P and Penrose, J. (eds) (1993a) *Constructions of Race, Place and Nation* London: UCL Press.

—— (1993b) 'Introduction: placing "race" and nation' in Jackson, P. and Penrose, J. (eds) *Constructions of Race, Place and Nation* London: UCL Press.

Jackson, P. and Smith, S. (eds) (1981) *Social Interaction and Ethnic Segregation* London: Academic Press.

Jacobs, J. (1996) *Edge of Empire: Postcolonialism and the City* London: Routledge.

—— (1993) ' "Shake 'im this country": the mapping of the Aboriginal sacred in Australia – the case of Coronation Hill' in Jackson, P. and Penrose, J. (eds) *Constructions of Race, Place and Nation* London: UCL.

—— (1988) 'Politics and the cultural landscape: the case of Aboriginal land rights' *Australian Geographical Studies* 26: 49–263.

Jacobs, S. W. (1922) *Official Report of Debates in the House of Commons* Ottawa: King's Publisher, Vol. III, 2,514–15.

Jenkins, R. (1997) *Rethinking Ethnicity: Arguments and Explorations* London: Sage.

—— (1996a) ' "Us" and "them": ethnicity, racism and ideology' in Barot, R. (ed.) *Theoretical Reflections on Race, Racism and Ethnicity: Essays Presented to Michael Benton* Lampeter: Edwin Mellen Press.

—— (1996b) *Social Identity* London: Routledge.

—— (1994) 'Rethinking ethnicity: identity, categorisation and power' *Ethnic and Racial Studies* 17: 197–223.

—— (1987) 'Countering prejudice – anthropological and otherwise', *Anthropology Today* 3, 2: 3–4.

—— (1986) 'Social anthropological models of inter-ethnic relations' in Rex, J. and Mason, D. (eds) *Theories of Race and Ethnic Relations* Cambridge: Cambridge University Press.

Jensen, A. (1969) 'How much can we boost IQ and scholastic achievement?' *Harvard Educational Review* 39: 1–123.

Jewson, N. and Mason, D. (1994) ' "Race", employment and equal opportunities: towards a political economy and an agenda for the 1990s' *Sociological Review* 42, 4: 591–617.

Jobanputra, S. (1995) 'Psychology and racism: views from the inside' Association for the Teaching of Psychology Resource Item: 125 Leicester: British Psychological Society.

Jones, A. M. (1997) 'A biography of ceramics: food and culture in late Neolithic Orkney' University of Glasgow: Unpublished Ph.D. Thesis.

Jones, M. A. (1976) *Destination America* London: Weidenfeld and Nicolson.

Jones, P. (1978) 'The distribution and diffusion of the coloured population in England and Wales 1961–1971' *Transactions of the Institute of British Geographers* 3, 4.

Jones, S. (1997) *The Archaeology of Ethnicity. Constructing Identities in the Past and Present* London: Routledge.

—— (1996) 'Discourses of identity in the interpretation of the past' in Graves-Brown, P., Jones, S. and Gamble, C. (eds) *Cultural Identity and Archaeology: The Construction of European Communities* London: Routledge.

Jones, T. (1993) *Britain's Ethnic Minorities* London: Policy Studies Institute.

Jordan, W. D. (1984) 'First impressions: initial English confrontations with Africans' in Husband, C. (ed.) *Race in Britain* London: Hutchinson.

—— (1974) *The White Man's Burden: Historical Origins of Racism in the United States* New York: Oxford University Press.

Joseph, G. G., Reddy, V. and Searle-Chatterjee, M. (1990) 'Eurocentrism in the social sciences' *Race and Class* 31, 4: 1–26.

Kabbani, R. (1989) *Letter to Christendom* London: Virago Press.

Kamin, L. (1974) *The Science and Politics of IQ* Potomac, MD: Erlbaum; London: Wiley.

Katz, D. S. (1994) *The Jews in the History of England, 1485–1850* Oxford: Clarendon.

—— (1982) *Philo-Semitism and the Readmission of the Jews to England, 1603–1655* Oxford: Clarendon.

Katzelson, I. (1973) *Black Men, White Cities* London: Oxford University Press.

Keith, M. (1993) *Race, Riots and Policing: Lore and Disorder in a Multi-racist Society* London: UCL Press.

—— (1991a) 'Policing a perplexed society? No-go areas and the mystification of police–black conflict' in Cashmore, E. and McClaughlin, E. (eds) *Out of Order? Policing Black People* London: Routledge.

—— (1991b) 'Knowing your place: the imagined geographies of racial subordination' in Philo, C. (ed.) *New Words, New Worlds: Reconceptualising Social and Cultural Geography* Lampeter: Social and Cultural Geography Study Group of the Institute of British Geographers.

—— (1988a) 'Racial conflict and the "No-Go Areas" of London' in Eyles, J. and Smith, D. (eds) *Qualitative Methods in Human Geography* Cambridge: Polity Press.

—— (1988b) 'Riots as "social problem" in British cities' in Herbert, D. and Smith, D. (eds) *Social Problems in the City* Oxford: Oxford University Press.

—— (1987) ' "Something happened": the problems of explaining the 1980 and 1981 riots in British cities' in Jackson, P. (ed.) *Race and Racism: Essays in Social Geography* London: Allen and Unwin.

Keith, M. and Pile, S. (eds) (1993) *Place and the Politics of Identity* London and New York: Routledge.

Keith, M. and Rogers, A. (eds) (1991) *Hollow Promises: Rhetoric and Reality in the Inner-City* London: Mansell.

Kellas, J. G. (1991) *The Politics of Nationalism and Ethnicity* Basingstoke: Macmillan.

Key, V. O. (1949) *Southern Politics in State and Nation* New York: Knopf.

Khan, S. (1991) 'Influences shaping relations between the East Indians and the Anglo-Canadians in Canada: 1903–1947' *Journal of Ethnic Studies* 19, 1: 106–16.

Kiernan, V. G. (1984) 'European attitudes to the outside world' in Husband, C. (ed.) *Race in Britain* London: Hutchinson.

Kincaid, J. (1991) *Lucy* London: Jonathan Cape.

Knowles, C. (1996) 'Race, biography and psychiatry' in Amit-Talai, V. and Knowles, C. (eds) *Re-Situating Identities: The Politics of Race, Ethnicity and Culture* Peterborough: Broadview Press.

—— (1992) *Race, Discourse and Labourism* London: Routledge.

Kohn, M. (1995) *The Race Gallery: The Return of Racial Science* London: Cape.

Kollman, W. and Marschalck, P. (1973) 'German emigration to the United States' *Perspectives in American History* Vol. 7.

Kuper, A. (1988) *The Invention of Primitive Society: Transformations of an Illusion* London: Routledge.

Kushner, T. (1989) *The Persistence of Prejudice: Antisemitism in British Society During the Second World War* Manchester: Manchester University Press.

—— (ed.) (1992) *Jewish Heritage in British History: Englishness and Jewishness* London: Frank Cass.

Kushner, T. and Lunn, K. (eds) (1990) *The Politics of Marginality: Race, the Radical Right and Minorities in Twentieth Century Britain* London: Frank Cass.

La Fontaine, J. (1986) 'Countering racial prejudice: a better starting point' *Anthropology Today* 2, 6: 1–2.

Labour Party (1933) *The Colonies* London: Labour Party.

Ladd, E. C. (1966) *Negro Political Leadership in the South* Ithaca, NY: Cornell University Press.

Lal, B. B. (1990) *The Romance of Culture in Urban Civilization* London: Routledge.

Lamming, G. (1995) 'The occasion for speaking' [extract from *The Pleasures of Exile* 1960] Reprinted in Ashcroft, B., Griffiths, G. and Tiffin, H. (1995) *The Post-colonial Studies Reader* London: Routledge.

Larick, R. (1986) 'Age grading and ethnicity in the style of Loikop Sanbura spears' *World Archaeology* 18: 269–83.

Leach, E. (1954) *Political Systems of Highland Burma: A Study of Kachin Social Structure* London: Athlone.

Leavis, F. R. (1973) *The Great Tradition: George Eliot, Henry James, Joseph Conrad* New York: New York University Press.

Lee, T. (1977) *Race and Residence: The Concentration and Dispersal of Immigrants in London* Oxford: Clarendon Press.

—— (1973) 'Ethnic and social class factors in residential segregation: some implications for dispersal' *Environment and planning* 5: 477–90.

Lees, L. H. (1979) *Exiles of Erin: Irish Migrants in Victorian London* Manchester: Manchester University Press.

Lentz, C. (1995) ' "Tribalism" and "ethnicity" in Africa: a review of four decades of anglophone research' *Cahiers des Sciences Humaines* 31: 303–28.

Leopold, J. (1974) 'British application of aryan theory of race to India, 1850–1870' *The English Historical Review* 80, 352: 578–603.

Lévi-Strauss, C. (1952) *The Race Question in Modern Science* Paris: UNESCO.

Levy, M. R. and Kramer, M. S. (1972) *The Ethnic Factor: How America's Minorities Decide Elections* New York: Simon and Schuster.

Lewontin, R. C., Rose, S. and Kamin, L. (1984) *Not in Our Genes* New York: Pantheon Books.

Ley, D. (1984) 'Pluralism and the Canadian state' in Clarke, C., Ley, D. and Peach, C. (eds) *Geography and Ethnic Pluralism* London: George Allen and Unwin.

Ley, D., Peach, C. and Clarke, C. (1984) 'Introduction: pluralism and human geography' in Clarke, C., Ley, D. and Peach, C. (eds) *Geography and Ethnic Pluralism* London: George Allen and Unwin.

Lieberson, S. (1981) 'An asymmetrical approach to segregation' in Peach, C., Robinson, V. and Smith, S. (eds) *Ethnic Segregation in Cities* London: Croom Helm.

Lijphart, A. (1994) Book review of Ted Robert Gurr *et al.* (1993) *Minorities at Risk, Comparative Political Studies* 27, 3: 448–51.

—— (1977) *Democracy in Plural Societies: A Comparative Exploration* New Haven, CT: Yale University Press.

—— (1968) *The Politics of Accommodation: Pluralism and Democracy in the Netherlands* Berkeley, CA: University of California Press.

Lipman, V. D. (1954) *Social History of the Jews in England 1850–1950* London: Watts and Co.

Livingstone, D. (1992) *The Geographical Tradition* Oxford: Blackwell.

—— (1994) 'Climate's moral economy: science, race and place in post-Darwinian British and American geography' in Godlewska, A. and Smith, N. (eds) *Geography and Empire* Oxford: Blackwell.

Luebke, F. C. (1990) 'Turnerism, social history and the historiography of European ethnic groups in the United States' in F. C. Luebke (ed.) *Germans in the New World: Essays on the History of Immigration*, Urbana and Chicago: University of Illinois Press.

—— (1974) *Bonds of Loyalty: German Americans and World War I* De Kalb, IL: Northern Illinois University Press.

—— (1969) *Immigrants and Politics: The Germans of Nebraska, 1880–1900* Lincoln, NB: University of Nebraska Press.

Lupton, G. *et al.* (eds) (1992) *Society and Gender: An Introduction to Sociology* Melbourne: Macmillan.

Mackie, D. and Hamilton, D. (eds) (1993) *Affect, Cognition and Stereotyping: Interactive Processes in Group Perception* New York: Academic Press.

MacKinnon, C. A. (1996) 'From practice to theory, or what is a white woman anyway?' in Bell, D. and Klein, R. (eds) *Radically Speaking, Feminism Reclaimed* London: Zed.

Manzo, K. A. (1995) *Creating Boundaries: The Politics of Race and Nation* Boulder, CO: Lynne Rienner.

Marable, M. (1985) *Black American Politics: From the Washington Marches to Jesse Jackson* London: Verso.

Marcus, G. (1992) 'Past, present and emergent identities: requirements for ethnographies of late twentieth-century modernities' in Lash, S. and Friedman, J. (eds) *Modernity and Identity* Oxford: Basil Blackwell.

Margoliouth, M. (1851) *The History of the Jews in Great Britain* 3 vols, London: Richard Bentley.

Marshall, T. H. (1950) *Citizenship and Social Class* Cambridge: Cambridge University Press.

Marx, A. W. (1998) *Making Race and Nation: A Comparison of South Africa, the United States and Brazil* Cambridge: Cambridge University Press.

Mason, D. (1995) *Race and Ethnicity in Modern Britain* Oxford: Oxford University Press.

—— (1994) 'On the dangers of disconnecting race and racism' *Sociology* 28, 4: 845–58.

—— (1992) 'Categories, identities and change: ethnic monitoring and the social scientist' *European Journal of Intercultural Studies* 2, 2: 41–52.

—— (1990) 'Competing conceptions of "fairness" and the formulation and implementation of equal opportunities policies' in Ball, W. and Solomos, J. (eds) *Race and Local Politics* London: Macmillan.

—— (1982) 'After Scarman: a note on the concept of institutional racism' *New Community* 10, 1: 38–45.

Mason, P. (1967) *Patterns of Dominance* Oxford: Oxford University Press.

Matthews, D. R. and Prothro, J. W. (1966) *Negroes and the New Southern Politics* New York: Harcourt, Brace and World.

McArthur, L. (1982) 'Judging a book by its cover: a cognitive analysis of the relationships between physical appearance and stereotyping' in Hastorf, A. and Isen, A. (eds) *Cognitive Social Psychology* New York: Elsevier.

McBride, T. C. (1923) *Official Report of Debates in the House of Commons* Ottawa: King's Publisher, Vol. V, 4,648.

McCann, W. J. (1990) ' "Volk and Germanentum": the presentation of the past in Nazi Germany' in Gathercole, P. and Lowenthal, D. (eds) *The Politics of the Past* London: Unwin Hyman.

McGarry, J. and O'Leary, B. (eds) (1993) *The Politics of Ethnic Conflict Regulation* London: Routledge.

McGuire, R. H. (1982) 'The study of ethnicity in historical archaeology' *Journal of Anthropological Archaeology* 1: 159–78.

McLemore, S. D. (1994) *Race and Ethnicity in America* fourth edition, Boston: Allyn and Bacon.

McLoughlin, C. and Koh, T.-H. (1982) 'Testing intelligence: a decision suitable for the psychologist' *Bulletin of the British Psychological Society* 35: 308–11.

McNeil, M. (1992) 'Pedagogical praxis and problems: reflections on teaching about gender relations' in Hinds, H., Phoenix, A. and Stacey, J. (eds) *Working Out: New Directions in Women's Studies* London: Falmer.

McWilliams, C. (1949) *North from Mexico: The Spanish-Speaking People of the United States* Philadelphia, PA: J. B. Lippincott.

Meier, A. and Rudwick, E. (1986) *Black History and the Historical Profession* Urbana and Chicago, IL: University of Illinois Press.

—— (1976) *Along the Color Line: Explorations in the Black Experience* Urbana, IL: University of Illinois Press.

—— (1973) *CORE: A Study in the Civil Rights Movement* New York: Oxford University Press.

—— (1970) *From Plantation to Ghetto* London: Constable.

Mercer, K. (1994) *Welcome to the Jungle: New Positions in Black Cultural Studies* New York: Routledge.

Miles, R. (1994) 'A rise of racism and fascism in contemporary Europe? Some skeptical reflections on its nature and extent' *New Community* 20, 4: 547–62.

—— (1993) *Racism After 'Race Relations'* London: Routledge.

—— (1989) *Racism* London: Routledge.

—— (1982) *Racism and Migrant Labour* London: Routledge and Kegan Paul.

Miles, R. and Phizacklea, A. (1984) *White Man's Country: Racism in British Politics* London: Pluto.

Mill, H. (1905) 'The present problems of geography' *Geographical Journal* 25, 1: 1–17.

Miller, A. (1982) *In the Eye of the Beholder: Contemporary Issues in Stereotyping* New York: Praeger.

Miller, D. (ed.) (1995) *Worlds Apart: Modernity Through the Prism of the Local* London: Routledge.

Mills, C. (1994) 'Non-Cartesian sums: philosophy and the African-American experience' *Teaching Philosophy* 17, 3: 373–93.

Mills, J. (1863) *The British Jews* London: Houlston and Stoneman.

Milner, D. (1991) 'Innocence, ignorance and belief' Inaugural Professorial Lecture 5 December, London: Polytechnic of Central London.

—— (1983) *Children and Race: Ten Years On* London: Ward Lock Educational.

Minard, R. (1952) 'Race relationships in the Pocahontas coal field' *Journal of Social Issues* 8: 29–44.

Mirza, H. S. (1992) *Young, Female and Black* London: Routledge.

—— (ed.) (1997) *Black British Feminism, a Reader* (London and New York: Routledge.

Misrow, J. C. (1915) 'East Indian immigration on the Pacific Coast' Stanford University, California: Unpublished Thesis.

Modood, T. (1994) 'Political blackness and British Asians' *Sociology* 28, 4: 859–76.

—— (1992) *Not Easy Being British* Stoke-on-Trent: Trentham Books.

—— (1988) ' "Black", racial equality and Asian identity' *New Community* 14, 3: 397–404.

Modood, T., Berthoud, R., Lankey, J., Nazrod, J., Smith, P., Virdu, S. and Beishon, S. (1997) *Ethnic Minorities in Britain* London: Policy Studies Institute.

Moerman, M. (1965) 'Ethnic identification in a complex civilisation: who are the Lue?' *American Anthropologist* 67: 1,215–30.

Mohanty, C. T. (1993) 'Under Western eyes: feminist scholarship and colonial discourses' in Chrisman, L. and Williams, P. (eds) *Colonial Discourse and Post-colonial Theory* London: Harvester Wheatsheaf.

Morgan, K. O. (1990) *The People's Peace* Oxford: Oxford University Press.

Morley, D. and Chen, K.-H. (eds) (1996) *Stuart Hall: Critical Dialogues in Cultural Studies* London: Routledge.

Morrison, T. (1992) *Playing in the Dark: Whiteness and the Literary Imagination* Cambridge, MA: Harvard University Press.

—— (ed.) (1993) *Race-ing Justice, En-gendering Power* London: Chatto and Windus.

Mosse, W. *et al.* (eds) (1991) *Second Chance: Two Centuries of German-speaking Jews in the United Kingdom* Tübingen: J. C. B. Mohr.

Mukherjee, A. P. (1995) 'Ideology in the classroom: a case study in the teaching of English literature in Canadian universities' reprinted in Ashcroft, B., Griffiths, G. and Tiffin, H. *The Post-colonial Studies Reader* London: Routledge.

Murray, C. (1984) *Losing Ground: American Social Policy, 1950–1980* New York: Basic Books.

Myrdal, G. (1944) *An American Dilemma: The Negro Problem and Modern Democracy* New York: Harper and Row.

Nadel, S. (1990) *Little Germany: Ethnicity, Religion and Class in New York City 1845–80* Urbana, IL: University of Illinois Press.

Neill, A. W. (1923) *Official Report of Debates in the House of Commons* Ottawa: King's Publisher, Vol. V, 4,643–9.

Nisbett, R. E. and Ross, L. (1980) *Human Inference: Strategies and Shortcomings of Social Judgement* Englewood Cliffs, NJ: Prentice Hall.

Odling-Smee F. J. (1990) 'The mistreatment of diversity' commentary on 'Are intelligence differences hereditarily transmitted?' (Pierre Roubertoux and Christiane Capron) *European Bulletin of Cognitive Psychology* 10, 6: 653–8.

Odner, K. (1985) 'Saamis (Lapps), Finns and Scandinavians in history and prehistory' *Norwegian Archaeological Review* 18: 1–12.

Olsen, B. (1985) 'Comments on Saamis, Finns and Scandinavians in history and prehistory' *Norwegian Archaeological Review* 18: 13–18.

Olsen, B. and Kobylinski, Z. (1991) 'Ethnicity in anthropological and archaeological research: a Norwegian-Polish perspective' *Archaeologia Polona* 29: 5–27.

Osofsky, G. (1968) *The Burden of Race: A Documentary History of Negro–White Relations in America* New York: Harper and Row.

—— (1966) *Harlem: The Making of a Ghetto* New York: Harper and Row.

Paddayya, K. (1995) 'Theoretical perspectives in Indian archaeology: an historical overview' in Ucko, P. J. (ed.) *Theory in Archaeology. A World Perspective* London: Routledge.

Panayi, P. (1995) *German Immigrants in Britain During the Nineteenth Century, 1815–1914* Oxford: Berg.

—— (1994) *Immigration, Ethnicity and Racism in Britain, 1815–1945* Manchester: Manchester University Press.

—— (1993) 'Anti-immigrant riots in nineteenth and twentieth-century Britain' in Panayi, P. (ed.) *Racial Violence in Britain, 1840–1950* Leicester: Leicester University Press.

—— (1991) *The Enemy in Our Midst: Germans in Britain during the First World War* Oxford: Berg.

—— (ed.) (1996) *Germans in Britain Since 1500* London: Hambledon.

Parenti, M. (1967) 'Ethnic politics and the persistence of ethnic identification' *American Political Science Review*, 61, 3: 717–26.

Parker, D. (1995) *Through Different Eyes: The Cultural Identities of Young Chinese People in Britain* Aldershot: Avebury.

Parker, I. (1992) *Discourse Dynamics* London: Routledge.

—— (1989) *The Crisis in Modern Social Psychology and How to End it* London: Routledge.

Parker, I. and Shotter, J. (1990) *Deconstructing Social Psychology* London: Routledge.

Parker, K. (1985) 'The revelation of Caliban: "the black presence" in the classroom' in Dabydeen, D. (ed.) (1985) *The Black Presence in English Literature* Manchester: Manchester University Press.

Paul, K. (1997) *Whitewashing Britain: Race and Citizenship in the Postwar Era* Ithaca, NY: Cornell University Press.

Peach, C. (1975a) 'Introduction: the spatial analysis of ethnicity and class' in Peach, C. (ed.) *Urban Social Segregation* London: Longman.

Peach, C. (ed.) (1975b) *Urban Social Segregation* London: Longman.

Peach, C., Robinson, V. and Smith, S. (eds) (1981) *Ethnic Segregation in Cities* London: Croom Helm.

Peach, C. and Rossiter D. (1994) 'Level and nature of spatial concentration and segregation' paper presented to OPCS Seminar, 5–6 September, University of Leeds.

Peach, C. and Smith, S. (1981) 'Introduction' in Peach, C., Robinson, V. and Smith, S. (eds) *Ethnic Segregation in Cities* London: Croom Helm.

Peller, G. (1995) 'Race consciousness' in Danielson, D. and Engle, K. (eds) *After Identity: A Reader in Law and Culture* New York: Routledge.

Pettigrew, T. F. (1958) 'Personality and socio-cultural factors in intergroup attitudes: a cross national comparison' *Journal of Conflict Resolution* 2: 29–42.

Pfeil, F. (1995) *White Guys, Studies in Postmodern Domination and Difference* London: Verso.

Phoenix, A. (1994) 'Positioned differently: issues of "race" difference and commonality' *Changes* 12, 4: 299–305.

—— (1987) 'Theories of gender and black families' in Weiner, G. and Arnot, M. (eds) *Gender Under Scrutiny* London: Hutchinson.

Piggott, S. (1965) *Ancient Europe. From the Beginnings of Agriculture to Classical Antiquity* Edinburgh: Edinburgh University Press.

Pinderhughes, D. M. (1987) *Race and Ethnicity in Chicago Politics: A Reexamination of Pluralist Theory* Urbana and Chicago: University of Illinois Press.

Piper, A. (1992) 'Passing for white, passing for black' *Transitions* 58: 4–32.

Portelli, A. (1991) *The Death of Luigi Trastulli and Other Stories* New York: State University of New York Press.

Porteous, J. (1984) 'Easter Island: pluralism and power' in Clarke, C., Ley, D. and Peach, C. (eds) *Geography and Ethnic Pluralism* London: George Allen and Unwin.

Potter, J. and Litton, I. (1985) 'Some problems underlying the theory of social representations' *British Journal of Social Psychology* 24: 81–90.

Potter, J. and Wetherell, M. (1987) *Discourse and Social Psychology* London: Sage.

Praetzellis, A., Praetzellis, M. and Brown III, M. (1987) 'Artefacts as symbols of identity: an example from Sacramento's Gold Rush Era Chinese community' in Saski, A. (ed.) *Living in Cities: Current Research in Historical Archaeology* Pleasant Hill: The Society for Historical Archaeology.

Pratt, M. L. (1992) *Imperial Eyes: Travel Writing and Transculturation* London and New York: Routledge.

Preston, M. B. and Woodard, M. (1984) 'The rise and decline of black political scientists in the profession' *PS* 17, 4: 787–92.

Prichard, J. C. (1813) [1973] *Researches into the Physical History of Man* Chicago, IL: University of Chicago Press.

Province of British Columbia (1927) *Report on Oriental Activities Within the Province* Victoria: Legislative Assembly.

*Queens Quarterly* 1927–8, 1930 and 1933 Kingston, Ontario: Queen's University.

Quinley, H. E. and Glock, C. Y. (1979) *Antisemitism in America* New York: Free Press.

Rabinow, P. (ed.) (1984) *The Foucault Reader: An Introduction to Foucault's Thought* Harmondsworth: Penguin.

Radcliffe-Brown, A. R. (1952) *Structure and Function in Primitive Society: Essays and Addresses* London: Cohen and West.

Rainwater, L. and Yancey, R. (eds) (1967) *The Moynihan Report and the Politics of Controversy* Cambridge, MA: MIT Press.

Rattansi, A. (1994) ' "Western" racisms, ethnicities and identities in a "post-modern" frame' in Rattansi, A. and Westwood, S. (eds) *Racism, Modernity and Identity* Oxford: Polity.

Rattansi, A. and Westwood, S. (eds) (1994) *Racism, Identity and Modernity on the Western Front* Cambridge: Polity Press.

Rea, A. (1988) *Manchester's Little Italy: Memories of the Italian Colony of Ancoats* Swindon: Neil Richardson.

Rees, P. and Phillips, D. (n.d.) 'Geographical spread: the national picture' draft paper, unpublished.

Reicher, S. (1993) 'Policing normality and pathologising protest: a critical view of the contribution of psychology to society' *Changes* 11, 2: 121–6.

—— (1988a) 'Psychology and apartheid' *Social Psychology Section Newsletter* Spring: 7–19.

—— (1988b) 'Reply to Markova' *Social Psychology Section Newsletter* Spring: 23–9.

—— (1986) 'Contact, action and racialisation: some British evidence' in Hewstone, M. and Brown, R. (eds) *Contact and Conflict in Intergroup Encounters* Oxford: Basil Blackwell.

—— (1982) 'The determination of collective behaviour' in Tajfel, H. (ed.) *Social Identity and Intergroup Relations* Cambridge: Cambridge University Press.

Reimers, D. M. (1985) *Still the Golden Door: The Third World Comes to America* New York: Columbia University Press.

Renfrew, C. (1979) *Problems in European Prehistory* Edinburgh: Edinburgh University Press.

—— (1972) *The Emergence of Civilisation. The Cyclades and the Aegean in the Third Millennium B.C.* London: Methuen and Co.

Retamar, R. F. (1989) *Caliban and Other Essays* trans. Edward Baker Minneapolis: University of Minnesota Press.

Rex, J. (1991) *Ethnic Identity and Ethnic Mobilisation in Britain* Warwick: ESRC Centre for Research in Ethnic Relations.

—— (1973) *Race, Colonialism and the City* London: Routledge and Kegan Paul.

—— (1970) *Race Relations in Sociological Theory* London: Weidenfeld and Nicolson.

Rex, J. and Mason, D. (1986) *Theories of Race and Ethnic Relations* Cambridge: Cambridge University Press.

Richards, G. (1997) *Race, Racism and Psychology: Towards a Reflexive History* London: Routledge.

Richardson, R. (1994) 'The underclass in our time' *The Runnymede Bulletin* 280: 2–3.

Ricoeur, P. (1992) *Oneself As Another* trans. Kathleen Blamey, Chicago, IL: University of Chicago Press.

Robertson, R. (1992) *Globalization: Social Theory and Global Culture* London: Sage.

Robinson, V. (1987) 'Spatial variability in attitudes towards "race" in the UK' in Jackson, P. (ed.) *Race and Racism: Essays in Social Geography* London: Allen and Unwin.

Rodriguez, R. (1992) *Days of Obligation: An Argument With My Mexican Father* New York: Viking Books.

Rose, N. (1989) *Governing the Soul: The Shaping of the Private Self* London: Routledge.

Rose, H. and Rose, S. (1978) 'The IQ myth' *Race and Class* 20, 1: 63–74.

Rose, P. I. (1968) *The Subject is Race* New York: Oxford University Press.

Rosenbaum, R. J. (1981) *Mexicano Resistance in the Southwest: 'The Sacred Right of Self-Preservation'* Austin, TX: University of Texas Press.

Roth, C. (1950) 'The rise of provincial Jewry; the early history of the Jewish communities in the English countryside' *Jewish Monthly*.

—— (1941) *A History of the Jews in England* Oxford: Clarendon Press.

Rothschild, J. (1981) *Ethnopolitics: A Conceptual Framework* New York: Columbia University Press.

Rubinstein, B. (1996) *A History of the Jews in the English Speaking World: Great Britain* Basingstoke: Macmillan.

Rushton, J. P. (1990) 'Race differences, r/k theory, and a reply to J. R. Flynn' *The Psychologist* 3, 5: 195–8.

Rutherford, J. (ed.) (1990) *Identity, Community, Culture, Difference* London: Lawrence and Wishart.

Said, E. (1978) *Orientalism* Harmondsworth: Penguin.

Samelson, F. (1978) 'From "race psychology" to "studies in prejudice": some observations on the thematic reversal in social psychology' *Journal of History of the Behavioural Sciences* 14: 265–327.

Samuel, R. (ed.) (1989) *Patriotism, the Making and Unmaking of British National Identity* London: Routledge.

San Miguel, G. (1987) *'Let Them All Take Heed': Mexican Americans and the Campaign for Educational Equality in Texas, 1910–1981* Austin, TX: University of Texas Press.

Satzewich, V. (1989) 'Racism and Canadian immigration policy: the government's view of Caribbean migration, 1962–1966' *Canadian Ethnic Studies* 11, 1: 77–97.

Schaible, K. H. (1885) *Geschichte der Deutschen in England* Strasbourg: Karl J. Trubner.

Schlee, G. (1989) *Identities on the Move: Clanship and Pastoralism in Northern Kenya* Manchester: Manchester University Press.

Schor, N. and Weed, E. (eds) (1994) *The Essential Difference* Bloomington: Indiana University Press.

Shanks, M. and Tilley, C. (1992) [1987] *Re-constructing Archaeology: Theory and Practice* London: Routledge.

Shennan, S. J. (1989) 'Introduction' in Shennan, S. J. (ed.) *Archaeological Approaches to Cultural Identity* London: Unwin and Hyman.

Sherratt, A. (1982) 'Mobile resources: settlement and exchange in early agricultural Europe' in Renfrew, C. and Shennan, S. J. (eds) *Ranking, Resource and Exchange: Aspects of the Archaeology of Early European Society* Cambridge: Cambridge University Press.

Shockley, W. (1972) 'Dysgenics, geneticity, raceology: a challenge to the intellectual responsibility of educators' *Phi Delta Kappan* January: 297–307.

Showalter, E. (1978) *A Literature of Their Own: British Women Novelists from Bronte to Lessing* London: Virago.

Simpson, G. E. and Yinger, J. M. (1965) *Racial and Cultural Minorities: an analysis of prejudice and discrimination* third edition, New York: Harper and Row.

—— (1985) *Racial and Cultural Minorities: An Analysis of Prejudice and Discrimination* fifth edition, New York: Plenum Press.

Sitkoff, H. (1981) *The Struggle for Black Equality, 1954–1980* New York: Hill and Wang.

Sivanandan, A. (1982) *A Different Hunger* London: Pluto Press.

Skellington, R. (1992) *'Race' in Britain Today* London: Sage.

Sklenár, K. (1983) *Archaeology in Central Europe: The First Five Hundred Years* Leicester: Leicester University Press.

Smaje, C. (1997) 'Not just a social construct: theorising race and ethnicity' *Sociology* 31, 2: 307–27.

Small, S. (1994) *Racialised Barriers: The Black Experience in the United States and England in the 1980s* London: Routledge.

Smith, A. D. (1994) 'The problem of national identity: ancient, medieval and modern?' *Ethnic and Racial Studies* 17: 375–99.

Smith, M. G. (1986) 'Pluralism, race and ethnicity in selected African countries' in Rex, J. and Mason, D. (eds) *Theories of Race and Ethnic Relations* Cambridge: Cambridge University Press.

—— (1965) *The Plural Society of the British West Indies* Berkeley, CA: University of California Press.

Smith, S. (1993) 'Bounding the Borders: claiming space and making place in rural Scotland' *Transactions, Institute of British Geographers* (New Series) 18: 291–308.

—— (1989a) *The Politics of 'Race' and Residence* Cambridge: Polity Press.

—— (1989b) 'Race and racism' *Urban Geography* 10, 10: 593–606.

Solomos, J. (1993) *Race and Racism in Britain* second edition Basingstoke: Macmillan.

Solomos, J. and Back, L. (1996) *Racism and Society* Basingstoke: Macmillan.

Sonenshein, R. J. (1993) *Politics in Black and White: Race and Power in Los Angeles* Princeton, NJ: Princeton University Press.

Soysal, Y. N. (1994) *Limits of Citizenship: Migrants and Postnational Membership in Europe* Chicago, IL: University of Chicago Press.

Spear, T. and Waller, R. (eds) (1993) *Being Maasai: Ethnicity and Identity in East Africa* London: James Currey.

Spencer, I. R. G. (1997) *British Immigration Policy: The Making of Multi-Racial Britain* London: Routledge.

Spivak, G. C. (1993) *Outside in the Teaching Machine* New York and London: Routledge.

—— (1987) *In Other Worlds* New York and London: Methuen.

Sponza, L. (1988) *Italian Immigrants in Nineteenth Century Britain: Realities and Images* Leicester: Leicester University Press.

Stampp, K. (1956) *The Peculiar Institution* New York: Alfred Knopf.

Stanley, L. (1993) 'On auto/biography and sociology' *Sociology* 27, 1: 41–52.

Stannard, D. E. (1992) *American Holocaust, The Conquest of the New World* New York and London: Oxford University Press.

Statistics Canada (1992) *Year Book* Ottawa: Statistics Canada.

Steele, S. (1990) *The Content of Our Character* New York: Harper.

Steinberg, M. (1995) ' "Identity" and multiple consciousness' paper delivered at the workshop 'Identity: do we need it?' sponsored by the Internationales Forschungszentrum Kulturwissenschaften, Vienna, Austria.

Stepan, N. (1982) *The Idea of Race in Science: Great Britain, 1800–1950* Basingstoke: Macmillan.

Stepan, N. L. and Gilman, S. L. (1993) 'Appropriating the idioms of science: the rejection of scientific racism' in Harding, S. (ed.) *The 'Racial' Economy of Science: Toward a Democratic Future* Bloomington and Indianapolis, IN: Indiana University Press.

Stocking, G. W. (1988) 'Bones, bodies, behaviour' in Stocking, G. W. (ed.) *Bones, Bodies, Behaviour: Essays on Biological Anthropology* Madison: University of Wisconsin Press.

—— (1987) *Victorian Anthropology* New York: The Free Press.

—— (1973) 'From chronology to ethnology. James Cowles Prichard and British Anthropology 1800–1850' in Prichard, J. C. [1813] *Researches into the Physical History of Man* Chicago, IL: University of Chicago Press.

—— (1968) *Race, Culture and Evolution: Essays in the History of Anthropology* London: Collier-Macmillan.

Stone, C. N. (1989) *Regime Politics: Governing Atlanta 1946–1988* Lawrence, KA: University Press of Kansas.

Stone, J. (1977) 'Race relations and the sociological tradition' in Stone, J. (ed.) *Race, Ethnicity and Social Change* North Scituate, MA: Duxbury Press.

Storr, A. (1979) *Human Aggression* Harmondsworth: Penguin.

Swift, R. and Gilley, S. (1989) *The Irish in Britain, 1815–1939* London: Pinter

—— (1985) *The Irish in the Victorian City* Beckenham: Croom Helm.

Tajfel, H. (1981) *Human Groups and Social Categories* Cambridge: Cambridge University Press.

—— (1978a) 'Intergroup behaviour: individualistic perspectives' in Tajfel, H. and Fraser, C. (eds) *Introducing Social Psychology* Harmondsworth: Penguin.

—— (1978b) *The Social Psychology of Minorities* London: Minority Rights Group Report no. 38.

—— (1969) 'Cognitive aspects of prejudice' *Journal of Social Issues* 25, 4: 79–97.

Tajfel, H. and Turner, J. (1979) 'An integrative theory of intergroup conflict' in Austin, W. G. and Worchel, S. (eds) *The Social Psychology of Intergroup Relations* Monterey, CA: Brooks Cole.

Takaki, R. (1993) *A Different Mirror: A History of Multicultural America* New York: Little, Brown and Co.

—— (1989) *Strangers from a Different Shore: A History of Asian Americans* New York: Little, Brown and Co.

Tallgren, A. M. (1937) 'The method of prehistoric archaeology' *Antiquity* 11: 152–64.

Taylor, C., Gutmann, A., Rockefeller, S. C., Walzer, M. and Wolf, S. (1992) *Multiculturalism and 'The Politics of Recognition'* Princeton, NJ: Princeton University Press.

Taylor, J. (1997) 'Racialised representations in British and American advertising' *Area* 29, 2: 160–71.

Taylor, K. W. (1991) 'Racism in Canadian immigration policy' *Canadian Ethnic Studies* 23, 1: 1–20.

Taylor, P. M. (1971) *The Distant Magnet: European Emigration to the USA* London: Eyre and Spottiswoode.

Taylor, S. (1981) 'A categorization approach to stereotyping' in Hamilton, D. (ed.) *Cognitive Processes in Stereotyping and Intergroup Behaviour* Hillsdale, NJ: Erlbaum.

Thernstrom, S. (ed.) (1980) *Harvard Encyclopedia of American Ethnic Groups* Cambridge, MA: Harvard University Press.

Thomas, J. (1996) *Time, Culture and Identity: An Interpretive Archaeology* London: Routledge.

Thomas, W. I. and Znaniecki, F. (1919) *The Polish Peasant in Europe and America* Boston, MA: Richard G. Badger.

Thompson, E. P. (1963) *The Making of the English Working Classes* Harmondsworth: Penguin.

Thompson, F. M. L. (1990) *The Cambridge Social History of Britain* three volumes, Cambridge: Cambridge University Press.

Thornton, S. and Gelder, K. (eds) (1996) *The Subcultures Reader* London and New York: Routledge.

Thorpe, E. (1979) *The Central Theme of Black History* Westport, CT: Greenwood Press.

Tilley, C. (1991) *Material Culture and Text: The Art of Ambiguity* London: Routledge.

Tiryakian, E. A. and Rogowski, R. (eds) (1985) *New Nationalisms of the Developed West* Boston, MA: Allen and Unwin.

Tolmie, S. F. (1926) *Official Debates of the House of Commons* Ottawa: King's Publisher Vol. I, 995–1,005.

Trigger, B. G. (1989) *A History of Archaeological Thought* Cambridge: Cambridge University Press.

—— (1984) 'Alternative archaeologies: nationalist, colonialist, imperialist' *Man* (n.s.) 19: 355–70.

—— (1978) *Time and Traditions: Essays in Archaeological Interpretation* Edinburgh: Edinburgh University Press.

Turner J. and Giles, H. (eds) (1981) *Intergroup Behaviour* Oxford: Blackwell.

Turner, J. and Oakes, P. (1986) 'The significance of the social identity concept for social psychology with reference to individualism, interactionism and social influence' *British Journal of Social Psychology* 25: 237–52.

Ucko, P. J. (1994) 'Museums and sites: cultures of the past within education – Zimbabwe some ten years on' in Stone, P. G. and Molyneux, B. L. (eds) *The Presented Past: Heritage, Museums, Education* London: Routledge.

—— (1983) 'The politics of the indigenous minority' *Journal of Biosocial Science* Supplement 8: 25–40.

van den Berghe, P. L. (1981) *The Ethnic Phenomenon* New York: Elsevier.

—— (1967) *Race and Racism: A Comparative Perspective* New York: Wiley.

van Dijk, T. (1993) 'Principles of critical discourse analysis' *Discourse and Society* 4, 2: 249–83.

—— (1992) 'Discourse and the denial of racism' *Discourse and Society* 3, 1: 87–118.

—— (1988) 'Social cognition, social power and social discourse' *Text*, 8: 1/2: 129–57.

—— (1987) *News as Discourse* Hillsdale, NJ: Erlbaum.

—— (1984) *Communicating Racism: Ethnic Prejudice in Thought and Talk* London: Sage.

van Teeffelen, T. (1994) 'Racism and metaphor: the Palestinian–Israeli conflict in popular literature' *Discourse and Society* 5, 3: 381–405.

Vecoli, R. J. (1973) 'European Americans: from immigrants to ethnics' in Cartwright, W. H. and Watson, R. L. Jr (eds) *The Reinterpretation of American History and Culture* Washington, DC: National Council for the Social Studies.

Veit, U. (1989) 'Ethnic concepts in German prehistory: a case study on the relationship between cultural identity and objectivity' in Shennan, S. J. (ed.) *Archaeological Approaches to Cultural Identity* London: Unwin and Hyman.

Verba, S. and Nie, N. H. (1972) *Participation in America: Political Democracy and Social Equality* New York: Harper and Row.

Verdery, K. (1994) 'Ethnicity, nationalism and state-making. Ethnic groups and boundaries: past and future' in Vermeulen, H. and Govers, C. (eds) *The Anthropology of Ethnicity: Beyond 'Ethnic Groups and Boundaries'* Amsterdam: Het Spinhuis.

Verkuyten, M., De Jong, W. and Masson, K. (1995) 'The construction of ethnic categories: discourses of ethnicity in The Netherlands' *Ethnic and Racial Studies* 18, 2: 251–76.

—— (1994a) 'Racial discourse, attitude, and rhetorical manoeuvres: race talk in The Netherlands' *Journal of Language and Social Psychology* 13, 3: 278–98.

—— (1994b) 'Similarities in anti-racist and racist discourse: Dutch local residents talking about ethnic minorities' *New Community* 20, 2: 253–67.

Waddell, P. (1993) 'Does Berg understand the relevance of race in urban America? A reply to Berg's comment' *Urban Geography* 14, 2: 201–3.

—— (1992) 'A multinomial logit model of race and urban structure' *Urban Geography* 13, 2: 127–41.

Wade, P. (1993) ' "Race", nature and culture' *Man* (n.s.) 28: 17–34.

Wallman, S. (1986) 'Ethnicity and the boundary process in context' in Rex, J. and Mason, D. (eds) *Theories of Race and Ethnic Relations* Cambridge: Cambridge University Press.

—— (1978) 'The boundaries of race: processes of ethnicity in England' *Man* (n.s.) 13: 200–17.

Walvin, J. (1984) *Passage to Britain: Immigration in British History and Politics* Harmondsworth: Penguin.

Ward, P. W. (1990) *White Canada For Ever* Montreal: McGill-Queens University Press.

Ware, V. (1992) *Beyond the Pale: White Women Racism and History* London: Verso.

Washburn, W. (1971) 'The writing of American Indian history: a status report' *Pacific Historical Review* 40: 261–81.

Ware, V. (1992) *Beyond the Pale: White Women, Racism and History* London: Verso.

Waters, M. (1995) *Globalization* London: Routledge.

Webster, Y. (1992) *The Racializing of America* New York: St Martins Press.

Weedon, C. (1987) *Feminist Practice and Poststructuralist Theory* Oxford: Basil Blackwell.

West, C. (1982) *Prophesy Deliverance!* Philadelphia: Westminster Press.

Wetherell, M. and Potter, J. (1992) *Mapping the Language of Racism* Hemel Hempstead: Harvester Wheatsheaf.

—— (1988) 'Discourse analysis and the identification of interpretive repertoires' in Antaki, C. (ed.) *Analysing Everyday Explanation: A Casebook of Methods* London: Sage.

Whitelam, K. W. (1996) *The Invention of Ancient Israel: The Silencing of Palestinian History* London: Routledge.

Wijworra, I. (1996) 'German archaeology and its relation to nationalism and racism' in Díaz-Andreu, M. and Champion, T. C. (eds) *Nationalism and Archaeology in Europe* London: London University Press.

Willey, G. R. and Phillips, P. (1958) *Method and Theory in American Archaeology* Chicago: University of Chicago Press.

Williams, B. (1976) *The Making of Manchester Jewry, 1740–1875* Manchester: Manchester University Press.

Williams, B. F. (1989) 'A class act: anthropology and the race to nation across ethnic terrain' *Annual Review of Anthropology* 18: 401–44.

Williams, D. (1989) *Blacks in Montreal 1628–1986: An Urban Demography* Cownasville Que: Les Editions Yvon Blais inc.

Williams, J. (1985) 'Redefining institutional racism' *Ethnic and Racial Studies* 8, 3: 323–48.

Willis, P. (1978) *Profane Culture* London: Routledge and Kegan Paul.

—— (1977) *Learning to Labour* London: Saxon House.

Wilson, A. (1978) *Finding a Voice: Asian Women in Britain* London: Virago.

Wilson, W. J. (1996) 'The poorest of the urban poor: race, class and social isolation in America's inner city ghettos' in Bulmer, M. and Rees, A. (eds) *Citizenship Today: The Contemporary Relevance of T. H. Marshall* London: UCL Press, 223–48.

—— (1987) *The Truly Disadvantaged* Chicago: University of Chicago Press.

—— (1978) *The Declining Significance of Race* Chicago: University of Chicago Press.

—— (1973) *Power, Racism and Privilege: Race Relations in Theoretical and Socio-historical Perspective* New York: Free Press.

Wittke, C. (1957) *The German-Language Press in America* Lexington, KT: University of Kentucky Press.

—— (1952) *Refugees of Revolution: The German Forty-Eighters in America* Cambridge, MA: Harvard University Press.

Wodak, R. and Matouschek, B. (1993) ' "We are dealing with people whose origins one can clearly tell just by looking": critical discourse analysis and the study of neo-racism in Austria' *Discourse and Society* 4, 2: 225–48.

Wolf, E. R. (1994) 'Perilous ideas: race, culture, people' *Cultural Anthropology* 35: 1–12.

Wolfinger, R. E. (1965) 'The development and persistence of ethnic voting' *American Political Science Review* 59, 4: 896–908.

Wong L. M. (1994) 'Di(s)-secting and dis(s)-closing "whiteness": two tales about psychology' *Feminism and Psychology* 4, 1: 133–54.

Woodsworth, J. S. (1924) *Debates, House of Commons* Ottawa: King's Publisher Vol. IV, 4,004–5.

Worsley, P. (ed.) (1987) *The New Introducing Sociology* Harmondsworth: Pelican Books.

Yee, A. H., Fairchild, H. H., Weizmann, F. and Wyatt, G. E. (1994) 'Addressing psychology's problems with race' *American Psychologist* 48, 11: 1,132–40.

Young, C. (1983) 'The temple of ethnicity' (review article) *World Politics* 35, 4: 652–62.

Young, I. (1990) 'The ideal of community and the politics of difference' in Nicholson, L. (ed.) *Feminism/Postmodernism* New York: Routledge.

Young, L. (1996) *Fear of the Dark, 'Race', Gender and Sexuality in the Cinema* London and New York: Routledge.

Young, R. (1995) *Colonial Desire: Hybridity in Theory, Culture and Race* London: Routledge.

—— (1991) *White Mythologies: Writing, History and the West* London: Routledge.

Zubaida, S. (ed.) (1970) *Race and Racialism* London: Tavistock.

# Index